"Greg Smith has written a timely book on a timeless question: 'What is the relationship of testing to temptation and suffering?' Smith rightly sees God's testing of his people as a theological theme woven through the warp and woof of Scripture. This work will be of immense help to scholars, pastors, and laypeople alike who must deal with the question of 'why' behind our suffering. Smith offers us a solidly biblical and theological basis for encouragement and hope. Buy it; read it; apply it!"

—**David L. Allen**, dean, School of Theology and Professor of Preaching, Southwestern Baptist Theological Seminary

"In a world where Christians are tempted to settle for easy answers to the difficult problems of life, this book comes as a breath of fresh air. Though directed at scholars, there is much in these pages that will benefit the lay Christian. The testing that we experience is confined not just to our student days, studying for midterms and finals, but occurs throughout our lives and is often extremely painful. As Greg Smith shows, God is behind that testing, not as a cosmic sadist enjoying us squirm, but as a loving father attempting to restore us and our fallen world. The sufferings we endure through testing are part of our redemption."

—**William Dembski**, senior fellow, Discovery Institute's Center for Science and Culture

"Gregory S. Smith in a serious academic study presents an impressive case for the Bible's view that testing is a divine means of confirming the authentic faith of his people. He shows that testing and its concomitant experience of suffering are a divine obligation in a covenant context that seals covenant commitment and achieves the good results promised by the Lord."

—**Kenneth Mathews**, professor of Divinity, Beeson Divinity School

THE
TESTING OF
GOD'S SONS

THE **REFINING OF FAITH** AS A BIBLICAL THEME

GREGORY S. SMITH

B&H
PUBLISHING GROUP

NASHVILLE, TENNESSEE

The Testing of God's Sons: The Refining of Faith as a Biblical Theme
Copyright © 2014 by Gregory S. Smith

B&H Publishing Group
Nashville, Tennessee

ISBN: 978-0-8054-6418-4

Dewey Decimal Classification: 234.2
Subject Heading: FAITH \ BIBLE. O.T. PENTATEUCH \ BIBLE.
O.T.—BIOGRAPHY

Printed in the United States of America

1 2 3 4 5 6 7 8 9 10 • 18 17 16 15 14

SB

For Mom

TABLE OF CONTENTS

LIST OF ABBREVIATIONS

AB   Anchor Bible

AHw   W. von Soden, *Akkadisches Handwörterbuch*, 3 vols., Wiesbaden, 1959–81

AnBib   Analecta Biblica

ANE   Ancient Near East

ANET   *Ancient Near Eastern Texts Relating to the Old Testament*, ed. J. B. Prichard, Princeton, 1969

BASOR   *Bulletin for the American Schools of Oriental Research*

BDB   Brown, F., S. R. Driver, and C. A. Briggs, *A Hebrew and English Lexicon of the New Testament and Other Early Christian Literature*. Chicago, 1961.

Bib   *Biblica*

BZAW   Beihefte zur Zeitschrift für die alttestamentliche Wissenschaft

CAD   *The Assyrian Dictionary of the Oriental Institute of the University of Chicago*, Chicago, 1956–

CBQ   *Catholic Biblical Quarterly*

CBQMS   Catholic Biblical Quarterly Monograph Series

COS   *The Context of Scripture*, ed. William H. Hallo, 3 vols., Leiden, 2003

DCH   *Dictionary of Classical Hebrew*, ed. D. J. A. Clines, Shef-
             field, 1993–

DOTP   *Dictionary of the Old Testament: Pentateuch*, InterVarsity,
             2003

DISO   C.-F. Jean and J. Hoftijzer, *Dictionary des inscriptions
             sémitiques de l'ouest*, Leiden, 1965

DNWSI   J. Hoftijzer and K. Jongeling, *Dictionary of the North-
             West Semitic Inscriptions*, 2 vols., Leiden, 1995

EA   *The Armarna Letters*, ed. and trans. William Moran. Bal-
             timore: Johns Hopkins University Press, 1992.

HALOT   *The Hebrew and Aramaic Lexicon of the Old Testament*, ed.
             and trans. M. E. J. Richardson. New York: Brill, 1994–

Int   *Interpretation*

JAOS   *Journal of the American Oriental Society*

JETS   *Journal of the Evangelical Theological Society*

JBL   *Journal of Biblical Literature*

JNES   *Journal of Near Eastern Studies*

JPS   Jewish Publication Society

JSOT   *Journal for the Study of the Old Testament*

JSOTSup   Journal for the Study of the Old Testament Supplement
             Series

KAI   H. Donner and W. Röllig, *Kanaanäische und aramäische
             Inschriften*, 3 vols., Wiesbaden, 1967–1969

KTU   *Die keilalphabetischen Texte aus Ugarit*, I, ed. M. Dietrich,
             O. Loretz, and J. Sanmartín, AOAT 24, Neukirchen-
             Vluyn, 1976

NICOT   New International Commentary on the Old Testament

NAC   New American Commentary

NIDNTT   *The New International Dictionary of New Testament Theol-
             ogy*, ed. C. Brown, 4 vols., Grand Rapids, 1975–1978 (ET
             of *Theologisches Begrifslexicon zum NT*, ed. L. Coenen
             et al., 4 vols., Wuppertal, 1965–1971)

NIDOTTE   *The New International Dictionary of Old Testament Theology and Exegesis*, ed. Willem A. VanGemeren, 6 vols., Grand Rapids, 1997

OBT   Overtures to Biblical Theology

OrAnt   *Oriens antiquus*

OTL   Old Testament Library

PRU   *Le Palais royal d'Ugarit*, ed. C. F.-A. Schaeffer and J. Nougayrol, Paris, 1956–

SVT   Supplements to Vetus Testamentum

TDNT   *Theological Dictionary of the New Testament*, ed. G. Kittel and G. Friedrich, tr. and ed. G. W. Bromiley, 10 vols., Grand Rapids, 1964–1976 (ET of *Theologisches Wörterbuch zum NT*, 10 vols., Stuttgart, 1933–1979)

TDOT   *Theological Dictionary of the Old Testament*, ed. G. J. Botterweck, H. Ringgren, and H.-J. Fabry, tr. J. T. Willis, Grand Rapids, 1974– (ET of *TWAT*)

TLOT   *Theological Lexicon of the Old Testament,* ed. Jenni Ernst and Claus Westermann, 3 vols., Peabody: Hendrickson, 1997.

UF   *Ugarit-Forschungen*

VT   *Vetus Testamentum*

WTJ   *Westminster Theological Journal*

WBC   Word Biblical Commentary

ZAW   *Zeitschrift für die alttestamentliche Wissenschaft*

ZDMG   *Zeitschrift der deutschen morgenländischen Gesellschaft*

FOREWORD

As a pastor, I deal with people who are hurting on an almost daily basis. In a fallen world, suffering is the common experience for most everyone with whom I cross paths. Thus, helping those people who are hurting is a huge ministry for the local church. For a church as large as Walnut Ridge, I have had to bring together a variety of specialists who help me and the rest of the pastoral team meet the needs of those who are hurting. More and more, the church needs technicians who have both the biblical knowledge and the life experience to help people who are asking very specific questions about the suffering they experience. This is a book that helps the technicians.

Greg's book *The Testing of God's Sons: The Refining of Faith as a Biblical Theme* defines testing and traces this theme through the entire Old and New Testaments. Pretty quickly, one discovers that God, as a Father, is very interested in the faith development of those in His family. What we fail to recall is that God uses testing as the primary means of refining faith. As a parent myself, I understand how we can assist in the faith development of our own children. God is no different. Greg explains how testing involves a range of intensities and is built on the basic metallurgical idea of the refinement of precious metals. Thus, the pain and suffering we encounter in life can also be the very means

THE TESTING OF GOD'S SONS

by which God accomplishes the necessary faith development in our lives. This basic concept offers some explanatory power for those who are in the work of helping hurting people. Does God allow pain in our lives in order to gain the attention of our faith? Absolutely! Does this sometimes involve the refinement of faith that is already present in the life of the believer? Yes! Testing is the biblical conversation that focuses on God's covenant obligations to a somewhat wayward and rebellious group of people. Their story is one that involves wilderness experiences, continuous harassment from opposing nations, and even exile from their land. In Israel, we are invited to see ourselves.

Randy Weeaks
Pastor, Walnut Ridge Baptist Church
Mansfield, Texas

PREFACE

The concept of testing has occupied a great deal of my thinking over the last few years. In researching and writing this volume I was surprised to find significant connections of testing with the much broader question of suffering, even amid a few of my personal experiences. We often say in contexts of suffering that God *tests* faith. I am absolutely confident that this is true. The difficulty, as we will see, is that testing often involves the experience of suffering. In conflict with this is a world that desperately seeks to avoid, and even eliminate, all pain and suffering. A *good* God would not allow such things to happen—or would he? More than ever, a biblically correct understanding of the idea of testing serves both to encourage and inform the believer who experiences suffering and equips those seeking to help others. It offers necessary perspective for one who is trying to make sense of it all. The Bible is not shy in presenting its heroes as they experience the refinement of their faith through suffering and trial. In fact, the Bible invites us to see ourselves in their stories. So in this volume we hope to present not just the facts about biblical testing but offer a practical and pastoral side for the theology of testing as well.

In the pages ahead the theme of testing will be explored as a theological theme that stretches across the pages of Scripture. Our investigation will include concepts from the ancient world that assist our understanding of the biblical concept. Our investigation of testing as a pentateuchal theme will begin with Joseph. It is our contention that Joseph's testing, in combination with the testing of his brothers, contributes a necessary theological link between the patriarchal history and Israel's history that follows. The relevance of this theme for Israel then, as well as for the modern believer today, will be appreciated. The biblical fact is that God tests his sons; Adam, Abraham, Joseph, Moses, Job, Israel, and even Christ were all tested. Through the experience of God's tested sons we are invited to understand more fully and deeply our own experience of testing.

Greg Smith
March 2013
Fort Worth, Texas

INTRODUCTION

At a pivotal moment in the Joseph narrative, Joseph accuses his brothers of being spies and challenges them with a test. In Genesis 42:15, he declares, "By this you will be tested: by the life of Pharaoh, you shall not go from this place unless your youngest brother comes here!" After putting his brothers in three days of solitary confinement, Joseph further declares, "Do this and live, for I fear God" (v. 18b). Joseph's words and actions at this critical juncture share a variety of interpretations among scholars,[1] who see him as both villain and hero in his dealings with the brothers. For some he is acting in kind. For others he is acting as a selfish brat out for revenge. The study ahead will focus on Joseph's significant role as both one tested *and* as a tester of others. Joseph's declared *fear* of God signals the climax of a testing cycle that began for him in Egypt. As we will see, Joseph also plays a pivotal role in the testing of the brothers.

---

[1] Claus Westermann summarizes the major interpretations of this phrase as follows: "international religious morality"; "a moral attitude"; "a guarantee among men that their word is reliable"; and "an ironic cut at his brothers." See Claus Westermann, *Genesis 37–50: A Commentary* (Minneapolis: Augsburg, 1982), 109–10.

1

For many, the basic idea of testing remains an often overlooked and somewhat clouded theological theme. For example, pastors, laymen, and students who locate the word *test* in biblical resources, such as dictionaries, are often redirected to the entries "tempt" or "temptation." From this one may come to the conclusion that *testing* and *tempting* are the same biblical concept.[2] As a means of clarification, this study will bring emphasis to the primary Hebrew testing terms, נסה, בחן, and צרף, and the unique nuances that each term holds.[3] It will show that the nuance "temptation" does not translate well in those contexts where testing occurs in the Old Testament.[4] Against this notion testing will be recognized as the divine means by which

---

[2] See, for example, Warren Carter, "Tempt, Temptation," in *The New Interpreter's Dictionary of the Bible* (Nashville: Abingdon, 2006), 5:516. This tendency is primarily due to the fact that the Septuagint translates the primary Hebrew testing term, נסה, with πειράζω, which carries with it the stronger New Testament nuance of "tempt, temptation." See also Larry Richards, *Expository Dictionary of Bible Words* (Grand Rapids: Regency Reference Library, 1985), 592–94. The 1611 version of the King James translation, for example, translates נסה in Gen 22:1 as "tempt" with the original meaning of "to test," as opposed to the idea of enticement to do wrong. It seems that the historical meaning of "tempt" has changed over its history.

[3] See, for example, Stephen D. Renn, ed. *Expository Dictionary of Bible Words* (Peabody: Hendrickson, 2005), 965–67. This dictionary, as an example, does a better job of maintaining the unique nuances for each of the primary Hebrew terms, נסה, בחן, and צרף but does so by separating out the terms בחן and צרף and the meaning of "test" from the term נסה and the meaning of "tempt, temptation." Our investigation will develop meaning for each of these terms under the single rubric of "test, testing" from the biblical context.

[4] Graham H. Twelftree solves this by using the word *temptation* in his definition for "testing" and defines *testing* as the "temptation to be unfaithful to God" arising "from internal enticement to sin and from external afflications." In our development of the language of testing in the next chapter, we will suggest that while this definition may work well for the Hebrew term נסה, it does not carry the nuance for the other two primary testing terms, בחן and צרף. See T. Desmond Alexander and Brian S. Rosner, eds., *New Dictionary of Biblical Theology* (Downers Grove: InterVarsity, 2000), 814–15.

God cultivates and establishes the faith and fidelity of his own people. Testing shares a strong covenantal and relational idea in the Old Testament that includes the testing of both individuals and groups.

After a look into the language and concepts of testing, our investigation of the biblical idea will begin with the Joseph narrative, which is often overlooked in the scholarly conversation. The Joseph narrative, however, has a significant and necessary contribution to make to this theme. It illustrates the role of testing in God's divine concern for the quality of faith and fidelity of his people. Moreover, Joseph demonstrates how the faithful respond amid the difficulties, trials, and sufferings of life. In fact, on a foundation of understanding from the Pentateuch's own presentation of testing, I will extend this theme across the entire biblical context. By doing so, I hope to offer greater clarity on a subject that churches today need to hear. Those in ministry or who are preparing for ministry often receive the "why?" question from those under their care. Thus, the theme of suffering emerges as a significant pastoral topic. Practically, biblical testing shares some common ground with the much broader theme of Christian suffering. Understood biblically, testing addresses some of the "why?" behind Christian suffering. As will be seen, both Moses and Paul addressed audiences who were asking essentially the same question. What was true for the wilderness generation and their experience of hunger, thirst, and hardship was also true for the persecuted church in Paul's day. In a fallen world hardship, exile, and suffering all work to produce the faith that a relationship with a loving Father requires—in a fallen world adopted sons must always be tested sons.

Thus, my hope is that a proper understanding of testing will assist the modern pastors, laymen, counselors, and teachers charged with the task of helping those who struggle to make sense of the suffering they experience. A proper understanding of testing offers a theological basis for encouragement and hope to anyone who is in the family of

God. James exhorts us to consider it all joy when we encounter testing, and there are strong biblical reasons to think he is right!

The Way Ahead

As a means of gaining greater clarity, this study will first explore the language and concepts for testing from both the biblical context and texts from the ancient world. We will seek to define the meaning of testing by exploring the nuances of the primary Hebrew testing terms נסה, בחן, and צרף.[5] We will then explore biblical contexts where testing occurs either explicitly (with the primary terms) or implicitly (without the terms but with the primary concepts). Our biblical investigation will begin with the Joseph narrative and argue for its significant (and necessary) contribution to the theology of testing the Pentateuch presents. We will then examine the Pentateuch as a whole for the theme of testing. Finally, we will explore the theology of testing in the rest of the biblical context, including several key New Testament texts. The title for chapter 4, "The Testing of God's Sons," parallels the title of this work and demonstrates that God is concerned for the establishment, cultivation, and even refinement of the faith of his sons (and daughters) at any age.[6] The biblical consensus on the idea of testing offers both understanding and hope to the faithful who struggle—even suffer—in their demonstration of fidelity both to God and to others in the community of faith.

---

[5] While these three terms are the most frequent, other terms that also share semantic overlap will be discussed along the way.

[6] We credit Birger Gerhardsson for inspiration for the title of this project. See Birger Gerhardsson, *The Testing of God's Son (Matt. 4:1–11 & Par.): An Analysis of an Early Christian Midrash*, Coniectanea Biblica New Testament Series 2 (Lund: Gleerup, 1966).

THE LANGUAGE
OF TESTING

This chapter seeks to establish a working semantic field for the main Hebrew testing terms נסה, בחן, and צרף, drawing primarily from biblical contexts and secondarily from the broader context of the ancient world.[1] Biblical authors did not write their inspired texts in a vacuum and often employed terms and concepts available from the world around them. Thus, the work of establishing meaning for biblical terms can be a tricky business, as James Barr rightly cautions, "Etymology is not, and does not profess to be, a guide to the semantic value of words in their current usage, and such value has to be determined from the current usage and not from the derivation."[2] Barr indicates that an understanding of a particular Hebrew root must

---

[1] D. A. Carson (*Exegetical Fallacies*, 2nd ed. [Grand Rapids: Baker, 1996], 27–64) warns of several specific interpretive fallacies related to word studies built from the work of James Barr and others. The semantic field approach applied here seeks to avoid such fallacies.

[2] James Barr, *The Semantics of Biblical Language* (Oxford: Oxford University Press, 1961), 107; Sue Groom, *Linguistic Analysis of Biblical Hebrew* (Carlisle, UK: Paternoster, 2003), 45–71.

be grounded in a semantic field established with other terms of the same historical period.[3] Thus, the work of establishing meaning must include sensitivity to the historical development of a term's meaning in both biblical and nonbiblical contexts.

The Biblical Language of Testing

The Root נסה

While נסה is the most frequent term for testing in the biblical context, the etymological origin for this root lacks consensus among scholars.[4] Of the theories proposed, its origins as a military term have received the most attention.[5] H. J. Helfmeyer argues for a link between נסה and a similar Hebrew term, נס, which means "standard, flag."[6] The military connection suggests that this word refers to the *training* of a soldier that validates the skills necessary for a battle. Helfmeyer extends the proposal of Otto Eissfeldt and supports his position on those biblical contexts where the root נסה occurs in military contexts

---

[3] James Barr, *Comparative Philology and the Text of the Old Testament*, 2nd ed. (Winona Lake, IN: Eisenbrauns, 2001), 89, 171.

[4] Bing Bayer ("The Testing of God in the Hebrew Bible," Ph.D. diss. [Louisville: The Southern Baptist Theological Seminary, 1987], 27–64) summarizes the history of the field with regards to the Syriac, Ethiopic, Arabic, and Ugaritic cognates for נסה but finds no solid explanations. See also Ernest Klein, *A Comprehensive Etymological Dictionary of the Hebrew Language for Readers of English* (New York: Macmillan, 1987), 418.

[5] The proposal of Adrian van Selms ("Yammu's Dethronement by Baal: An Attempt to Reconstruct Texts UT 129, 137 and 68," *Ugarit-Forschungen* 2 [1970]: 264) for the Ugaritic *nsy* and the Hebrew נסה is rendered speculative at best. See G. Gerleman, "נסה *Nsh* Pi. to Test," trans. Mark Biddle in *TLOT* 2:741.

[6] H. J. Helfmeyer, *TDOT*, 9:443. Ludwig Koehler and Walter Baumgartner ("נסה," in *HALOT*, ed. and trans. M. E. J. Richardson [New York: Brill, 1995] 2:702) also render נסה in a secondary definition as "to give experience, train."

(cf. Judg 3:1; 1 Sam 17:39).[7] Moshe Greenberg applies this military idea in his translation of נסה in Exodus 20:20 and associates נסה with other Hebrew terms for seeing, knowing, and learning.[8]

In other biblical contexts the root נסה occurs most frequently in texts that refer to the testing of individuals (e.g., Abraham). Deuteronomy employs a high usage of this term in its theological evaluation of Israel's wilderness experience.[9] Deuteronomy 8:2 offers the purpose of Israel's wilderness experience as *testing* and states,

> You shall remember all the way which the LORD your God
> has led you in the wilderness these forty years, that He
> might humble you, *testing* you, to know what was in your
> heart, whether you would keep His commandments or not
> (emphasis added).

In further analysis, it will become evident that God tests loyalty or fidelity because covenant relationship demands loyalty.[10] However,

---

[7] Otto Eissfeldt, "Zwei verkannte militär-technische Termini im Alten Testament," *VT* 5 (1955): 232–38; see also "נסה," *DCH* 5:907.

[8] While Moshe Greenberg ("נסה in Exodus 20:20 and the Purpose of the Sinai Theophany," *JBL* 79 [1960]: 276) does not relate נסה to the root נס, he does find the military contexts in 1 Samuel 17:39 as supporting his view. Brevard Childs, *The Book of Exodus: A Critical, Theological Commentary*, OTL (Philadelphia: Westminster, 1974), 344 opposes this interpretation.

[9] Occurrences of this root: Gen 22:1; Exod 15:25; 16:4; 17:2, 7; 20:20; Num 14:22; Deut 4:34; 6:16; 8:2, 16; 13:4[3]; 28:56; 33:8; Judg 2:22; 3:1,4; 6:39; 1 Sam 17:39; 1 Kgs 10:1; Pss 26:2; 78:18, 41, 56; 95:9; 106:14; Job 4:2; Eccl 2:1; 7:23; Isa 7:12; 2 Chr 9:1; 32:31; Dan 1:12, 14. See *BDB*, 650; Abraham Even-Shoshan, ed., *A New Concordance of the Old Testament Using the Hebrew and Aramaic Text*, 2nd ed. (Jerusalem: Kiryat Sefer, 1990), 763. Interestingly, Israel's wilderness experience also dominates the wisdom context for this term (Pss 78:18, 41; 95:9; 106:14).

[10] Birger Gerhardsson (*The Testing of God's Son [Matt. 4:1–11 & Par.]: An Analysis of an Early Christian Midrash*, New Testament Series 2 [Lund: Berlingska Bibtryckeriet, 1966], 25–26) argues against Greenberg's meaning of "to experience something," on the grounds that the term has obvious covenantal meaning in half of its biblical uses. T. Brensinger ("נסה," *NIDOTTE* 3:112) identifies the key testing texts as: the sacrifice of Isaac (Gen 22:1), wilderness

in other contexts where God is not the tester, testing occurs merely
because of an established relationship between two individuals or
groups of people, such as a family. These examples serve to illustrate
what faithfulness and fidelity should look like in Israel. Yahweh
reserves the exclusive role as tester of his *own* people. In other words,
God remains the subject of the verb in many contexts. Contexts where
individuals, such as Gideon (Judg 6:39), and the nation Israel (Mal
3:10) test God, demonstrate either lack of faith or a situation where
God invites testing because of Israel's lack of faith and covenant infidelity (Exod 17:2, 7; Num 14:22; Deut 6:16; Pss 78:18, 41; 95:9; 106:14).
Biblical authors commonly use נסה in contexts where God's words
are spoken or commanded, with the expectation of obedience (cf. Gen
22:1–2; Exod 15:25–26; 16:4; 20:20; Num 14:22; Deut 6:16–17; 8:2).
Thus, God tests the covenant community and those in special relationship to him *by means of* his spoken word or command.[11] The term
נסה occurs frequently in combination with the Hebrew term ידע, "to
know," which suggests a cognitive nuance for the biblical idea of testing (cf. Gen 22:1, 12; Deut 8:2; 13:4[3]; Judg 3:4; 6:37, 39; 2 Chr 32:31).
Finally, נסה occurs in parallel with other similar terms, such as בחן, "to
test, authenticate" (Pss 26:2; 95:9), צרף, "to refine" (Ps 26:2) and ראה,

---

instructions (Exod 15:25; 16:4), theophany at Sinai (Exod 20:20), the wilderness
wonderings (Deut 8:2, 16), false prophets (Deut 13:3[4]), unconquered nations
(Judg 2:22; 3:1, 4), and individual temptation (2 Chr 32:31). He summarizes the
goals of these testing devices as follows: to measure obedience (Exod 15:25; 16:4;
Deut 8:2; Judg 2:22), to create fear (Exod 20:20), to hinder sinning (Exod 20:20),
to discern the heart (Deut 13:3[4]; 2 Chr 32:31) and to create future prosperity
(Deut 8:16). While these categories are useful, the broader concern remains the
fidelity or faithfulness of the covenant member.

[11] Each of these texts contains God's word either spoken, as in Gen 22:1–2, or
written, as in Exod 20:20. This idea is fundamental to a basic understanding of
the "testing" of an inferior's loyalty by a superior in a covenant or treaty context.
Normally the quality of the loyalty of the inferior covenant member is tested
(revealed or authenticated) by means of a defined stipulation.

"to see" (Eccl 2:1). This observation suggests that a semantic range for biblical testing includes subtle nuances of testing derived from its association with other testing terms: נסה, בחן and צרף.[12]

The Root בחן

Like נסה, the etymology of the root בחן is uncertain. However, some have compared this term to Syriac, baḥen, which means "to examine, to scrutinize."[13] Further evidence suggests other possible comparisons, such as with Aramaic terms that convey the meaning of "to examine."[14] Some evidence links the functional idea of *examination* to the world of metallurgy and the use of the ancient touchstone for the examination of the quality of precious metals such as gold.[15]

---

[12] Gerhardsson, *Testing of God's Son*, 32. Helfmeyer (*TDOT* 9:455) notes five occurrences of the root נסה in Qumran texts and discusses the single occurrence where בחן and נסה are in parallel (1 QH 2:14; 11QTemple 54:12=Deut 13:4[3]). He comments that the "sign" (נס) is the means by which God examines (בחן) "men of truth" and tests (נסה) "friends of discipline."

[13] Carolo Brockelmann, *Lexicon Syriacum* (Halis Saxonum: Sumptibus Max Niemeyer, 1928), 35; Bayer, "Testing of God," 186; Ernst Jenni, "בחן *Bhn* to Test," trans. Mark Biddle, *TLOT* 1:207. Edward W. Lane, *Arabic-English Lexicon* (New York: Frederick Ungar, 1956), 7:3018.

[14] J. Hoftijzer and K. Jongeling, *Dictionary of The North-West Semitic Inscriptions* (Leiden: E. J. Brill, 1995), 1:150. The Septuagint translates בחן with the Greek δοκιμάζειν twelve times, ετάζειν three times, and εκετάζειν two times. See M. Tsevat, "בחן," *TDOT* 2:69.

[15] For a full discussion see Appendix A: Testing as "Touchstone." By "touchstone" we are referring to the more ancient method of checking the quality of gold and other precious metals. By taking a gold sample and rubbing it on certain types of hard, black stones, called touchstones, ancient metallurgists could determine the quality of a sample by a simple examination of the shade or color of the streak left behind on the touchstone. More will be said on this in the analysis ahead.

In contrast to נסה, the root בחן occurs with much more frequency in the prophetic and wisdom texts.[16] The two occurrences in Genesis will be the primary focus in our discussion of Joseph's testing of his brothers. It is significant to our development of testing as "touchstone" that God appears as the primary subject, or active agent, behind testing in these contexts. As previously mentioned, in a few usages of נסה, individuals test God in a context of rebellion or lack of faith.[17] For בחן, the heart frequently occurs as the object of testing (Jer 11:20; 17:10; Ps 7:9; Prov 17:3; 1 Chr 29:17). This use of בחן parallels ancient texts that describe the examination of one's heart and will offer further support for our biblical discussion of testing and the metallurgical idea of "touchstone."[18]

Syntactically, בחן is commonly paired with ידע ("to know") and in contexts where deeper or concealed knowledge of an individual is sought. This pairing resonates well with the metallurgical idea of the touchstone, where the removal of the surface of precious metals

---

[16] All occurrences of this root are Gen 42:15–16; 1 Chr 29:17; Job 7:18; 12:11; 23:10; 34:3; 34:36; Pss 7:10[9]; 11:4–5; 17:3; 26:2; 66:10; 81:8; 95:9; 139:23; Prov 17:3; Isa 28:16; 32:14; Jer 6:27; 9:6[7]; 11:20; 12:3; 17:10; 20:12; Ezek 21:18[13]; Zech 13:9; Mal 3:10,15. Of these occurrences, only three occur outside of prophetic, Psalms, and wisdom contexts. See Even-Shoshan, *New Concordance*, 163; *TDOT* 2:69–79; *TLOT* 1:207.

[17] God is subject of the verb in the following texts: Pss 7:10[9]; 11:4–5; 17:3; 26:2; 66:10; 81:8; 139:23; Job 7:18; 23:10; 34:3, 36; Prov 17:3; Jer 9:6[7]; 11:20; 12:3; 17:10; 20:12; Zech 13:9; 1 Chr 29:17. In Gen 42:15–16 Joseph "tests" the sons of Jacob. Likewise, the prophet Jeremiah "tests" Judah in Jer 6:27 as a function of his prophetic role. In Ps 95:9 Israel is "testing" God in the wilderness out of rebellion, and in Mal 3:10, 15 the prophet challenges Israel to test God in response to her state of spiritual infidelity.

[18] Raymond C. Van Leeuwen ("A Technical Metallurgical Usage of Yṣ'," *Zeitschrift für die alttestamentliche Wissenschaft* 98, no. 1 [1986]: 112–13) has demonstrated the metallurgical/testing sense for יצא that parallels בחן and this same metallurgical/testing idea in several biblical contexts, such as Prov 25:4b, "Take away the dross from the silver, And there comes out (יצא) a vessel for the smith." Job 23:10b also parallels both בחן and יצא in a single verse and a testing context, "*When* He has tried (בחן) me, I shall come forth (יצא) as gold" (emphasis added).

parallels the same idea of a touchstone used to authenticate the human heart (Gen 42:16; Jer 6:27; 12:3; 17:9–10; Ps 139:23; Job 23:10).[19] This idea finds additional support in the pairing of בחן with לב ("heart"), where the idea of knowing or authenticating the heart is clear (see Jer 11:20; 12:3; 17:10; Pss 7:9; 17:3; Prov 17:3; 1 Chr 29:17).[20] These frequent links of בחן with verbs of "seeing" and "knowing" highlight the cognitive nuance of the term and support the etymological link of בחן to the "touchstone" suggested here.

The Root צרף

Unlike the terms נסה and בחן, the etymology of צרף is more certain. In Akkadian texts, verb, noun, and attributive forms all convey the basic meaning "to refine metals, to burn, refine."[21] The Syriac cognate

---

[19] The idea of knowing is presented both in consequence to testing (Jer 6:27; Ps 139:23) and in coordination with testing (Jer 12:3; 17:9–10). All three Jeremiah texts imply that the tested person is known first and emphasize the link of בחן and its cognitive nuance.

[20] בחן occurs in six of seven texts as a participle, two of which link לב ("heart") with כליות ("kidneys"). This nuance of *seeing the heart/mind* occurs with other terms for "seeing, searching," such as ראה (Jer 20:12), חקר (Jer 17:10), דרש (1 Chr 28:9), and תכן (Prov 21:2). Proverbs 21:2 describes Yahweh as a *"weigher* of hearts." The term בחן pairs with other words that help expand and refine its semantic range: צרף (Pss 17:3; 26:2; 66:10; Prov 17:3; Jer 9:6; Zech 13:9; see also Jer 6:27, 29), ידע (Ps 139:23; Job 23:10; Jer 6:27; 12:3; 17:9), נסה (Pss 26:2; 95:9), ראה (Jer 12:3; 20:20), חקר (Jer 17:10; Ps 139:23).

[21] This metallurgical meaning of צרף and the Akkadian cognate ṣarāpu is evident in the following text: "He refined (ṣarāpu) the amūtu-metal and a lump (weighing) two-thirds of a shekel came out (of the kiln), through the refining (ṣarāpu) or through the . . . (there occurred) a loss of four shekels." See *CAD*, 16:59. Christfried Baldauf ("Läutern und Prüfen," 917–18) recognizes the link to the Akkadian ṣarāpu and the particular metallurgical meaning of "refining by melting." The denominative form of the root represents the *melting pot*. Baldauf cites Isa 1:25 as an example of the theological application where the exilic experience functions to remove unfit members of the covenant community.

ṣerap means "to torture, to put into a vat, to refine."[22] The Aramaic phrase אבן צרף, "stone of testing," parallels the Hebrew phrase אבן בחן, "testing stone, touchstone," and supports a possible parallel to our proposed meaning of "touchstone" for בחן.[23] Of the occurrences of צרף, all but five are found in the Psalms, wisdom, and prophetic books.[24] Almost half of its occurrences are in contexts where a metal is named as the object of the verb צרף.[25] This term also serves as the favorite of prophets who compare Israel and Judah's experience of exile to Israel's historic wilderness experience.[26] While צרף occurs in

---

[22] Brockelmann, *Lexicon*, 308. Imperial Aramaic uses the root צרף as a passive participle for "refined silver," much like the biblical usage of צרף. See texts 5:15; 9:20; 10:11; 11:6; 12:30 cited in Emil Kraeling, *The Brooklyn Museum Aramaic Papyri: New Documents of the Fifth Century B. C. from the Jewish Colony at Elephantine* (New Haven: Yale University Press, 1953).

[23] See A. Cowley, *Aramaic Papyri of the Fifth Century B.C.* (Oxford: Clarendon, 1923), 135–36. J. Hoftijzer and K. Jongeling (*DNWSI*, 2:976) offer a different translation for the Aramaic phrase אבן צרף and render it as "colored/dyed stone." G. Lete and J. Sanmartin (*A Dictionary of the Ugaritic Language in the Alphabetic Tradition*, vol. 67 of *Handbook of Oriental Studies*, ed. and trans. G. E. Watson [Leiden: Brill, 2004], 2:790–91) render the same Ugaritic phrase as "reddish dye," suggesting a kind of alum.

[24] In the historical books: Judg 7:4; 17:4; 2 Sam 22:31; Neh 3:8, 32; wisdom books: Pss 12:7; 17:3; 18:31; 26:2; 66:10; 105:19; 119:140; Prov 25:4; 30:5; and prophetic books: Isa 1:25; 40:19; 41:7; 46:6; 48:10; Jer 6:29; 9:6[7]; 10:9; 10:14; 51:17; Mal 3:2–3; Zech 13:9; Dan 11:35; 12:10. Even-Shoshan, *New Concordance*, 996.

[25] The term is used with other terms that share a refining nuance. See, for example, אש ("fire"; Jer 6:29; Zech 13:9; Mal 3:2), עליל ("furnace"; Ps 12:6), כור ("furnace"; Isa 48:10), זהב/כסף ("silver/gold"; Judg 17:4; Ps 66:10; Prov 25:4; Isa 40:19; 46:6; 48:10; Jer 6:29; 10:9; Zech 13:9; Mal 3:3).

[26] Significantly, Ps 105:19 characterizes Joseph's Egyptian experience as a צרף ("testing"). This text informs the idea behind the reference to the Egyptian experience as a מכור הברזל ("iron furnace") for Israel in Deut 4:20. Often the context is one of judgment. See נקם (Isa 1:24–25; Jer 9:6–9); בכור עני ("furnace of affliction"; Isa 48:10); פקד ("visit"; Jer 9:6–9); הבאתי את השלשית ("to put into the fire"; Zech 13:9); כאש מצרף ("a refiner's fire"; Mal 3:2).

parallel with בחן and נסה, the term צרף carries the strongest refining nuance that is supported by a clear metallurgical background.[27]

Conclusion

Our examination of Hebrew expressions for testing suggests that a range of meaning is shared among the primary biblical terms בחן, נסה, and צרף that describe the full concept of testing. This range of meaning includes both common ground and unique nuances of meaning for each term. These unique nuances are evident and supported from both biblical and nonbiblical contexts.[28]

From our investigation thus far, we can make several helpful observations regarding the nuances for each of the primary biblical testing terms נסה, בחן, and צרף. First, "testing" includes a range of *intensity* shared across these terms. Testing ranges from mild, medium, and hot in degree of intensity; and this range of intensity tracks closely with the metallurgical background for testing, especially for the Hebrew terms בחן and צרף (see figure 1 on next page). Thus, while testing may involve the "revealing" of faith or fidelity (נסה), a divinely assigned quality check, it may also involve the refining (צרף) or authenticating (בחן) of faith. These last two categories of testing will normally involve the application of external pressure (or heat) in the life of the one being tested. Testing as revealing of faith normally occurs after refinement has already occurred in the life of the tested individual. Somewhere

---

[27] Unlike בחן, which occurs frequently with terms of "knowing" and "seeing," צרף does not occur at all with cognitive terms. The root צרף is more likely to occur in contexts where the focus is on the refinement processes, whereas בחן occurs in contexts where authentication as a prerefinement step is required. However, this is only a general observation.

[28] The Septuagint maintains the distinction in terms by translating נסה with πειραζειν ("to test"), בחן with δοκιμαζειν ("to test by trial, harden"), and צרף with πυρουν ("to test by fire, purge") with a high degree of consistency. See Gerhardsson, *Testing of God's Son*, 25–27.

Figure 1. Range of Intensity for Testing

נסה   בחן   צרף

←——————————————————————————————————→

Reveal   Authenticate   Refine

Testing as . . .

"Quality Check"   "Quality Improvement"

between these two extremes of revealing and reliving is the authentication of faith, and this stems from the basic metallurgical idea of the touchstone. Thus, biblical testing is concerned about the revealing and improvement of the faith and fidelity of the family of God.

Second, we have observed that each of these terms contributes a unique nuance to the broader idea of "testing" in the biblical context (see figure 2). Thus biblical testing reveals, authenticates, and refines; and the context, as well as the term employed, determines the precise interpretation. For example, in covenant or noncovenantal relationships, testing will validate or authenticate the fidelity or faith of an individual (or group), as well as refine and improve the quality of the desired faith of an individual (or group). Testing, primarily refining, also occurs in contexts of divine judgment. Normally, testing requires an experience of hardship (and even suffering) for the one undergoing the refinement of faith. These general observations will be demonstrated as the biblical texts are discussed in the chapters ahead.

Testing to authenticate or reveal often involves the faithful response to a spoken word or command and the *visual* sign or verification of the fidelity or loyalty expressed—the alignment of *word* and *deed*. This testing establishes the quality of the faith or fidelity of

Figure 2. Semantic Field for Testing

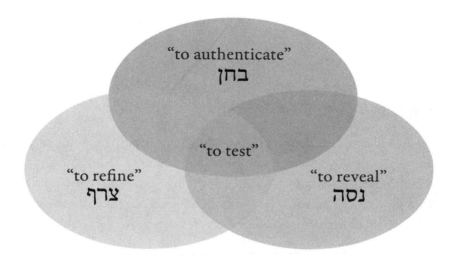

the individual—thus, a quality check. Testing to refine also involves, at times, a specific *experience* of an individual or group. The desired product or result will be the improved faith or fidelity of the individual or group—thus, a quality improvement. Before we move into the Joseph narrative and other biblical contexts where testing occurs, additional ancient texts will be examined for their discussion and presentation of testing. The general categories for testing that have just been discussed, such as the aural response, the visual examination, and the experience of refinement, will prove helpful in our examination of these texts.

The Concept of Testing in the Ancient World

In ancient literature, the testing of faith or loyalty occurs mostly in texts that involve some relationship, including texts with covenant or treaty language.[29] Though not exhaustive, the following texts represent a broad chronological and geographical range, including the Mari, Amarna, and ancient Babylonian periods. It should be no surprise to discover that the biblical authors discussed and presented the idea of the testing in much the same way as their ancient counterparts.

Testing by Examination

Significantly, several Akkadian terms that occur in both treaty and metallurgical contexts exhibit semantic nuances similar to Hebrew בחן. The common term, *amāru*, shares similar meaning with both biblical terms נסה and בחן.[30] Akkadian *amāru* conveys the idea of loyalty examined and confirmed between two members in relationship. The following examples illustrate this usage with the term *amāru* translated in italics:[31]

> [F]rom this I will *come to know* whether you behave like a
>   brother.
> [F]rom this *we will see* whether you love (us).

---

[29] The foundation of terms and concepts used in the ancient world to discuss treaty or covenant relationships, as will be seen, are drawn from the household or family. Thus, loyalty within a household or family was essential to its stability. It will be seen that the biblical authors draw from this same common pool of familial terms to discuss faith or loyalty as it relates to the vertical relationship with God.

[30] The term is defined as "to come to know, realize, see, to learn by experience, to examine (a person)." See *CAD* 1.2.5. Wolfgang Heimpel (*Letters to the King of Mari: A New Translation, with Historical Introduction, Notes and Commentary* [Winona Lake, IN: Eisenbrauns, 2003], 170) notes the difficulty of translating words related to the semantic field of *seeing* verbs, especially the Akkadian root *amārum* "to see, regard, have a vision, watch, view." He observes the difficulty of distinguishing this term from the related terms *naplusum* "observed, behold," and *naṭālum* "have before the eyes, look, perceive." In the Hebrew text, the root ידע or its equivalent is found in the immediate context of בחן six times (cf. Jer 6:27; 12:3; 17:9–10; Ps 139:23; Job 23:10).

[31] *CAD* 1.2.13.

[L]*et me see* your love and the constancy of your heart.

[M]ay the king, my lord, *come to know* (my) faithfulness such as
a servant has to his lord (emphasis added).[32]

These examples also demonstrate how terms of family relationship,
such as "brother," "father," and "love," were all employed in treaty
correspondence between kings to convey the idea of covenant solidarity.[33] It seems that the family commonly illustrated how covenant
members were to behave toward one another. This functional use of
amāru parallels בחן and supports the meaning of *authentication* suggested previously.

Another Akkadian term, *naṭālu*, conveys the nuance of "to see, to
look at/inspect, to look for support, to judge and to face."[34] A second-
century Babylonian hymn parallels the use of בחן in Jeremiah:

Of all the lands of varied speech; You know their plans, you
scan/inspect their way (emphasis added).[35]

Notice the similarity to Jeremiah 6:27:

I have made you an assayer *and* a tester among My people,
That you *may know and assay* their way (emphasis added).

---

[32] In this text one equal member of a covenant agreement requests a demonstration of fidelity from another member. The party *Warḥum-ma-gir* requests
from his covenant partner to send "1 shekel of silver or 1 fattened ram for the
Adad-festival" as a demonstration or authentication of his continued loyalty.
Albrecht Goetze, "Fifty Old Babylonian Letters from Harmal," *Sumer* 14
(1958): 40–41.

[33] Paul Kalluveettil (*Declaration and Covenant*, AnBib 88 [Rome: Biblical
Institute, 1982], 93–103) discusses the use of these terms that signal covenant
relationship.

[34] *CAD* 11.2.121.

[35] W. G. Lambert, *Babylonian Wisdom Literature* (Oxford: Clarendon, 1960),
120. Benjamin Foster (*COS*, 1.117.125) translates this line and the next as follows: "The nay-sayers' speeches are before you, You quickly analyze what they
say. You hear and examine them, you see through the trumped-up lawsuit."

The juxtaposition of the Hebrew terms ידע and בחן in this text conveys the nuance of "authentication" for testing. It may even be helpful to understand Jeremiah's role as a prophetic "touchstone" for the people in this context. Deryck Sheriffs notes that ידע and the Akkadian term *idû* operate similarly to confirm the quality of loyalty between two covenant members. He comments:

> Corporate and individual aspects of covenant membership
> cannot really be separated, and political covenant membership
> cannot really be separated, and political treaty-making as well
> as biblical covenant rituals both use language which pinpoints
> the heart of the individual who is taking oath. Political and
> biblical documents are hypersensitive to a divorce between the
> heart and the lips, between going through the motions of the
> ritual and making a wholehearted commitment.[36]

The connection between the heart and its examination for loyalty will become more evident as we explore additional texts.[37]

Testing by Verification

Ancient treaty texts also discussed the authentication of loyalty in terms of the examination of the individual. This particular activity often employed the visual and aural examination of a person's

---

[36] Deryck Sheriffs, *The Friendship of the Lord* (Carlisle: Paternoster, 1996), 18n20. For full discussion on ידע and its covenant background, see H. B. Huffmon, "The Treaty Background of Hebrew *Yāda*," *BASOR* 181 (1966): 31–37; H. B. Huffmon and S. B. Parker, "A Further Note on the Treaty Background of Hebrew *Yāda*," *BASOR* 184 (1966): 36–38.

[37] The context of Jer 6:27–30 suggests a two-step testing process that supports the distinctions made between בחן and צרף earlier. The *authentication* stage is indicated in v. 27 by the use of the term בחן. Once the dross is identified in vv. 28–29a, the second testing process of refining or purging is mentioned with the appropriate term צרף.

words—the basic idea of the alignment of word and deed. Amarna texts speak of this kind of authentication in terms that convey both activities of hearing and sight. William Moran recognizes this connection in his translated text:

> Moreover, note that I *heard and verified* this, there has been waging of war against him (emphasis added).[38]

Moran comments that the juxtaposed terms in this line, *šemû-amāru*, "hear-see," signal the idea of personal verification. This link recurs in another Amarna text:

> Why has my lord not heeded the word of his servant? My lord should know that there is no evil in the words of his servant. I do not speak any treacherous word to the king, my l[ord]. The king, my lord, has *examined* the words and has *heard* the words (emphasis added).[39]

Here the loyal activity of the servant authenticates the words of relationship previously spoken. In another Mari text the loyalty of a servant is validated by examining his deeds which are linked to his words:

> Now, I do not know whether that man (Ibni-Addu) is dead or alive. My lord must *check* on that man. Now if it pleases my lord—that man is truly your servant; that man is not committing a wrong (for which he must pay) with his life— dispatch me *a reliable man*, a rider of donkeys, *who does not*

---

[38] EA 364:17–28. William Moran, "The Ancient Near Eastern Background of the Love of God in Deuteronomy," *CBQ* 25 (1963): 362.

[39] EA 94:4–18, trans. Moran ("Love of God," 168); see also Samuel A. B. Mercer, *The Tell El-Amarna Tablets* (Toronto: Macmillan, 1939), 329. This is also verified in yet another text from Mari: "I do not write any news that I *hear* and my eyes *see* here and there to my lord, until [I] [check on] such news. I hope that [I] [can continue checking] on [news] in the future, and [ ] a single false word." See Text 26:302, translated in Heimpel, *Letters to the King*, 289.

mince words, and may that man (Ibni-Addu) live (emphasis added).[40]

In Amarna texts, this verification of loyalty also involves the direct examination of the individual. Moran offers one example:

> Being a loyal servant of the king, the Sun, with my mouth I speak words to the king that are nothing but the truth. May the king, my lord, heed the words of his loyal servant. May the archer-commander stay in Sumur, but fetch Ḫa'ip to yourself, examine him, and find out about [his] affai[rs] (emphasis added).[41]

This text links the examination of the individual with the investigation of his deeds. A similar phenomenon occurs in a text from Mari:

> The day [I sent] this tablet of mine to [my lord], those messengers [kept shouting] in the gate of the palace, [and with] both hands [they tore their] clothes. [They] (said), 'We came to (deliver) *good words*, so why can we not [ ], or else (why) can we not enter and [meet] with the king?' These things and many more they proclaimed in the gate of the palace. [ ] nobody answered them, and they retreated. The next day the vizier Erra-Nada and the personal secretary Sin-Iddinam came out from the palace and brought those messengers into the

---

[40] 26:312, trans. Heimpel (*Letters to the King*, 295, 304). This idea of the examination of an individual is similarly observed in text 26:326: "[He keeps writing denunciations about me to my lord [ ]. There is no fault whatsoever [from straw] to gold. And that man is biting me for (eliciting) untoward words, so that I make myself a pain to the person of my lord. My lord would sooner or later check on my words, and who would save me from the hands of my lord if I write untowards things to my lord?"

[41] EA 107:8–19, trans. Moran ("Love of God," 107–8). This text reveals some interesting parallels with Genesis 42. First, in line 7, Rib-Addi is said to bow "seven times (and) seven times." Second, "words" function as external means of testing. Third, a single member of the party is held back to guarantee that loyalty is demonstrated.

warehouse of the vizier and had a word with them as follows:
They (said), "Why do you keep shouting in the gate of the
palace [and] ripping your clothes? Your lord transgressed the
oath (sworn) by his gods and is determined to do harm and
ungood things. Let him come, and that Enlil *may see yes or
[no] [in] his [heart]*. And [until that is] so, you will not enter
and [meet] with the king." They rebuffed them. [ ] they (the
messengers) receive their former provisions (emphasis added).[42]

According to this text, the inferior king, represented by the messengers, has committed infidelity against Babylon. Here this same king is
summoned to return to Enlil, the Babylonian deity, who will examine
the heart of the accused.

Testing by Lifting One's Head

Some have recognized the nuance of "to examine" in the idiomatic expression, *rêša našû*, "lift the head," found in several Akkadian
texts.[43] This ancient concept offers a close parallel to the Hebrew idea
of "touchstone" explored previously for בחן. One example follows
closely with the functional idea of the touchstone presented earlier in
this chapter:

When the first-class gold has arrived I shall *examine* [*rêša našû*]
it in their presence and whatever is of bad quality I shall muster
(out); then I shall send an exact report to the king my lord
(emphasis added).[44]

This text hints at a prerefining step necessary to determine the quality of precious metal. As we have suggested, the touchstone was used
for this prerefinement examination in the ancient world. Thus, the

---

[42] Text 26:370, trans. Heimpel (*Letters to the King*, 324).
[43] A. Leo Oppenheim, "Idiomatic Accadian," *JAOS* 61 (1941): 253.
[44] Ibid.

idiom "lift the head" parallels the basic function of the touchstone in that as a gold sample is rubbed on a touchstone, its "head" is "lifted," or authenticated, and its value determined.[45] For treaty or covenant contexts, the concept of baring one's head conveys the confirmation of loyalty in the ancient world. To reveal one's head revealed one's loyal disposition in a similar way that a touchstone takes the top layer from the surface of a precious metal. A Nabonidus inscription describes two officers demonstrating loyalty by baring heads before their king:

> [C]onfirm the royal dictum, stand by his words, they (even) bare their heads and pronounce the oath.[46]

A similar phrase occurs in a line from a text from Mari:

> [May the god] of [our lord go by our side]! May the name of our lord be invoked [ ], and [we], the servants [of our lord], who [are staying] here—let our *heads be (carried) [high]* (emphasis added)![47]

These examples continue to support our basic observation that ancient authors borrowed metallurgical terminology to communicate and to discuss the quality of loyalty between covenant or treaty members.

---

[45] This Akkadian expression may have influenced later Tannaitic exegesis of such texts as Gen 22:1 and Exod 20:20, where the root נסה is translated in the sense of exaltation. Greenberg ("Theophany," 273) suggests a possible borrowing from the root נשא. Gerleman (*TLOT* 2:741) doubts any relationship to נשא on the grounds that it would require that the concept of "lifting" or "weighing" be understood as a test.

[46] See Moshe Weinfeld, "The Loyalty Oath in the Ancient Near East," *Ugarit-Forschungen* 8 (1976): 411; for the text, see 5:22–27 in Sidney Smith, trans., *Babylonian Historical Texts Relating to the Capture and Downfall of Babylon* (London: Metheun and Company, 1924), 86.

[47] Heimpel, *Letters to the King*, 329.

Testing by Examining the Heart

Two Akkadian terms function like בחן to convey both testing of precious metals and the loyalty of individuals. The first term, *ḫâṭu*, means "to explore, penetrate into, survey, examine, investigate, to search, to weigh (out), pay" and occurs in both metallurgical and treaty contexts.[48] Like בחן, *ḫâṭu* conveys the examination of the heart of the individual to confirm a loyal disposition.[49] Two examples illustrate this concept:

> [Marduk] my lord, *examines* the word, inspects the heart (emphasis added).

> (Shamash) who *examines* the heart of men, inspects the liver portents (emphasis added).[50]

Again, we find a parallel to Jeremiah's use of בחן in 11:20a:

> But, O Lord of hosts, who judges righteously,
> Who tries [בחן] the feelings and the heart.

This relationship of testing and the human heart finds significant parallel to the testing context developed in greater detail in our discussion of the Joseph narrative. In response to Joseph's testing (בחן) of his brothers for truth (Gen 42:16), Genesis 42:28 states, "And their hearts *sank* [lit. "went out"], and they *turned* trembling to one another, saying, 'What is this that God has done to us?'" In this context יצא

---

[48] *CAD* 6:159. See also Vladimire E. Orel and Olga V. Stolbova (*Hamito-Semitic Etymological Dictionary Dictionary: Materials for a Reconstruction* [Leiden: E. J. Brill, 1995], 305) for proto-Semitic background.

[49] Akkadian *ḫâṭu* also shares a metallurgical background with בחן. See two examples in *CAD* 6:161. Akkadian *ḫâṭu* parallels the Egyptian idea of Maat and the weighing of the heart of the deceased.

[50] *CAD* 6:160.

parallels בחן to convey the metallurgical sense of testing as it relates
to the heart.[51]

Another Akkadian term, *barû*, resembles בחן and the concept of
the examination of the heart. The following phrases with the translated term in italics illustrate this parallel:

My lord Marduk *inspects* the word, *examines* the heart.

Examine my heart!

Looking into the mind of man (emphasis added).[52]

Both of these Akkadian terms parallel biblical contexts where the
heart is *tested* or *examined* (cf. Jer 11:20; 12:3; 17:10; Pss 7:9; 17:3;
1 Chr 29:17).[53]

Texts from Egypt present a concept that parallels the examination of the heart. In Egypt the heart of the deceased was *examined* or

---

[51] Raymond C. Van Leeuwen has argued for the metallurgical/testing sense
for יצא in biblical contexts such as Prov 25:4, "Take away the dross from the
silver, and there comes out (יצא) a vesssel for the smith." Job 23:10b also parallels
both Hebrew בחן and יצא in a single verse and a testing context, "When He has
tried (בחן) me, I shall come forth (יצא) as gold." Raymond C. Van Leeuwen, "A
Technical Metallurgical Usage of Yṣʾ," in *Zeitschrift für die alttestamentliche Wissenschaft* 98, no. 1 (1986): 112–13.

[52] *CAD* 2:115. This cognitive meaning of "to see, examine, learn, know" is
supported in other proto-Semitic roots. See Orel and Stolbova, *Hamito-Semitic
Etymological Dictionary*, 55–56.

[53] The linkage between terms used for testing or sight and the idea of *examining exta* (extispicy) is evident in other terms, such as *amāru*, that is used in
reference to the examination of the exta. The use of בחן in the biblical texts as
a reference to the examination of the heart parallels this ancient Near Eastern
idea. See *CAD* 1.2.14. H. W. F. Saggs observes that the examination of internal
organs, or extispicy, is widely attested in Babylonian literature of the second millennium BC. While Israel may have borrowed this concept and the terms that
describe the divine examination of the individual from their neighbors, Saggs
(*Encounter with the Divine in Mesopotamia and Israel* [London: Athlone, 1978],
128) rightly cautions that the Mesopotamian practice was limited to determining
good or poor decisions with respect to the future.

weighed as a means to confirm its righteousness against the Egyptian standard of Maat, as is illustrated in this text:

> The Doorkeeper of this Hall of Maāti saith: "I will not
> announce thee unless thou tellest my name." [And I reply],
> "*Discerner* of hearts, *searcher* of bellies" is thy name. [The
> Doorkeeper saith]: "Thou shalt now be announced" (emphasis
> added).[54]

The setting of this dialogue is the Hall of Maat, where twelve gods are seated as judges and the conscience of the deceased is *weighed* or *balanced* against the feather of Anubis, which symbolizes law and justice. Thus, the Egyptian concept that conveys the authentication of individual righteousness through the examination of the heart parallels other examples from the ancient world where the heart is examined for loyalty.[55]

Testing by Demonstrated Word

The verification of loyalty by *doing* the commanded word is common among ancient Near Eastern treaty documents, as one might expect. Treaty correspondence from Amarna provides just a few examples:

---

[54] E. A. Wallis Budge, trans., *The Book of the Dead: The Hieroglyphic Transcript of the Papyrus of ANI* (New York: Bell, 1960), 593–96. See lines 36 and 37. This text demonstrates that the idea of "testing the heart" exists in both Semitic and non-Semitic contexts. This reference to both "hearts" and "bellies" parallels Jer 17:10, where it is said that Yahweh searches the *kidneys* and tries the *heart*.

[55] A relief from the tomb of Mereruka (c. 2300 BC) depicts the early processing of gold and includes two scribes weighing gold on a scale before it is melted and processed. The scale common to both metallurgical and cultic contexts suggests a cultic adaptation of the metallurgical practice of weighing precious metals for the religious weighing of an individual's heart. The Egyptian idea of Maat may have developed from this basic idea. For a diagram of the relief, see T. G. H. James, "Gold Technology," *Gold Bulletin* 5 (1972): 39.

One must not change another's words. [*Whatever be the things
that I say*], my brother [*should*] do, and whatever the things be
that my brother [*says, I will do*]. One [*shall not cause*] distress to
the ot[her] in anything whatsoever. [. . .] We [must] love and we
must rejoice as long as we live.[56]

   I read and reread the tablet that he brought to me, and I
listened to its words . . . (14–17). I will carry out my brother's
eve[ry] word [t]hat Mane brought to me. I will now, t[hi]s year,
del[iver] my brother's wife, the mistress of Egypt, and they will
bring her to my brother. On t[hat] day shall Ḫanigalbat and
Egypt be [one].[57]

These texts link loyalty to the consistency between the spoken words of
a superior and the specified actions of an inferior in treaty or covenant
relationship.[58] Additional Mari texts demonstrate this same concept:

They [said], "Besides Nahur before Haya-Sumu, there is no
second lord and father. *We will do* what our lord Zimri-Lim
says (emphasis added)."

Send this tablet quickly, and he [the king] must *act according to
the text* of the tablet (emphasis added)!

If you are truly my brother, do what is necessary to remove that
man from the district (emphasis added).[59]

Loyalty in the ancient world required the alignment of one's spoken
words and actions. The link between the spoken command and demonstrated deed as a verification of individual loyalty will inform our

---

[56] EA 29:130–32, trans. Moran (*Amarna Letters*, 95); see also Mercer, *El-
Amarna*, 175–76.
[57] EA 20:8–11, trans. Moran (*Amarna Letters*, 47); see also Mercer, *El-
Amarna*, 73.
[58] Kalluveettil (*Declaration*, 153) catalogs a number of documents that contain the basic formula, "Whatever my lord will say, I will do."
[59] 26:347, 414, and 27:36, trans. Heimpel (*Letters to the King*, 303, 356, 424).

understanding of Joseph's testing of his brothers in Genesis 42. As will be seen, Joseph's command carries this basic idea, "Send one of you that he may get your brother, while you remain confined, *that your words may be tested*, whether there is truth in you" (Gen 42:16a, emphasis added). The concept of testing as the authentication and subsequent refinement of individual or corporate fidelity is a central theme in other biblical contexts as well.

Testing by an Inferior

One interesting Akkadian text introduces the idea of testing in reverse. Instead of the superior member of covenant relationship testing for the loyalty of the inferior member, the inferior member tests the superior as a demonstration of disloyalty.[60] One text from Mari demonstrates this unique nuance:

> Say to my lord: Thus [says] Shibtu, your handmaid. All is in order in the palace. Shelebum fell into ecstasy in the temple of Anunitum on the third day [of the month]. Anunitum spoke thus: Zimrilim, people will *put you to the test* [latāku] by a rebellion. Be careful! Take to yourself trusty(?) servants in whom you have confidence [and] appoint them to watch over you. Do nothing alone! I will give into your hands the men who [want to put you] to the test! [With this message] I have sent the lock of hair [and the fringe of the eun(uch) (my lord)] (emphasis added).[61]

Biblical texts also present this type of testing as an example of the lack of faith of the inferior member of a covenant relationship (e.g., Judg 6:39; Mal 3:10). The most vivid example of this reverse testing occurs in the biblical account of Israel's rebellion in the wilderness, where

---

[60] *CAD* 11.2.125–26.

[61] Walter Beyerlin, *Near Eastern Religious Texts Relating to the Old Testament*, trans. John Bowden (Philadelphia: Westminster, 1978), 124.

נסה communicates Israel's putting Yahweh to the test (Num 14:22; Exod 17:2). This kind of testing also occurs on an individual basis, such as Gideon's testing of the Lord through the repeated fleece episodes (Judg 6:39) and the postexilic context where God invites Israel to *test* him in response to the withholding of their tithes (Mal 3:10).[62]

Testing by Refinement

The Akkadian term *ṣâdu* parallels צרף and conveys both the testing of metals and the refining of individual faith or loyalty, often in contexts of judgment. The following example demonstrates this nuance:

> At the onslaught of whose terrible weapons all countries
> writhe as if in labor, suffer [and] *melt* like [metal in] an oven
> (emphasis added).[63]

Scholars have observed the contrast between the ancient concept of individual suffering as the means of divine punishment and the biblical covenantal concept where God disciplines and corrects Israel "just as a man disciplines his son" (Deut 8:5b).[64] Covenant relationship uniquely obligates Yahweh both to demand and cultivate the fidelity of his people, even if a wilderness experience becomes the necessary means to accomplish both. Moses summarizes the divine purpose of the wilderness experience for Israel, "You shall remember all the way which the LORD your God has led you in the wilderness these forty years, that He might humble you, *testing you*, to know what was in your heart, whether you would keep His commandments or not" (Deut 8:2, emphasis added). While the wilderness certainly involved

---

[62] Malachi invites rebellious Judah to test (בחן) the Lord and offers a unique exception to this general rule. As Israel was already in violation of the covenant mandate to tithe, this invitation to *test* God actually offers Judah a step toward obedience (vv. 10, 15).

[63] *CAD* 16:59.

[64] Saggs, *Encounter with the Divine*, 122–23.

suffering and hardship, Moses describes the wilderness experience in language that conveys paternal discipline and love (v. 5). Again this is family activity. Thus, the more ancient concept of divine judgment stands in contrast to Israel's understanding of *divine testing*, where a divine concern exists for the faith development of both nation and individual.[65] Biblical testing occurs in the context of Israel's unique and privileged relationship with Yahweh and represents a radical departure from the pagan understanding of how the gods punished the infidel.[66] Israel's understanding of her relationship with Yahweh with regard to the idea of testing was somewhat radical in contrast to the ancient world!

Conclusion

This chapter has explored the meaning of testing from terms and concepts drawn from both biblical and extrabiblical contexts. While the primary biblical testing terms נסה, בחן, and צרף all convey the basic idea of testing, we also determined that each term carries a unique nuance that plays an important interpretive role in its context. We have suggested that the testing nuances best be thought of as a range of intensity. While testing as revealing (נסה), testing as authentication (בחן), and testing as refining (צרף) may cover the breadth of the overall concept of testing, the application of the more precise nuance

---

[65] Ibid., 123. Good parents know that some contexts for raising children require tough love. Biblically, as will be seen, the enactment of tough love always stems from the overflow of covenant commitment; and, thus, good parents are in a sense obligated to respond to rebellious children and enact suffering of some kind.

[66] Saggs (ibid., 123) states concerning the idea of "testing" in Israel, "This specifically Israelite development out of the old general ancient Near Eastern doctrine of divine retribution gave a new dimension to the problem. Suffering could be not only punishment, but also a mark of God's molding and testing the individual by bringing the suffering to him."

of testing will require a closer examination of the terms as they are employed in context.

From the ancient world we observed a variety of categories for testing. Most common was the demonstration of fidelity in response to the verbal (*aural*) demands of the superior. Second was the testing of *experience*. This testing often involves a harsh experience for the covenant member. While the ancients understood this experience as judgment only, the biblical portrayal remains unique in the ancient world. As will be seen, biblical authors adopted this category for testing to explain the divine purpose behind harsh experiences, such as the wilderness, the Babylonian exile, and even Joseph's Egyptian captivity. In contrast to the angry gods of the ancient world, Yahweh acts as covenant suzerain (father) and acts both to call for and to cultivate the faith and fidelity of his people. The testing terms and concepts identified in this chapter will assist our examination of biblical contexts where testing may even occur without the primary terms, such as the Joseph narrative.

Pastors and teachers should appreciate the breadth of terms and concepts used from both biblical and nonbiblical sources that illustrate the basic idea of testing. The variety of terms and concepts illustrate for congregations and classrooms how testing works on a personal level—especially important for those who are suffering. The idea of testing as *refinement* may come across as harsh to some. But the unique discovery is that God, as King, employs such hardship as a means of testing for the faith and fidelity of his own people because he is obligated to do so by covenant relationship—and *this* is the loving and gracious God of both the Old *and* New Testament. The intersection of covenant relationship with a fallen world demands it to be so!

CHAPTER 2

TESTING IN THE JOSEPH NARRATIVE

This chapter explores the role of the Joseph narrative and its unique contribution to the theme of testing in the Pentateuch. Building on the work of other biblical scholars, this investigation seeks to expand the discussion of Joseph's role among the *tested* patriarchs in Israel's history. Our goal is to demonstrate how testing in the Joseph narrative contributes uniquely to Israel's understanding of her own experience of testing and serves to establish testing as a significant theological theme that runs throughout Israel's covenant relationship with God.

Historical Investigation

The theme of testing in the Joseph narrative is an underdeveloped theological idea, especially as it contributes to the Pentateuch as a whole. In the Pentateuch the ideas of "testing" and the "fear of God" often occur together when the faith or fidelity of individuals is the focus. While scholars have identified the theological and semantic links between fear of God and testing in other pentateuchal contexts, these same links in the Joseph narrative have not generally received the full development they deserve. Our investigation will first focus on the scholarly discussion concerning these two concepts in the Joseph narrative and how interpreters have recognized their relationship with other pentateuchal contexts where fear and testing are presented.

Hermann Gunkel

Hermann Gunkel established the early interpretive baseline for the relationship between fear and testing upon which later scholarship built. Gunkel recognized the relationship of the concepts of fear and testing for Abraham in Genesis 22. Gunkel explained the meaning of נסה as a test for obedience "to see what condition someone or something is in . . . whether someone will obey God's command or not" (Exod 16:4; Deut 8:2; 13:4).[1] He recognized that Abraham's God-fearing status in Genesis 22:12 marks and defines the intended outcome of God's test and comments:

> God wanted to test Abraham as to whether he is God fearing.
> . . . This has now been determined. The performance of the
> sacrifice is, then, unnecessary: God does not want the procedure
> itself, but the attitude resolved to perform the procedure—an
> advanced concept of spirituality.[2]

Gunkel's recognition of the theological relationship between fear and testing in Genesis 22 and the basic meaning of "to test for obedience" has influenced later interpreters who have expanded the relationship between these two ideas.

While his analysis is helpful, Gunkel limits it to the theological relationship between fear and testing in Genesis 22. With regard to

---

[1] Hermann Gunkel, *Genesis*, trans. Mark Biddle, Mercer Library of Biblical Studies (Macon: Mercer University Press, 1997), 233.

[2] Ibid., 236.

Joseph's fear in Genesis 42:18, he believes, "'I fear the deity' refers to the fact that God punishes the upper class individual who treats the unprotected foreigner as guilty merely on the basis of suspicion . . . the real reason, in the legend's opinion, that Joseph refrains from chastising his brothers too harshly."[3] In Gunkel's analysis Joseph's fear of God explains the motive behind the *less* severe treatment of his brothers—the idea is that Joseph expressed a degree of kindness toward his brothers because of a commonly practiced international morality. But Gunkel's recognition of Joseph's test (בחן) as an intentional (and mean) punishment for his brothers in Genesis 42:15, 20 fails to take into consideration the breadth of the meaning of testing. Gunkel's connection of Joseph's fear of God to the *motive* behind his less severe test misses the possibility that the phrase identifies one who has experienced individual testing (42:19–20; cf. vv. 15–16).

Gerhard von Rad

Gerhard von Rad expands Gunkel's observations on the relationship between fear and testing by bringing more of the biblical context into his discussion. In his analysis of Genesis 22, von Rad prefers the idea of "temptation" for נסה to describe Abraham's test. He defines the concept of temptation as follows: "The idea of temptation, i.e., of a pedagogical test which God permits men to endure in order to probe their faith and faithfulness, is not really new in the patriarchal stories."[4]

Von Rad identifies this kind of testing for both individuals (cf. 12:1ff.; 15:1ff.; 12:10ff.; 18:1ff.) and the nation of Israel (cf. Deut 13:3; also Judg 2:22).[5] Regarding Abraham's fear of God in Genesis 22:12, von Rad moves away from the idea of "fear" as some kind of personal

---

[3] Ibid., 424.

[4] Gerhard von Rad, *Genesis: A Commentary*, rev. ed., trans. John H. Marks (Philadelphia: Westminster, 1973), 239.

[5] Ibid., 240.

religious experience to the covenantal idea where "fear" signals personal loyalty and fidelity. It does not refer "to a particular form of strong emotions but rather to their consequence, i.e., to obedience (Gen 20:11; 42:18; 2 Kgs 4:1; Isa 11:2; Prov 1:7; Job 1:1, 8)."[6]

In his analysis of the Joseph narrative, von Rad appreciates the link between Genesis 22:12 and 42:18 in their shared reference to the phrase "fear of God." In the Joseph narrative von Rad interprets "fear" as Joseph's "reliability" and comments, "He cannot allow himself to break his word, but he is bound to absolute divine commands; the brothers can therefore trust him. Fear of God, therefore, is here, as in 20:11 or 22:12, a term for obedience to commands."[7]

Thus, von Rad expands Joseph's testing (בחן) of the brothers to include more than Gunkel's punitive idea. Von Rad suggests that Joseph is seeking to verify the truth of their words and character.[8] While von Rad advances the understanding of the relationship of fear and testing in the Pentateuch, more needs to be said with regard to the specific Hebrew terms נסה and בחן as they function in the broader pentateuchal context.

Hans Walter Wolff

Wolff's development of a unified theology of the "fear of God" establishes the continuity of this theological theme throughout the Pentateuch (cf. Gen 20:1–18; 22:1–19; 42:1–20; Exod 1:15–21; 18:21;

---

[6] Ibid., 241–42. While "fear" in other contexts may certainly convey the sense of "religious awe" and the nuance of *mysterium tremendum et fascinans* developed by Rudolph Otto (*The Idea of the Holy* [New York: Oxford University Press, 1958]), in contexts where testing occurs, "fear" conveys the loyal status of the inferior covenant member.

[7] Ibid., 383.

[8] Ibid.

20:18–21).[9] Following Gunkel and von Rad, Wolff interprets Abraham's "fear of God" as the demonstration of obedience. Like von Rad, Wolff recognizes that Abraham was tested (נסה) to probe or examine his faith or fidelity. Wolff examines further the link between Genesis 22 and Exodus 20, where the expressions נסה, "test," and ירא אלהים, "fear of God," both occur. He comments:

> When God began to speak to Israel his will was the same as it was when he declared it to Abraham and as it had been in the other narratives: God tests his people through hard trials (*nissāh* in Gen. 21:1 as here in Ex. 20:20). God's normative word from Mount Sinai to all Israel is directed toward the same goal that he had set for the Patriarchs: fear of God, which produced obedience through trust in God's promise (Gen. 22) and which obediently accepts God's assurances.[10]

In addition, Wolff recognizes the significance of the phrase "fear of God" in the Joseph narrative (Gen 42:18) to signal the reliability of Joseph's word.[11] Wolff recognizes the unique use of בחן, as opposed to נסה in Genesis 42:15–16 to convey Joseph's unique treatment of his brothers. In his analysis Wolff agrees with von Rad and the notion that Joseph's test (בחן) was a means of validating the *words* of the brothers, as well as their *character*.[12]

But Wolff only briefly alludes to the theological implications of testing for Joseph and his status as God fearer, and he limits the meaning of Joseph's "fear of God" to the sense of one who is *trustworthy*. He comments:

---

[9] Hans W. Wolff, "The Elohistic Fragments in the Pentateuch," *Int* 26 (1972): 161–67.

[10] Ibid., 167.

[11] Ibid., 164.

[12] Ibid.; see also von Rad, *Genesis*, 238–39.

He tells them: "Fear not, for am I in the place of God" (50:19)? For him the fact that God meant for good the evil which the brothers had done was decisive. Here the theme of Joseph's fear of God reaches its climax. God brings salvation even out of the most serious human transgressions; anyone, therefore, who in obedience reflects on God's leading and acts not only for reasons of common humanity but also is able to make inhumanity serve his purpose can certainly *be trusted by even guilt-ridden brothers* (emphasis added).[13]

While Wolff advances the discussion by bringing attention to Joseph's role as a patriarch who is both *tested* and *tester* of the sons of Israel, more needs to be said on this role in the broader context of the Pentateuch.

Claus Westermann

Claus Westermann also recognized the theological links between Genesis 22 and Exodus 20 concerning the themes of "testing" and "fear." In an excursus on the meaning of נסה, Westermann readily acknowledges, "The testing is concerned with obedience, as here (Ex. 16:4; Judg 2:22), or the fear of God (Ex. 20:20)."[14] Westermann argues:

Gen. 22:12 and Ex. 20:18b–21 seem to be close to each other; in both cases God tests (נסה), and it is a question of proving the fear of God. . . . However, God's testing in Ex. 20 is directed towards the people, in Gen. 22 towards the individual. The idea that God tries his people is certainly older than that of trying an individual.[15]

Westermann differs from Wolff in his analysis of the theme of testing and fear in the Joseph narrative. Westermann follows the earlier

---

[13] Wolff, "Elohistic Fragments," 165–66.
[14] Claus Westermann, *Genesis 12–36: A Commentary*, 2nd ed., trans. John J. Scullion (Minneapolis: Augsburg, 1985), 356.
[15] Ibid., 362.

interpretation of Gunkel and his understanding of "fear of God" as *general morality*. He comments:

> Joseph gives the reason for the change in his orders in v. 18b: "I fear God," I am a God-fearing man. This is not to be understood as an objective statement about the piety of the foreign potentate; it is functional, giving the reason why he mitigates the measures he has taken. In the background is the widespread notion, at work in many religions, that God or the gods protects the defenseless stranger.[16]

Westermann recognized the variety of interpretations offered for the phrase "fear of God" and solved the interpretive problem by suggesting that a literary device of doubling is at work. He suggests that the second set of instructions for Joseph's test (20–42:18) (בחן), signaled by the addition of Joseph's "fear," may reveal, on the one hand, his real concern for the family of Jacob. On the other hand, this repetition may reflect the reality that it was really God who was concerned for the poor and hungry.[17] While Westermann advances the discussion of the continuity between "fear" and "testing" in Genesis 22 and Exodus 20, the impact of the Joseph narrative on the theology of testing remains outside of his analysis.

Walter Moberly

In a more recent work Walter Moberly writes:

> Within the context of the Old Testament, the linkage between Genesis 22 and Exodus 20:20 is probably the primary resonance of Genesis 22, and is one which can plausibly be argued to be a resonance intended by the writers of the Pentateuch. The linkage

---

[16] Westermann, *Genesis 37–50*, 109.
[17] Ibid., 110.

is both terminological and conceptual. In Genesis 22, Abraham's fear (*yare'*) is the purpose of God's test (*nissah*). The only other passage in the Old Testament where we find the conjunction of these two terms, and in the same sequence, is Exodus 20:20.[18]

Like Wolff and Westermann before him, Moberly observes the theological links between Genesis 22 and Exodus 20, but he sees the primary theological concern for Genesis 22:1, 12 and Exodus 20:20 as the testing for obedience. He comments:

> First, the overarching concern of the story is God's test of Abraham (v. 1) which is completely resolved by Abraham's obedience (v. 12). The meaning of this is illuminated when it is appreciated that the two key words, test (*nissah*) and fear (*yare'*) occur in conjunction in one other context of fundamental theological importance, that is Exod. 20:20.[19]

Moberly argues that Exodus 20 sets the theological agenda for both texts, that is, "God seeks by his commandments to draw out his people into fuller obedience and righteousness."[20] Moberly does not attribute this theological continuity to a single documentary source. Instead, he argues that the patriarchal stories of Abraham, Isaac, and Jacob express the theological perspective of Mosaic Yahwism. For Moberly, Mosaic Yahwism represents the deliberate way in which the patriarchal stories were retold through the theology and language of Torah-obedience first expressed at Sinai—thus, through a theological vantage point.[21] In this view Abraham functions in Genesis 22 as a

---

[18] R. Walter L. Moberly, *The Bible, Theology, and Faith: A Study of Abraham and Jesus* (Cambridge: Cambridge University Press, 2000), 81.

[19] Idem, "The Earliest Commentary on the Akedah," in *From Eden to Golgotha: Essays in Biblical Theology*, ed. Jacob Neusner (Atlanta: Scholars, 1987), 57.

[20] Ibid.

[21] Moberly, *Abraham and Jesus*, 83. For the purposes of this work, the phrase "Mosaic Yahwism" refers to the post-Sinai vantage point from which the

model of covenant fidelity for Israel. Moreover, Moberly takes a serious view of the narrative sequence and recognizes that the charge to *fear Yahweh* was essential to the delivery of Torah at Sinai. He believes that this sequence results from a premeditated theological retelling of the patriarchal stories. Though he holds firmly to this theological arrangement, Moberly claims that "the significance of Exodus 20:20 in context is sufficiently clear for the importance of the links with Genesis 22:1, 12 to be appreciated."[22] Moberly adds to previous scholarship and assigns a significant theological role to Genesis 22:15–18:

> If our interpretation of 22:15–18 as a profound theological
> commentary on the story of 22:1–14, 19 is correct, it becomes
> peculiarly appropriate that this earliest, and canonically
> recognized, commentary should be given a position of climactic
> significance within the Abraham cycle as a whole.[23]

Moberly's conclusion regarding the theological relationship between Genesis 22 and Exodus 20 raises the question of whether his understanding of relationship between the themes of fear and testing ought to include even more of the Pentateuch. While Moberly advances the discussion of such links beyond Westermann and von Rad, he stops short of Wolff's preliminary discussions of the theological links of the Joseph narrative to Exodus 20 and Genesis 22.[24] In light of the

---

patriarchal narratives were retold theologically. This study builds on Moberly's theological reading of the patriarchal narratives as a unity.

[22] Ibid.

[23] Moberly, "Earliest Commentary," 73.

[24] Moberly recognizes the concepts of fear and testing in other pentateuchal texts even where the primary terms do not occur. He limits this discussion to Exod 16:4; Deut 8:2; 13:3 [Hebrews 4]; 33:8–9; and Judg 2:22; 3:4. Against Westermann (*Genesis 12–36*, 356), Moberly (*Genesis 12–50*, Old Testament Guides [Sheffield: Sheffield Academic, 1995], 41–43) recognizes that the testing of an individual (cf. Genesis 22) could represent a unified theological vantage point, where the corporate testing of Israel as a nation is in view.

question of how the Joseph narrative fits into his theological reading of the Pentateuch, Moberly's proposals warrant further investigation.

Testing and Fear at Moriah and Sinai

Scholars provide various reasons for not connecting the theological contribution of the Joseph narrative to the rest of the Pentateuch. First, some suggest that the meaning of "fear of God" in Genesis 42 differs from the same phrase used in Genesis 22 and Exodus 20.[25] Second, some have suggested that the Joseph narrative belongs to a different genre or category of text altogether, thus relegating the Joseph narrative's origin to a time much later than the patriarchal narratives that precede it.[26] In response to each of these concerns, this study presents a case for a more unified theological reading of the Pentateuch based on the theme of testing that necessarily includes the Joseph narrative.[27]

The case for this theological continuity is built on the relationship of fear and testing in the context of Abraham on Mount Moriah and Israel at Mount Sinai. An interpretation of Genesis 22:1–18 identifies נסה ("test") in verse 1 with the theologically loaded expression

---

[25] For example, Moberly (*The Old Testament of the Old Testament: Patriarchal Narratives and Mosaic Yahwism* [Minneapolis: Augsburg, 1992], 189) interprets Joseph's fear of God in Genesis 42 as "general morality" (cf. Gen 20:11; Exod 1:17, 21; 18:21).

[26] Ibid., 7.

[27] Duane Garrett (*Rethinking Genesis: The Sources and Authorship of the First Book of the Pentateuch*, 2nd ed. [Grand Rapids: Baker, 1991], 169–82) argues that the Documentary Hypothesis and the traditionally understood Yahwist and Elohist sources do not sufficiently explain the Joseph narrative. Garrett recognizes a chiastic unity to the entire Joseph narrative and suggests that the genre of "migration epic" best explains how the narrative functioned in Israel's history. His analysis of the unity of the narrative challenges the view that the Joseph narrative is a composite of both Yahwist and Elohist sources. In their place he suggests that the "migration epic" of Joseph existed in a unified form before its incorporation into the text of Urgenesis, an edition of Genesis he attributes to the hand of Moses.

ירא ("fear") in verse 12. In this context "fear" signals Abraham's loyal status that is revealed through his demonstration of fidelity to the demands of verse 2. Similar to Joseph's story, the announcement of Abraham's "fear" comes at the climax of a period of time when Abraham experiences the refinement and development of the faith God calls for in Genesis 22. For Israel the account of Abraham's testing informs Israel's own experience at Sinai, where testing and fear also came together in a similar context of covenant response. The relationship between those two significant terms informs our understanding of the covenant relationship and warrants further investigation.

The proximity of these terms in the context of Genesis 22 amplifies the key theme of covenant loyalty. The term ירא ("fear") finds its primary meaning in the religious life of Israel and describes the disposition of one who is in healthy and vibrant covenant relationship with Yahweh—a term that "concerns doing rather than feeling."[28] The central event that defined Israel's faith life was the revelation of the Decalogue in Exodus 20:1–20, which served as the defining moment for the religion of Israel and set forth the interpretive framework for understanding the faith life of the patriarchs, such as Abraham and his test in Genesis 22.[29] At Sinai, Moses declared to the people, "Do not be afraid; for God has come in order to *test* you, and in order that the *fear* of Him may remain with you, so that you may not sin" (Exod 20:20, emphasis added). At Sinai the נסה "test" serves as the means

---

[28] Moberly (*Genesis 12–50*, 40–41) cites Deut 5:29 and Job 28:28 as support for the meaning of "fear" as "obedience" in Genesis 22 and Exodus 20. See also idem, *Abraham and Jesus*, 92–97.

[29] Moberly, *Genesis 12–50*, 41. Westermann (*Genesis 12–36*, 362) cautions against this linkage on grounds that the idea of the corporate testing of Israel (e.g., Exodus 20) is older than that of the testing of individuals (e.g., Genesis 22). Deryck Sheriffs (*The Friendship of the Lord* [Carlisle: Paternoster, 1996], 70) follows Moberly and recognizes that the "emotionally and theologically" charged Sinai event resonates theologically with the testing of Abraham at Moriah because both events signify demonstrations of loyalty.

by which Yahweh challenges Israel to a deeper future obedience and expression of covenant loyalty as they leave Sinai.[30] Thus, from Moses' theological vantage point, Abraham illustrates for Israel the faith that is *tested* but remains faithful to the commands of Yahweh.

Scholars have established even stronger links between Exodus 20 and Genesis 22 by noting the *conditionality* of blessing at Sinai and this same emphasis in the messenger's address in Genesis 22:15–18. For example, Moberly comments:

> A promise which previously was grounded solely in the
> will and purpose of Yahweh is transformed so that it is now
> grounded *both* in the will of Yahweh *and* in the obedience
> of Abraham. It is not that the divine promise has become
> contingent upon Abraham's obedience but that Abraham's
> obedience has been incorporated into the divine promise.[31]

In Genesis 22, the conditional aspects of the covenant are limited to the phrases "because you have done this thing" (v. 16) and "because you have obeyed My voice" (v. 18). This suggests that while the promises are *explicitly* linked to the fidelity displayed by Abraham, they are also "*implicitly* grounded in the character and purposes of YHWH himself."[32] Thus, Abraham becomes a "model of Israel's Torah-shaped obedience to God" and one who "offers sacrifice on the site

---

[30] The "words" (דברים) function as the mechanism by which Yahweh tests Israel. Joseph will soon "test" (בחן) his brothers by means of their words in Genesis 42. Chapter 2 will show that testing by means of words was common in the ancient Near East.

[31] Moberly, "Commentary," 320–21. T. Desmond Alexander ("Genesis 22 and the Covenant of Circumcision," *JSOT* 25 [1983]: 17–22) argues that Gen 22:15–18 records the divine oath offered to Abraham to reward him for his obedience and ratifies the covenant offered in Genesis 17.

[32] Moberly, *Genesis 12–50*, 48. The expression דבר, "word," in Gen 22:16 and דברים, "words," in Exod 19:6–7; 20:1 represent the aural demand of the "test" for Abraham and Israel. Thus, both Abraham and Israel are tested by means of

of Israel's worship on the mountain of the Temple in Jerusalem."[33] This theological coherence between Genesis 22 and Exodus 20 causes one to wonder if other passages in the Pentateuch fit this pattern. In our study ahead we will explore the question of whether Joseph could not also function as an example of a tested patriarch who demonstrates faith amid difficulty. Before this question is addressed, we must consider the historical and semantic concerns that lead scholars to exclude the Joseph narrative as a significant theological contributor to the Pentateuch's theology of testing.

The Joseph Narrative and the Meaning of "the Fear of God"

The Hebrew terms for "fear" and "testing" both function theologically in the Joseph narrative in much the same way we have observed for Abraham in Genesis 22 and for Israel in Exodus 20. The relationship between the concepts of testing and fear, and the terms נסה and ירא, clearly suggest the covenantal meaning of "loyal obedience" in the contexts of both Genesis 22 and Exodus 20. In addition to Genesis 22 and Exodus 20, this same theological emphasis may be found in texts where נסה occurs explicitly but "fear" occurs implicitly (e.g., Exod 16:4; Deut 8:2; 13:3 [4]; 33:8–9). Regarding this implicit option, Moberly comments, "It should be noted, moreover, that although the specific words 'test' and 'fear' are not found in conjunction elsewhere, the concept that they represent is."[34] In the discussion that follows, I

---

their faithfulness to these aural stipulations. The Joseph narrative will also present testing in this same manner.

[33] Moberly, *Genesis 12–50*, 49–50; see also Jo Milgrom, *The Binding of Isaac: The Akedah—a Primary Symbol in Jewish Thought and Art* (Berkeley, CA: BIBAL, 1988), 26–30.

[34] Moberly (*Genesis 12–50*, 41) makes the semantic link between נסה used in Genesis 22 and בחן used in Proverbs 17, though he does not seriously consider the link to בחן that occurs in Gen 42:15–16.

will argue that "fear" and "testing" occur both implicitly *and* explicitly in the Joseph narrative in a way that contributes to the same covenantal meaning that was observed for Genesis 22 and Exodus 20.[35]

In short, the explicit and implicit concepts of "fear" and "testing" occur in all three contexts of Genesis 22, Exodus 20, *and* Genesis 42, and each of these contexts contributes to the same theological pattern. Two primary objections are offered for the exclusion of Genesis 42:18 and its participation with the broader discussion of Genesis 22 and Exodus 20.[36] First, in other biblical contexts "fear" represents a moral restraint against the possibility of harming a weaker party.[37] Thus, Joseph's "refusal to take advantage of his brothers when he has them entirely at his mercy is what gives meaning to his claim to 'fear God.'"[38] Second, the meaning of "fear" as "general morality" includes both the faithful Israelite as well as the foreigner. Thus, in Genesis 42 Joseph acts as a foreigner. Moberly cites Deuteronomy 25:18 as a parallel example where "fear of God" conveys this sense of *general morality* being attributed to a foreigner.[39] This raises the question of whether Joseph is portrayed as a "foreigner" or a brother. Does he "fear God" in a manner that is consistent with and open to any non-Israelite,

---

[35] The Joseph narrative has been compared with other non-pentateuchal texts where testing occurs. Alfred Jespen (" אמן *'Aman,*" in *TDOT,* 1:297) recognizes the link of דבר and אמן in Gen 42:20, where Joseph requires that his brothers prove their words, to the parallel accounts of 1 Kgs 8:26 and 2 Chr 6:17, where God's word or promise to David is requested to be demonstrated true.

[36] Moberly, *Abraham and Jesus*, 92–94.

[37] Moberly (*Abraham and Jesus*, 93) cites Gen 20:11; Lev 19:14; 25:17, 36, 43; Deut 25:18; and Gen 42:18 as examples; see also Moshe Weinfeld, *Deuteronomy and the Deuteronomic School* (Winona Lake, IN: Eisenbrauns, 1992), 274.

[38] Moberly, *Abraham and Jesus*, 93.

[39] Ibid. Weinfeld (*Deuteronomic School*, 274) cites Deut 25:18 as the "classic example of יראת אלהים in the sense of general morality ... where Amalek's unforgettable crime of cutting down all the stragglers in the rear is motivated by a lack of fear of God." Weinfeld also cites Gen 20:11; 42:18; Exod 1:17, 21; Lev 19:14, 32; 25:17, 36, 43 as examples of this universal sense of morality, accessible to both Israelite and pagan.

or does he "fear God" and thus demonstrate loyalty in response to his familial obligations?[40] It seems evident from the narrative that Joseph's "fear of God" is announced only after a period where his faith and loyalty is both *authenticated* and *refined* in Egypt. This appears consistent with the pentateuchal presentation of the tested Patriarch, in whom Yahweh both refines and reveals faith. It can also be observed that "God-fearer" in Genesis 42:18 refers to Joseph's loyal response to his family. While Joseph will soon demonstrate loyalty in response to Jacob's specific command to care for his brothers, Joseph's tested loyalty is better understood in the context of a *brotherhood* (Gen 37:14).[41] Thus, Abraham *and* Joseph are designated "God-fearer" for the *same* reason—obedience or loyalty demonstrated under extreme circumstances—love or loyalty under fire. Thus, both Abraham and Joseph can serve as models of Torah obedience for Israel. The relationship of Joseph to Abraham on the concepts of "fear" and "testing" and as examples for Israel of covenant fidelity will be the primary focus in the investigation to come.

Scholars will also argue that "fear of God" in Genesis 42 conveys the sense of "general morality" because Genesis 42:18 uses the more generic term אלהים for God (see also Gen 20:11; Deut 25:18). The suggestion is that when אלהים is combined with ירא, it is more common to understand "fear" to mean this universal or general moral sense.[42] Moberly, for example, suggests that the switch between אלהים and יהוה occurs for theological emphasis, where אלהים is used when one responds to God in a *general* sense and יהוה occurs when one responds

---

[40] Moberly (*Abraham and Jesus*, 93) recognizes the possible interpretation of Joseph's fear as covenantal obedience but does not pursue this interpretation in the context of his discussion of testing in Genesis 22 and Exodus 20.

[41] Von Rad (*Genesis*, 383) suggests that in v. 18 Joseph's fear reflects his reliability or his obedience to commands. He links Gen 42:18 to Gen 20:11 and Exod 22:12 and suggests that all three contexts convey the nuance of obedience. Von Rad's interpretation of "fear" is close to the proposal suggested here.

[42] Moberly, *Abraham and Jesus*, 93.

to God in a *covenantal* sense.[43] Therefore, Joseph acts *morally* but not *loyally* (in the covenant sense) in Genesis 42 because ירא occurs with אלהים and not יהוה, the recognized covenant name for Yahweh.[44] It is interesting that both אלהים and יהוה occur in the context of Abraham on Mount Moriah. The argument is made that in Genesis 22, the alternation between יהוה (22:11, 14–16) and אלהים (22:1, 8, 12) affects the meaning of Abraham's fear of God. Traditional Jewish interpretation understands the names יהוה and אלהים to refer to different characteristics of God. Source-critical scholars have understood this same alternation of names to reflect stages in the history of and sources behind the text. Some more recent scholars argue that the divine names reflect the intentionality of the author. Moberly comments:

> The alternation between *'elohim* and *yhwh* is not evidence of different sources with different conceptions of when the divine name *yhwh* was first known, but rather evidence of two conceptual levels within Genesis 12–50. On the one hand, the context is prior to Moses, Sinai, Israel and a knowledge of God as YHWH, so within its one context the writers naturally refer to God either with the generic *'elohim* or with various titles compounded with *'el*. On the other hand, the patriarchal traditions have been appropriated and retold within a Yahwistic

---

[43] Moberly (ibid., 94) cites the example of Job, who was not an Israelite but who responded to God as a model for the faith community (יהוה in Job 1:21) and as a model for humanity (אלהים in Job 1:1, 8–9).

[44] According to Gordon Wenham ("Religion of the Patriarchs," in *Essays on the Patriarchal Narratives*, ed. A. R. Millard and D. J. Wiseman [Leichester: InterVarsity, 1980], 181), the editor of the Joseph narrative restricts the use of "Yahweh" to the narrative framework (eleven times in the framework compared to zero in the dialogue; this compared to thirty times in the dialogue for "Elohim"). He suggests that the author intentionally maintained the patriarchal reference to the name "Elohim," while he himself knew Yahweh. Consequently in the Joseph narrative, Joseph, like Abraham, functions as a model of Torah obedience for Israel.

context, where the writers have felt free to use Israel's name for
God because of their conviction that it is Israel's God of whom
the patriarchal stories tell.[45]

Moberly compares the use of the phrase ירא אלהים in Genesis 22:12
with Job 1:1–2:10 and suggests that here the "fear" demonstrated by
Abraham is of the "generic category" and that the "logic and dynam-
ics of what is portrayed is *not* peculiar to Yahwism" (emphasis added).[46]
In other words, the story of Abraham's "fear of God" in the original
telling portrayed a man who demonstrated proper *moral response* to
the generic God known to all. However, the covenantal meaning of
obedience for Abraham's fear is signaled by the messenger of Yahweh,
who represents the covenantal vantage point for the retelling of the
story.[47] Moberly observes that the juxtaposition of the phrase "אלהים

---

[45] Moberly (*Abraham and Jesus*, 95) notes the general lack of scholarly consensus with regard to the placement of the patriarchal promises within the history of Israel. He mentions the extreme position of John van Seters (*Abraham
in History and Tradition* [London: Yale University Press, 1975], 310–11), locates
a sixth-century exilic context for the promises made to the exiles, and von Rad
("The Form-Critical Problem of the Hexateuch," in *The Problem of the Hexateuch and Other Essays*, trans. E. W. T. Dicken [London: SCM, 1966], 55) argues
for a tenth-century "Yahwist" of the Solomonic enlightenment. Arguing for an
early date for the patriarchal narratives, Wenham ("Religion of the Patriarchs,"
184–85) notes the complete absence of "Baal" from the patriarchal narratives.
The fact that "Baal" usurped "El" in the west Semitic pantheon around 1500 BC
suggests an earlier date for the patriarchal narratives.

[46] Moberly, *Abraham and Jesus*, 96.

[47] Moberly ("Commentary," 308ff.) summarizes several of the arguments
against his position that Gen 22:15–18 represents a later addition to the narrative. George W. Coats ("Abraham's Sacrifice of Faith: A Form-Critical Study of
Genesis 22," *Interpretation* 27 [1973]: 389–400) has argued that the reward in v. 18
forms an inseparable part of the story in vv. 1–14, where the primary focus is on
Abraham's obedience. Alexander ("Genesis 22," 21) argues from the wider context of the patriarchal narratives and suggests that the promise of the covenant
made in Gen 17:1 was not fulfilled until Abraham's demonstrated obedience
in 22:12 and the offer of sacrifice in v. 13. Thus, the confirmation of Abraham's
obedience in vv. 15–18 is necessary to the immediate context. Wenham (*Genesis*

will see/provide" (v. 8) with "יהוה will see/provide" (v. 14) highlights the vantage point of Torah obedience and repositions Abraham's fear of אלהים ("God)" as a *covenantal fear* of יהוה ("the LORD").[48]

This last method of interpreting the divine names in the patriarchal narratives will prove helpful in the discussions that follow. This interchange of names may indeed reflect the sensitivity of the author to sources derived from historical periods much older than his own. Moberly's conclusions raise the question whether ירא אלהים could designate one who is obedient in a covenantal sense, even in a context where the term יהוה is not immediately present.[49] While יהוה does *not* occur in the immediate context of Genesis 42, where Joseph's fear of God is announced, the term *does* occurs earlier in the Joseph narrative, where Joseph experiences testing. During Joseph's captivity in Egypt, Yahweh (יהוה) remains with Joseph and prospers him (39:2, 23). In Genesis 39:7–18, Joseph's loyalty to his master is tested. Through a series of hardships, Joseph matures, trusts in Yahweh, and is transformed into a leader who has learned how to manage power and authority for the benefit of others (Gen 41:55–57)—a quality soon

---

16–50, 112) agrees with Moberly's theological observations on Gen 22:1–19 noting that in this narrative, the "faithful human response to God is taken up and incorporated within the purposes and activity of God."

[48] The narrative uses the covenant name "Yahweh" at the climactic moment of Abraham's demonstrated fidelity in v. 10. Abraham then confirms the fidelity of Yahweh by *seeing* the ram. Appropriately, Abraham names the place "Yahweh will see" in v. 14. Moberly (*Abraham and Jesus*, 96) is correct in his interpretation of Abraham's "fear" as indicative of his covenant response to Yahweh.

[49] Wenham ("Religion of the Patriarchs," 157–88) suggests that the divine names were signals employed by the author to describe either divine activity (where "Yahweh" is used) or to report divine speech (where "El" names are used). He argues that the editor of the patriarchal narratives demonstrates great faithfulness to an early tradition, and only where it suited his theological purpose did he substitute "Yahweh" in the divine speeches. Based on his statistical analysis, Wenham demonstrates that the name "Yahweh" was revealed originally to Moses at Sinai.

to be managed on behalf of the sons of Jacob. Joseph's fear of God (ירא
אלהים) in Genesis 42:18 represents a continuation of the fidelity that
Joseph previously demonstrated to Yahweh *throughout* his Egyptian
experience. The use of אלהים instead of יהוה in verse 18 also fits the
context of Joseph talking to his brothers as an *Egyptian*. While this
explanation does not solve all the problems, the following discussion
on Joseph's testing will provide further evidence to support the interpretation of ירא אלהים in Genesis 42:18 as a term that signifies the idea
of faith or fidelity.

Testing and Fear in the Joseph Narrative

Testing in the Joseph narrative expresses both the *aural* and *experiential* categories for testing discussed earlier. Our analysis of testing
in this account will be applied to the remainder of the Pentateuch in
the next chapter. This will show that the Joseph narrative presents a
consistent theology of testing with the rest of the Pentateuch: Joseph
stands as a tested patriarch and serves as a model of covenant fidelity
for Israel.

The Meaning of Testing

Of particular importance for the Joseph narrative is the key Hebrew
term בחן, used in Genesis 42. Our investigation suggested the meaning of "authenticate" for this term, drawn from the metallurgical idea
of the ancient "touchstone." I will argue that the sons of Jacob (Israel)
experience testing in both the sense of *authentication* and the sense of
refinement. The divine concern for the sons of Jacob (Israel), expressed
on the foundation of Joseph's already tested fidelity, is that their fidelity be refined and subsequently (like Joseph) be improved. I will demonstrate that בחן, rather than צרף and נסה, best conveys this overall
idea of testing in the Joseph narrative. Central to our analysis will be

the application of the testing categories of both *aural* and *experience* where testing occurs both explicitly and implicitly.[50]

Joseph's Testing in Egypt

The narrative of Genesis 37–41 sets up an implicit testing experience for Joseph that will parallel the more explicit testing soon to be experienced by Joseph's brothers. Joseph and his brothers will experience testing that involves both the authentication and improvement of their faith. Testing, both explicit and implicit, remains a highly integrated theme throughout the Joseph narrative. Early in the story Jacob's command for Joseph to "go" and "see" about the general welfare of the brothers and the family flocks offers the basis for an implicit aural test for the younger Joseph (Gen 37:13–14).[51] Joseph's faithfulness demonstrates *brotherhood* or family loyalty to this initial command—the older brothers will be tested for this same brotherhood. The implications of this demonstrated brotherhood become pivotal in the later events of Genesis 42 and contribute significantly to Joseph's statements

---

[50] Von Rad (*Genesis*, 383) proposes two levels of understanding for Joseph's test in Genesis 42. First, the immediate context probes the brothers for the truth or authenticity of their words. Second, the wider context tests and authenticates the character and loyal inclinations of the brothers toward Benjamin. This second test intends both to authenticate and to refine. Von Rad's emphasis on the disciplinary nature of Joseph's test parallels the divine intentions of the wilderness event according to Deut 8:5 and suggests that the testing of the brothers was a test of *experience*, similar to the wilderness experience for corporate Israel.

[51] Coats (*From Canaan to Egypt*, 15) recognizes the irony in the fact that while Joseph is sent to seek the שלום of his family in 37:14, he will encounter just the opposite. The word שלום in this context may serve a dual meaning and convey the familial sense of "loyalty." This sense of "loyalty" also recurs through the repeated motif of "bowing" first introduced in Genesis 37. In an ironic ending to the Joseph narrative, God himself will extend his שלום to the family of Jacob through the faithfulness of Joseph.

in Genesis 45:7 and 50:19–21.[52] Joseph's loyal response to his father also falls in line with Abraham and Moses and the key Hebrew term הנני, "behold, I," which signals for them a readiness and willingness to obey (37:13b; cf. 22:1–3; Exod 3:4). Like Abraham and Moses, Joseph's faithfulness allows divine blessing to be mediated to the sons of Jacob (Israel), despite their failure to demonstrate firm loyalty in return.

Joseph's dreams in Genesis 37:7, 9b anticipate the testing of his older brothers and serve to aggravate and thus expose the quality of their family loyalty (brotherhood) toward Joseph.[53] The narrative of Genesis 37:8b signals the status of their brotherhood, "So they hated him even more for his dreams and for his words." Clearly the brothers' loyal disposition toward Joseph that will become the object of further authentication and refinement. Joseph will create an intentional scenario in Genesis 42:18–20 by which this testing will be accomplished. In that context בחן signals the purpose of the test—Joseph creates a living "touchstone" that will authenticate the loyalty of this "brotherhood."[54] Joseph's dreams also emphasize the power and

---

[52] Walter Brueggemann (*Genesis*, Interpretation [Atlanta: John Knox, 1982], 290–93) recognizes a link to "bowing" and the ultimate fulfillment of this dream in Genesis 50:18 (cf. 42:6; 43:26, 28). He regards the fulfillment of this dream as the key interpretive link to the entire narrative. The statements in 45:5–8 and 50:19–20 provide the theological "big idea" to the whole narrative, that is, "God's way will triumph without the contribution of any human actor, including even Joseph himself."

[53] Bruce Waltke (*Genesis: A Commentary* [Grand Rapids: Zondervan, 2001], 500) recognizes that dreams were understood to convey divine communication in the ancient world.

[54] On the designation of the brothers as "ten brothers of Joseph," Robert Alter (*The Art of Biblical Narrative* [New York: Basic, 1981], 161) comments: "Though the ten are quite naturally identified as 'the sons of Israel' when they arrive in Egypt, emissaries of their patriarchal father, as they set out they are called 'Joseph's brothers.' They are headed, of course, for an ultimate test of the nature of their brotherhood with Joseph, a bond which they have denied by selling him into slavery and which they will now be forced to recognize in a new way."

influence he gains in Egypt through personal experience of refinement that results in transformation.[55] Joseph's Egyptian experience
anticipates the climactic encounter that he will soon have with his
brothers.[56] The contrast between the younger Joseph at home and
the Joseph who emerges from Egypt is striking. Joseph receives the
dreams as an immature younger brother, who perhaps saw them as a
divine mandate for power and control in the family.[57] However, as he
emerges from his refining experience with all the power and control
of Egypt at his fingertips, we see a radically different Joseph. Having been left to die, and with every reason to seek revenge against his
brothers, Joseph's encounter in Genesis 42 will reveal the quality of
his loyalty to his entire family. Similar to the account in Genesis 22
of Abraham on Mount Moriah, Genesis 42 reveals the testing of faith
amid a familial context. However, for this climactic chapter, scholars
differ on their interpretation of Joseph's actions. Brueggemann, for
example, paints a more dismal picture for Joseph's character at this
juncture and comments:

---

[55] Regarding Joseph's implicit testing or refinement experience in Egypt, see
my discussion above.

[56] Coats (*From Canaan to Egypt*, 13) recognizes the link between Joseph's
dreams and Genesis 42, and comments, "But the dream also anticipates the
brothers' subjugation to Joseph's power and foreshadows the account in Gen 42
that brings the brothers in humble submission to an 'unknown' but powerful
administrator in the court of Egypt."

[57] Waltke (*Genesis*, 499) suggests that the "bad report" from 37:2b portrays
the young Joseph as a "pestering, tattletale little brother." Coats (*From Canaan
to Egypt*, 19) regards Joseph as "the typical spoiled child, favored by his father,
hated by his brothers. He reports his dreams to his brothers, almost as if in con-
descension to taunt them with his superiority." While this characterization of
Joseph as a youth is certainly correct, it raises the question of what Joseph will
do with the power he obtains in Egypt. *Who* will emerge from the experience
of testing in Egypt, a pestering, spoiled little brother bent on revenge, or a more
tempered and mature little brother still seeking the שלום of his family?

He is presented as ruthless, cunning, and vengeful. He is
prepared to return to his brothers some of the grief caused him.
He has forgotten nothing. There is nothing noble about him.
There is no hint that he has any awareness of a larger vocation.
The God-fearing cliché of 42:18 does not touch much of what
follows. He remembers the dream (cf. 42:9), but he sees it only
in terms of power, not vocation or fidelity.[58]

This interpretation takes too lightly Joseph's experience in Egypt
and the transformative impact that it had on him. Joseph emerges from
Egypt not as a vengeful brother—or he would have killed them on the
spot! Instead, in Egypt he learns that power must not be wielded flip-
pantly when it emerges as a divine provision. Joseph learns humility
and trust in the Lord amid the suffering he endured in Egypt. In Genesis 42, Joseph demonstrates fidelity toward his brothers as one who
has learned this lesson. The test of authentication (בחן) that he creates
for the brothers demonstrates both grace and tough love and recognizes that their more significant immediate need is not famine relief
but a change of heart. As a tested patriarch, Joseph's actions toward
his brothers illustrate even more for Israel the divine balance of grace
and tough love that work together in testing experiences intended
to bring necessary humility and refinement. As an agent of Yahweh,
Joseph seeks to *authenticate* the brothers for brotherhood (loyalty) and
to refine for the loyalty that is not evident at first. Are they scoundrels
to the core, or can they be changed? Neither נסה nor צרף conveys the
uniqueness of Joseph's test, for he creates a "touchstone" by which
their loyalty will be authenticated.[59] Thus, Joseph's test in Genesis 42

---

[58] Brueggemann, *Genesis*, 340.
[59] Ibid. Coats (*From Canaan to Egypt*, 37–38) recognizes Joseph's test as a
means to test the honesty of the brothers and secure Benjamin's safe passage to
Egypt but regards the motivation behind the test as Joseph's means of torturing
his brothers. His portrayal of Joseph as a tyrannical "anti-legend" in Genesis 42
fails to take into consideration the statement of Joseph's "fear of God."

parallels Genesis 22; both Abraham and Joseph demonstrate fidelity at a climactic moment after they had emerged through testing experiences of their own. Each demonstrates the role of the tested patriarch for Israel.

The Climax of Testing

At the story level Joseph's test intends to expose and to remove the fratricidal tendencies of the ten—fratricide being the antithesis of brotherhood.[60] Scholars have varied in how Joseph's motivation is to be interpreted. Sternberg, for example, summarizes the scholarly opinions as "punishing, testing, teaching and dream fulfillment" and comments:

> [E]ach line is wrong because all are right. In characteristic biblical fashion, no hypothesis can bridge the discontinuities and resolve the ambiguities by itself; nor can the joint explanatory power of all four—and a few others to be suggested—unless brought to bear on the narrative in a certain order and shifting configuration.[61]

---

[60] Alter (*Biblical Narrative*, 161) observes that the movement in Genesis 42:3–4 from "Joseph's brothers" to "Joseph's brother" and to "his brothers" emphasizes the *brotherhood* Joseph will soon test. Westermann (*Genesis*, 106) suggests that the reference to בני ישראל in v. 5 is displaced from its original sequence with Genesis 41:57. Victor P. Hamilton (*The Book of Genesis,* NICOT [Grand Rapids: Eerdmans, 1995], 515–16) argues that this shift in reference is intentional by the author.

[61] After his analysis of all four possible interpretations, Meir Sternberg (*The Poetics of Biblical Narrative: Ideological Literature and the Drama of Reading* [Bloomington: Indiana University Press, 1987], 286) prefers to view the test as a means of revealing the brotherhood or loyalty of the sons of Jacob. Sternberg is correct in his assessment that the brothers are never fully rehabilitated. Westermann (*Genesis*, 107) rightly cautions against placing Joseph's motives as punitive and suggests that the wider narrative reveals Joseph's true intent.

In language common to the ancient Near East, the brothers declare their familial loyalties in the repeated statements, "We are all sons of one man," and "Your servants are twelve brothers" (Gen 42:11, 13). In response to their suspicious claims to familial loyalty, Joseph devises his specific "test" (בחן) that functions to expose their true inclinations and *authenticate* their loyalty.[62] The details of verse 15 declare the terms of the test—the procurement of Benjamin.[63] Verse 16 adds to the stipulation the condition that nine brothers will remain in confinement while one leaves to fetch the younger; the testing of brotherhood lies at the heart of this intentionally devised scenario. The three-day confinement recalls Joseph's confinement in Egypt (cf. Gen 40:4, 7).[64] After three days Joseph modifies the stipulations of the test (42:19).[65]

---

[62] In 2 Kgs 10:5ff., Kalluveettil (*Declaration*, 141) identifies a twofold structure that parallels Genesis 42. Kalluveettil recognizes the intimidating force of Jehu's letter and calls it a "subtle way indeed of frightening the nobles into submission and subservience!" The response of the nobles includes their declaration of subservience: "We are your servants," and their declaration of loyalty, "All these things we will do." These phrases parallel Gen 42:10 and 18–20 respectively. Jehu's second letter required a demonstration of loyalty that was linked to a specific demand (i.e., the bringing back of heads; cf. the bringing back of Benjamin). Kalluveettil (citing Weinfeld, "Oath," 379–414) points out that these loyalty oaths functioned to demonstrate loyalty in covenant relationship.

[63] Robert Longacre (*Joseph: A Story of Divine Providence: A Text Theoretical and Textlinguistic Analysis of Genesis 37 and 39–48* [Winona Lake, IN: Eisenbrauns, 1989], 36–37) recognizes the chiastic structures of both of Joseph's speeches in Gen 42:14–16 and 18–20.

[64] A parallel to the three-day period occurs in Mari text 26 368: "And about the sons of Mutiabal [who] ran away from battle and entered Yamutal, Hammu-Rabi had written to Rim-Sin about calling those men to account, and he answered as follows: He (said), 'Don't you know that I love life? Those [men]— once, twice, I have . . . them to the interior of my land. *I will give them time to calm their hearts* and send them back to you.' This he wrote to him" (Heimpel, *Letters to the King*, 322 [emphasis added]). Joseph gives his brothers three days to calm their hearts after he accuses them of being spies. The lingering fear or terror experienced by the brothers reflects their guilt.

[65] Sternberg (*Poetics*, 288) comments, "The trumped-up charge makes sense not only as a prelude to retribution but also as the first step in the tit-for-tat

His new arrangement demands that *one* brother be left behind, while
the remaining *nine* retrieve the youngest brother—a scenario that
comes closest to the original event of Joseph's abandonment (v. 20).
Joseph clearly intends to authenticate the brotherhood through this
test and, if necessary, move the brothers through a refinement experience of their own. The details replicate Joseph's own experience.[66]
His test demands an active (obedient) answer to the question, "Will
they abandon yet another brother?"[67] While the conversation of the
brothers in verses 21–22 acknowledges the events of the past, their
words fall short and mean little. Joseph's "test" (בחן) intends to move
the brothers toward an authentic loyalty.[68]

The nature of Joseph's test receives further clarification in the
immediate context. First, the *testing* (בחן) of the *words* (דברים) for *truth*
(אמת) in 42:16 and 20 examines the sincerity of their claim to familial
loyalty (42:11, 13). Alter comments,

---

process itself, for it reenacts the final phase of Joseph's own suffering: vilification,
by Potiphar's wife, leading to imprisonment."

[66] Weinfeld ("Covenant Grant," 194) comments that the gift of land to
Abraham and kingship to David is formulated in familial language that reflects
diplomatic vocabulary of the second millennium (i.e., fathership=suzerainty,
sonship=vassalship, and brotherhood=parity relationship). This study recognizes that the idea of testing as it is portrayed in the ancient Near East is also
contemporary to this same period.

[67] Longacre calls Benjamin an "echo or reflection of Joseph himself" and
suggests that the macrostructure of Genesis 42–44 requires that the testing of
the brothers must precede their reconciliation with Joseph—this would not have
been accomplished by means of just their salvation from starvation (*Joseph*, 50).

[68] According to Gen 37:25, after the fratricidal event the brothers sit down
to have a meal (lit. "eat bread"). The possible allusion to the common ancient
Near Eastern practice of sealing a covenant with a meal seems clear. Walter
McCree, "The Covenant Meal in the Old Testament," *JBL* 45 (1926): 120–28; see
also Dennis J. McCarthy, "Three Covenants in Genesis," *CBQ* 26 (1964): 184–85,
189. After dissolving brotherhood with one brother, they reconfirm their brotherhood to each other. This demonstration of brotherhood functions as a foil to
the brotherhood Joseph asks for in Genesis 42.

But the test has a profound logical function in the oblique interrogation of brothers: if in fact they have left Benjamin unharmed all these years, the truth of their words will be confirmed, that, despite past divisiveness, "we are twelve . . . brothers, the sons of one man."[69]

In this context an understanding of בחן as "touchstone" assists in our understanding of Joseph's intended test.[70] The occasion Joseph creates by the demands of Genesis 42:18–20 links to the original loyalty that was alluded to in Joseph's dream (cf. 37:5–7). While Joseph's actions may be interpreted as harsh, it is important that this test not be completely disassociated with Joseph's own refinement experience. The text offers clues that this association be made. The first phrase in 42:18–20, "Do this and live, for I fear God," forms an inclusio with the last phrase, "and you will not die," that highlights the potential *life and well-being* of Jacob's family. Clearly Joseph emerges from his Egyptian experience with loyal intentions toward his family, fulfilling Jacob's initial charge to "go now and see about the welfare (שלום) of your brothers" (37:14). Now he is ready to act and extend שלום to his family as an extension from that first command. Joseph's concern for Benjamin demonstrates his familial loyalty. Sternberg asks, "What fate (Joseph asks himself) has this gang of fratricides devised for Benjamin,

---

[69] Alter, *Biblical Narrative*, 165. Commenting on Gen 42:20, Jespen (*TDOT* 1:297) states, "Here Joseph has his brothers prove that their word to him was 'true, reliable,' thus that a person could rely on their word."

[70] Waltke (*Genesis*, 541) recognizes that Joseph both *tests* and *disciplines* his brothers. In chapter 2, we demonstrated that בחן can bear both of these nuances. Joseph's strategy encompasses the metallurgical activities of both refining and testing/authenticating. Hamilton (*Genesis*, 522) recognizes the metallurgical implications of the term בחן in this text and suggests that Joseph's test intends to determine the value of something—in this case the truthfulness of the brothers and their words. Joseph authenticates his brothers just as metals are tested and authenticated (cf. Jer 6:27; Ps 66:10).

his full brother and the next object of jealousy, allegedly at home now but quite possibly likewise put out of the way?"[71]

Joseph's words "Do this and live!" carry the divine agenda for himself, through whose fidelity the household of Jacob (Israel) will ultimately experience divine blessing and provision in Egypt. Joseph's test shows some similarities with Israel's wilderness experience, where it was Yahweh who led the nation through the wilderness for the purpose of humbling, testing, and determining what was in their hearts (Deut 8:2). The Joseph narrative illustrates for Israel that the fullness of life in covenant relationship requires faith that is accompanied by the demonstration of obedience to God's word (cf. Deut 8:3). Thus, Joseph's words in Genesis 42:18 are similar to the climatic words that Moses delivers to Israel in Deuteronomy 30:15, 19: "See, I have set before you today *life* and prosperity (טוב), and death and adversity. . . . So choose life in order that you may live, you and your descendants" (emphasis added).

Like Moses, Joseph declares the prospect of good to his family in Genesis 50:20: "As for you, you meant evil against me, *but* God meant it for good (טוב) in order to bring about this present result, to preserve many people alive."

Both Joseph and Moses deliver the words of life and blessing to the people of God. Both contexts bring emphasis to the fact that God extends the blessings of life, peace, and good (טוב) to his faithful people (cf. 50:24).[72] Joseph operates like Moses in serving as a mediator of divine blessing to the household of Jacob (Israel).

---

[71] Sternberg, *Poetics*, 289. See also Hamilton, *Genesis*, 522.

[72] In contrast to Joseph, the brothers were unable to trust a brother in Gen 50:15 and apparently fabricated *false words* in vv. 16–18. The theological point is that God works to preserve and maintain his promise of care and blessing despite the group of ambiguously transformed brothers.

Joseph's Fear of God

As we have already said, the "fear of God" attributed to Joseph in Genesis 42:18 designates the positive result for Joseph's refining experience in Egypt. While Joseph may enter Egypt as a spoiled and brattish younger brother, he emerges with a newly forged concern for the *brotherhood* of his family—this entire experience was an implicit test of refinement for Joseph. While our interpretation suggests that Joseph's "fear of God" signals the *loyal* motives behind his treatment of the brothers, others have interpreted this "fear" to suggest that Joseph is merely acting out of a general sense of morality.[73] On this interpretation Joseph acts in moral goodness or kindness toward the brothers by allowing *nine* to carry grain home instead of just *one*.[74] Thus, Joseph's decision is a benevolent gesture—nine mules carry more famine relief grain than one. However, Joseph's actions cannot be interpreted apart from his Egyptian prison experience. Clearly Joseph demonstrates kindness by sending home nine brothers but even more by his decision

---

[73] Westermann (*Genesis*, 109–10) suggests that the functional interpretation for Joseph's "fear" is that it offers "the reason why he mitigates the measures he has taken." He suggests that this fear was "a widespread notion, at work in many religions, that God or the gods protects the defenseless stranger." He links this "fear" to Gen 20:11. Weinfeld (*Deuteronomic School*, 274–75) links יראת אלהים in Deut 25:18 and the sense of general morality to Elohistic passages such as Gen 20:11 and 42:18. Weinfeld contends that it was Joseph's general sense of morality that prevented him from arresting *all* ten of his brothers. While Joseph certainly acted morally, his fear describes his *obedience* before Yahweh, who was with him throughout his testing in Egypt.

[74] Wenham (*Genesis 16–50*, 408) comments that "the God-fearing man is one who cares for the needy and hungry." On one level Wenham is certainly correct. However, the broader context brings together "test" and "fear," and the mediatorial role of Joseph aligns him too closely with Abraham in Genesis 22 for "fear" here to mean only general morality. Hamilton (*Genesis*, 525) links Genesis 22 and Genesis 42 on the idea of testing but not fearing. This study recognizes that both concepts function necessarily in Genesis 42. While in the past it took *ten* brothers to enact a covenant against Joseph, now Joseph intends to see if *nine* will do the same.

not to take revenge against the brotherhood.[75] This brotherly encounter reverses the previous one where Joseph was left for dead. Instead of revenge Joseph's actions demonstrate consistency with his status as one who fears God, a loyal disposition forged through Joseph's Egyptian experience.[76]

Wolff expressed similar theological concerns for the relationship between fear and testing in the patriarchal development of the theme of "fear." He posits an intentional transformation from the older idea of "fear" as *general morality* to the more specific covenant idea of *obedience*.[77] Though using source critical assumptions, Wolff credits the Elohist with the shift from נסה in Genesis 22:1 to בחן in Genesis 42:15, 20 as an intentional way to describe Joseph's treatment of his brothers. He comments,

> They are to be tested to see whether or not they are spies,
> whether they are still ruled by their old animosity, or whether
> they can be reformed.[78]

---

[75] Joseph is portrayed as both Jacob, whose faith is transformed and then tested in the encounter with Esau, and Esau, who emerges from personal and implied transformation and demonstrates loyalty to the family of Jacob.

[76] In personal conversation at the University of Durham in 2005, Professor Walter Moberly commented that Joseph's Egyptian experience was transformative and the reason Joseph treats his brothers kindly in Genesis 42. He recognized further links between Joseph's experience and Israel's experience in the wilderness. Whereas Israel learned fidelity through deprivation, Joseph learned fidelity through captivity.

[77] Westermann (*Genesis*, 109–10) recognizes ambiguity in Joseph's "fear" but remains with the majority view that regards Joseph as acting in kind toward his brothers. He summarizes the four basic positions as general universal morality (e.g., Gunkel, Skinner, Weinfeld, Moberly, Westermann), loyalty to one's word (e.g., Wolff), contextually in the theology of history (e.g., Schmitt, Ruppert), and an ironic statement (e.g., Redford). We concur with Wolff.

[78] Ibid.

I appreciate Wolff's recognition of the theological links between Genesis 22 and 42, for his interpretation of בחן in this context supports the metallurgical nuance that was developed earlier for this same term.

On further analysis the interpretation of Joseph's fear as *general morality* does not seem to be supported by the details of the narrative. Joseph's decision to send *nine* brothers intentionally (and necessarily) involves *all* the brothers in the test of brotherhood. It is significant that any hope of the test restoring the loyal disposition of the brotherhood requires that *all available* brothers experience the conditions set by Joseph. Certainly any *kind* intentions that Joseph may have had for his brothers are quickly dashed when the returned money is discovered (v. 42:28).[79] Furthermore, the question of whether the brothers will again leave behind one of their own can only be answered if the remaining nine brothers are sent. Joseph intends to authenticate the loyalty of all the brothers, who have already offered their hollow *words* of brotherhood: "We are all sons of one man" (42:11) and "Your servants are twelve brothers" (42:13a).[80] The loyal inclinations of the brotherhood remain Joseph's primary concern. Joseph not only wants to know how the brothers have treated Benjamin, *his* brother, but he intends to determine their loyalty toward one of their *own*.[81] Sternberg recognizes that the "role-reversal" created by Joseph duplicates the

---

[79] Sternberg (*Poetics*, 293) notes that the return of all the money was not a *kind* gesture on Joseph's part. He suggests that the returned money moves the scenario closer to the circumstances that surrounded the original sale of Joseph into slavery and raises a new question: "Will they now opt for the brother or for the money?"

[80] Waltke (*Genesis*, 546) argues that Joseph tests the claim of honesty and loyalty. He states, "A covenant family must be more than honest; it must show loving loyalty toward one another. Nevertheless, Joseph will test this claim."

[81] Recall the rivalry between these brothers already established due to the fact that they come from different mothers—Joseph and the younger Benjamin come from the mother (Rachel) who shared greater favor and affection from Jacob. Alter (*Biblical Narrative*, 167) notes that after Joseph hears the remorse of the brothers in v. 22 he still cannot trust them and must go on with his test.

earlier scenario and *tests* whether they will repeat their actions in the choice of brotherly abandonment.[82] Joseph's (and God's) theological lesson is not, "Be *nice* to your brother," but, "Be a *loyal* brother." The questions of "What will the brothers do?" and "What will *a* brother do?" are brought together in the climactic events of Genesis 42. Early evidence for the effectiveness of Joseph's testing scenario appears in the response of the brothers—Joseph's distress has now been transferred to his brothers (v. 21). The comment of Genesis 42:28 offers another significant clue, "And their hearts sank (יצא), and they *turned* trembling to one another, saying, 'What is this that God has done to us?'" Scholars have recognized the metallurgical background for יצא and the meaning of "to come out, lift up."[83] Thus, this term in the context of Joseph's test suggests the exposing or uncovering of the plans and intentions of the brothers, who now felt fully exposed. The net effect appears similar to the ancient touchstone discussed previously. Joseph's test is having an immediate impact on the brothers and anticipates their next move.

Thus, the Joseph narrative makes a vital contribution to the themes of "fear" and "testing" in the Pentateuch. For Israel, Joseph illustrates the quality of faith and loyalty that would have been vital for success in the land. Certainly the idea of brotherhood and loyalty would have been of great theological concern to Israel on the plains

---

[82] Sternberg, *Poetics*, 294. Waltke (*Genesis*, 547) states, "They taste for three days what Joseph had tasted for thirteen years!"

[83] Raymond C. Van Leeuwen ("A Technical Metallurgical Usage of Yṣ'," 112–13) has argued for the metallurgical/testing sense for יצא that parallels the meaning of בחן developed in the last chapter. The metallurgical sense for יצא occurs in biblical contexts such as Prov 25:4b, "Take away the dross from the silver, and there comes out (יצא) a vessel for the smith." Similar to the context of Genesis 42, Job 23:10b also parallels both בחן and יצא in a single verse and a testing context, "*When* He has tried (בחן) me, I shall come forth (יצא) as gold." The fact that it is the *heart* of the brothers that is being *lifted up* also parallels the ancient Near Eastern background concept of the testing of the heart discussed in the last chapter.

of Moab in preparation to enter the land. (In the land it is vital that brothers get along!) Thus for Israel the Joseph narrative illustrates both themes of testing and loyalty that are woven masterfully into the entire narrative of Genesis 37–50. Finally, the Joseph narrative illustrates for Israel the *quality* of covenant faith and fidelity necessary to be prosperous in the land.

Testing in Genesis 43–50

The ambiguity created by the apparent time lapse between Jacob's last words in Genesis 42:38 and the fact that further famine came upon the land (Gen 43:1) before the brothers returned casts doubt on the brotherhood. In this context the inactivity of the brotherhood warrants cause for concern. Joseph's prior words, "Do this and live," are met with the pathetic words of Jacob, "If *it must be* so, then do this" (43:11a). One may ask if this group is *really* concerned about the brother left behind. Jacob's gift list mimics the Ishmaelite gift list of Genesis 37:25 and suggests that a reversal of plot is underway.[84] While Judah's appeal to brotherhood (43:8–10) appears as a ray of hope and signals that the rest of the brothers may also be on the road to recovery as well, the immediate concern of the brothers seems more about famine relief than for a brother in need.

Upon the return to Egypt with gifts and Benjamin in hand, it becomes clear that Joseph plans to escalate the test (בחן) previously enacted (Gen 43:15, 23). This may indeed be because the apparent lapse of time has alerted Joseph to the lack of brotherly concern for Simeon. According to Sternberg, the test of brotherhood regarding Simeon has been "too easy" and inconclusive:

> Too easy, because Simeon is no object of general hatred. Also inconclusive, because the (to Joseph, suspiciously) long delay

---

[84] See also Alter, *Biblical Narrative*, 172.

in the brothers' return to Egypt leaves their motive ambiguous
between starvation and affection. . . . Viewed in the most
charitable light, the test proves only the solidarity among the
ten malcontents. But does fraternal solidarity now extend to
Rachel's sons as well?[85]

The accusation of being spies intensifies to the accusation of being
thieves (44:4–5), and the "words" of the brothers are again tested for
truth (44:10; cf. 42:16). Joseph expands his test to include the additional
option of abandoning yet another of Rachel's sons.[86] The terms of the
test now include Joseph's brother Benjamin.

The narrative signals that a transformation may have begun in the
brothers; they leave the city as "men," but they return to Joseph's house
in apparent solidarity as "Judah *and his brothers*" (Gen 44:14).[87] Judah's
speech appears to extend loyalty to the young Benjamin in verse 16,
"[W]e are my lord's slaves, both we and the one in whose possession
the cup has been found." Joseph appears unmoved by the initial words
of Judah and may even regard Judah to be motivated more by guilt
than by brotherhood (44:17).[88] This new ambiguity warrants further
testing of the brotherhood. Joseph's command in verse 17 forces the
brothers to leave Benjamin behind as a slave. Joseph's command also

---

[85] Sternberg, *Poetics*, 302; see also Waltke, *Genesis*, 559.

[86] Westermann (*Genesis*, 134) comments, "Joseph has thus achieved what
he had intended from the beginning, to restore the original grouping.
In Genesis 37, the event that brought about the breach took place between the
father, the brothers, and the youngest son. It is so again. What will the brothers
do? Judah gives the answer in his address."

[87] Sternberg, *Poetics*, 305.

[88] Alter (*Biblical Narrative*, 174) interprets Judah's speech positively, calling
it "a point-for-point undoing, morally and psychologically, of the brothers' earlier violation of fraternal and filial bonds." Westermann (*Genesis*, 137) is satisfied
that the brothers have changed based on Judah's admission of their corporate
guilt in v. 16. However, the mere admission of guilt may not reflect the fundamental change Joseph seeks in his brothers. He wants to see *proof* of brotherhood, and this strong desire fuels the strong words of v. 17.

moves the brotherhood to make a clear choice: the sons of Jacob must demonstrate loyalty to another son of Rachel or commit fratricide all over again. Judah's speech expresses the long-awaited fidelity hoped for by Joseph (44:18–34). Judah's willingness to sacrifice himself for a brother *authenticates* his brotherhood before Joseph.[89] Alter comments:

> Twenty-two years earlier, Judah engineered the selling of
> Joseph into slavery; now he is prepared to offer himself as a
> slave so that the other son of Rachel can be set free. Twenty-two
> years earlier, he stood with his brothers and silently watched
> when the bloodied tunic they had brought to Jacob sent their
> father into a fit of anguish; now he is willing to do anything in
> order not to have to see his father suffer that way again.[90]

Joseph responds kindly. With an overwhelming display of emotion toward his family, he reveals his true identity (45:2–3). Joseph declares his fidelity toward his brothers as he comforts them and reveals to them that despite their evil intentions, the kind intentions of the Lord would prevail and be demonstrated through Joseph's actions:

> I am your brother Joseph, whom you sold into Egypt. Now do
> not be grieved or angry with yourselves, because you sold me
> here, for God sent me before you to preserve life. (vv. 4b–5)

Joseph now stands before his brothers as a *tested* mediator of the divine blessing of God (45:12). Although he demonstrates faithfulness, he

---

[89] Sternberg, *Poetics*, 308. Everett Fox (*In the Beginning: A New English Rendition of the Book of Genesis* [New York: Schocken, 1983], 202) comments, "Only by recreating something of the original situation—the brothers are again in control of the life and death of a son of Rachel—can Joseph be sure that they have changed. Once the brothers pass the test, life and covenant can then continue." Longacre (*Joseph*, 51) observes that Judah's reactions remove all of Joseph's doubts concerning the integrity of his brothers and that Joseph must now convince his brothers that he has forgiven them.

[90] Alter, *Biblical Narrative*, 175.

declares God to be the true hero of the story. What remains to be seen is the full resolution of Joseph's test and concern for the brotherhood in Genesis. Will these brothers ever change?

Joseph's Theological Contribution to Pentateuchal Testing

Genesis 50:20–21 summarizes the primary theological theme for the Joseph narrative:

> As for you, you meant evil against me, *but* God meant it for good in order to bring about this present result, to preserve many people alive. So therefore, do not be afraid; I will provide for you and your little ones.

In verse 24, Joseph continues to assure his brothers of God's blessing and care that he intends to provide for the entire family:

> I am about to die, but God will surely take care of you and bring you up from this land to the land which He promised on oath to Abraham, to Isaac and to Jacob.

Throughout the narrative Joseph fulfills the role of the faithful mediator of God's grace and blessing to a group of unworthy recipients. Furthermore, Joseph's own fidelity to this role was tested at significant junctures. He passed his most severe test in Genesis 42, when he demonstrated loyalty toward the brotherhood despite the temptation to do otherwise. The test Joseph imposed on the brothers illustrates the concern of Yahweh for the loyalty that is demanded by covenant relationship. It is significant to our investigation that the entire testing cycles for both Joseph *and* his brothers are designated as "good" (Gen 50:20). Thus the cycles of testing in the Joseph narrative illustrate that the fires caused by hardship and difficulties— even suffering—are *good* in that they function to produce a more purified and refined loyalty in the life of the covenant member.[91] Thus, it will be important in our later study to note those contexts where testing may be assigned a covenantal function, as a means of refining for the loyalty demanded by covenant relationship. In those contexts suffering and hardship can rightly be identified as good. The Joseph narrative makes significant contributions to the Pentateuch's understanding of testing. First, and in retrospect, Joseph's climactic test in Genesis 42 parallels and extends Abraham's testing described in Genesis. Both contexts portray the testing of a patriarch in an extraordinary situation. Second, and in prospect, Joseph's experience in exile parallels and informs Israel's experience of exile in the wilderness. Both exiles involve the lesson of obedience or loyalty, that "man lives by everything that proceeds out of the mouth of the LORD" (Deut 8:3). In both cases individual (Joseph) and corporate (Israel) testing yield the same result.[92]

Conclusion

The Joseph narrative demonstrates an affinity with the rest of the Pentateuch and its presentation of testing. It demonstrates both implicit and explicit testing. Joseph's time in Egypt represents the implicit

---

[91] This basic idea will be developed more fully in the upcoming chapters. For a full discussion of the meaning of טוב and its function in covenant contexts, see "Appendix B: Covenant *Good* as Functional *Good*." There we explore ancient and biblical contexts for those occurrences where covenants and treaties are described as *good*.

[92] Genesis leaves the loyalty of the brotherhood somewhat ambiguously. The brothers failed by never fully trusting Joseph (Gen 50:15–17). Furthermore, the grudge (שׂטם) that the brothers fear may still remain in Joseph clearly suggests that they cannot yet trust him. Clearly Judah's words of repentance and brotherhood in Gen 44:16 are not shared by all. While Judah appears to speak for his brothers in Gen 44:16ff., by using the first-person plural, the actions of the brothers speak to the contrary. Joseph's response of remorse may reflect his personal realization that his experiment of brotherhood refinement failed.

experiential test of refinement intended to bring about the necessary enhancement of faith and fidelity in Joseph. Through his experience the spoiled younger brother of Genesis 37 transforms into the mature and tempered leader of Genesis 42. While he has the power to exact full retribution against his brothers, Joseph acts loyally toward his family and seeks to help the sons of Jacob (Israel) learn the lesson of brotherhood themselves. This lesson for the brotherhood occurs in the midst of a testing scenario that begins with Joseph's properly executed commands as an Egyptian and concludes with Joseph fulfilling the role of the faithful (and tested) mediator of divine grace and blessing as a brother. Joseph's declaration in Genesis 50:20 attributes *good* to the testing cycle that involved hardship and even suffering for both Joseph and his brothers.

Theologically the Joseph narrative contributes to the unified theme of testing for the remainder of Genesis. First, Joseph's experience parallels Abraham's testing in Genesis 22 in that both patriarchs model covenant fidelity for Israel in response to an experience of refinement. Second, the next chapter will demonstrate how Joseph's experience anticipates Israel's wilderness experience and again serves as a model of covenant fidelity for Israel, who also has experienced national refinement in the wilderness and is preparing for its next big test of faith. This aspect of the Joseph narrative will be consistent with Deuteronomy's theological vantage point that states the divine purpose behind Israel's testing experience. In his context Moses addresses this new *authenticated* generation as having learned obedience through the experience of hardship and humility—lessons vital for their journey ahead. The Joseph narrative illustrates and confirms two significant covenant themes for Israel. First, the unique relational status of God's faithful often involves the testing of their faith; such testing often requires that the faithful (and unfaithful) endure hardship and suffering—and according to Joseph, this aspect of covenantal testing is *good*. Second, the Joseph narrative demonstrates how God extends covenant blessing to his people (Israel) through the faithfulness of an individual (Joseph). Both of these themes will be explored further in the next chapter.

Practically, modern believers need to hear the encouraging message of Joseph on the theme of testing. Those struggling with difficulties, such as loss of job or rejection by family members, need an invitation to identify with Joseph's situation. What does it look like to remain faithful amid great trials? Where is God when I am struggling? How might God use my present circumstances, though harsh, to advance his agenda for my life and even in the lives of others? The Joseph narrative's focus on testing addresses these questions for the modern reader.

CHAPTER 3

TESTING AS A UNIFIED PENTATEUCHAL THEOLOGICAL THEME

This chapter examines the Pentateuch's presentation of testing. Examples are organized along the broad categories for testing discussed in chapter 1: tests that check for faith and tests that refine and enhance faith. These categories will allow for an examination of a much broader biblical context where testing can occur both explicitly and implicitly. This examination demonstrates that the Pentateuch as a whole shares an internal consistency with regard to its presentation of this significant biblical theme.

Testing that Authenticates Faith

This category of testing anticipates the loyal response of the faithful to the verbally delivered demand of a superior member of the relationship. In the biblical context this faith or loyalty is confirmed through demonstrated obedience and often in the context of covenant relationship. Testing that authenticates faith will occur in contexts that demonstrate explicit use of key terminology, as well as in contexts where testing must be identified implicitly through more subtle use of testing concepts.

The Testing of Abraham

The theology of testing in the Abraham narrative begins with one of the most significant commands in Scripture, "Go forth from your country, and from your relatives and from your father's house, to the land which I will show you" (Gen 12:1). This verbal command represents the aural component of Abraham's test of faith. From this context two key terms emerge that signal patriarchal testing in later narratives. First, the imperative לֵךְ ("go"), which occurs repeatedly in the patriarchal narratives (e.g., Gen 12:1, 19; 22:2; 24:51; 27:3, 9; 42:33; see also Exod 12:32; Num 17:11), signals the fundamental test of loyalty. In the Pentateuch the command to "go" often leads to a response by which the quality of one's loyalty is both demanded and measured. The blessing of seed and land frequently requires this demonstration of fidelity by the covenant member, which is often directly linked to the fidelity of the patriarch.[1] Thus, the unique mediatorial role of the tested patriarch is central to patriarchal testing as was evident in Joseph, and now Abraham.[2] Both tested patriarchs will be used by God to extend blessing to their respective families.

---

[1] This phrase in Gen 12:1 forms an inclusio with Gen 22:2 and links the promises of Gen 12:3 and Gen 22:18 with regards to seed. See Bruce Waltke, *Genesis: A Commentary* (Grand Rapids: Zondervan, 2001), 196. T. Desmond Alexander ("Abraham Re-Assessed Theologically: The Abraham Narrative and the New Testament Understanding of Justification by Faith," in *He Swore an Oath: Biblical Themes from Genesis 12–50*, ed. Richard S. Hess, Gordon J. Wenham, and Philip E. Satterthwaite [Grand Rapids: Baker, 1994], 9n4) recognizes that the divine speeches in 12:1–3 and 22:15–18 form an inclusio and frame the entire unit of chapters 12–22.

[2] David Clines (*The Theme of the Pentateuch*, JSOTSup 10 [Sheffield: JSOT, 1978], 29) finds unity within the Pentateuch on this theme of the faith of the

The second key term is ראה ("to see"), which signals a visual confirmation of the loyalty that Yahweh demonstrates in response to Abraham's obedience (cf. Gen 12:1; 13:14–15; 22:2, 13; 24:63; 27:1; 33:1). We have seen that authentication of loyalty in the ancient world often involved the *visual* examination of an individual's words or deeds. In the Abraham narrative, as well as other biblical contexts, the ideas of *seeing* and *lifting one's eyes* often focus attention on the divine fidelity demonstrated through signs and miraculous events—in them, the covenant member is reminded of God's covenant faithfulness. These themes of "testing" and "seeing" are closely linked in the Abraham narrative. The climax of Abraham's testing cycle in Genesis 22, for example, will include seven references to sight or visual examination.

Abraham demonstrates immediate fidelity to the aurally delivered command of Genesis 12:4.[3] However, Abraham's faith, similar to that of younger Joseph in Egypt, is also tested and refined through a series of hardships and difficulties.[4] Early in his testing cycle Abraham

---

patriarch and promised blessing. Deryck C. T. Sheriffs ("Faith," in *Dictionary of the Old Testament Pentateuch*, ed. T. Desmond Alexander and David W. Baker [Downers Grove, IL: InterVarsity, 2003], 282) recognizes the theme of "faith" throughout the Abraham, Isaac, Jacob, and Joseph narratives that begins with the promise of Gen 12:1–3. He regards Gen 12:1 and Gen 50:24 as bookends to this theme.

[3] Waltke (*Genesis*, 206, 216) observes that Abraham's response aligns with the command in Gen 12:1. Gordon Wenham ("The Face at the Bottom of the Well: Hidden Agendas of the Pentateuchal Commentator," in *He Swore an Oath: Biblical Themes from Genesis 12–50*, ed. Gordon J. Wenham, Richard S. Hess, and Phillip E. Satterthwaite [Grand Rapids: Baker, 1994], 204) notes that despite his failure, the divine promise of Gen 22:16–18 assures that the rewards of Abraham's obedience in Gen 12:7 are secure (cf. 13:14–17).

[4] Jo Milgrom (*The Binding of Isaac: The Aḳedah-A Primary Symbol in Jewish Thought and Art* [Berkeley, CA: BIBAL, 1988], 60–62) develops this visual emphasis in the midrashic interpretations of the ten trials of Abraham. Sheriffs (*The Friendship of the Lord* [Carlisle: Paternoster, 1996], 47–48) recognizes that Abraham's covenant relationship was tested at every juncture throughout the narrative.

fails to demonstrate the quality of faith necessary to stand against the potential threats to the divine promise of seed.[5] Unlike Joseph, who emerges positively from his Egyptian (exilic) experience, Abraham will, for the moment, remain as a floundering patriarch. Significantly, it takes the words of a pagan king in Genesis 12:19, "Take . . . and go," to repeat the divine mandate of Genesis 12:1 and thus redirect Abraham to his divinely mandated destination. However, and just like Joseph's, Abraham's faith is necessarily tested and refined through a process *before* it is called upon at another pivotal moment in his life.[6]

As with Joseph, Yahweh remains *with* Abraham throughout his period of refinement and hardship. Yahweh visits Abraham at a time of personal struggle and reminds him of his loyalty in dramatic fashion.[7] In Genesis 15:1–6, Abraham receives encouragement in two ways. First, Yahweh affirms his loyalty to Abraham with the words "Do not fear" (15:1). This phrase is common in ancient treaty language to encourage fidelity in covenant relationship (e.g., 1 Sam 23:17; Jer 30:10; 46:27), often in the context of the threat that the vassal would transfer his allegiance to another covenant partner.[8] Second, Yahweh counters Abraham's doubt in Genesis 15:2–3 with a confirmation of

---

[5] Israel's own history parallels the testing cycles of both Abraham and Joseph and the refinement of faith that was necessary prior to the climactic testing event—for Abraham, the offering of Isaac; for Joseph, his encounter with the brothers; and for Israel, the conquest of the land.

[6] The expressions in Gen 13:14–15, "Lift up your eyes and look" and "The land which you see," signal that Yahweh has not wavered on his promises. Paul Kalluveettil (*Declaration and Covenant: A Comprehensive Review of Covenant Formulae from the Old Testament and the Near East*, AnBib 88 [Rome: Biblical Institute, 1982], 180ff) recognizes that this command parallels the initial imperative in Gen 12:1.

[7] Waltke (*Genesis*, 239) recognizes that the conditional aspects of Yahweh's commitment to Abraham are transformed into unconditional commitments toward Israel in Gen 15:1–21, and to the nations in Gen 17:1–27. The unconditionality of Yahweh's fidelity and the extent of his blessing will be dramatically portrayed in the metaphors of the night sky, as well as the sands of the ocean.

[8] Kalluveettil, *Declaration*, 127. See also H.-P. Stähli, *TLOT*, 2:573–74.

loyalty that involved both words (15:4) and the visual demonstration and reminder of divine faithfulness (15:5). Yahweh's command to "now look to the heavens" signals the visual demonstration of divine fidelity emphatically captured by the night sky.[9] This divine confirmation aligns with Abraham's inner confirmation in Genesis 15:6a, "Then he believed (הֶאֱמִן) in the LORD; and He reckoned it to him as righteousness."[10] Abraham's response parallels the prophetic words in Nehemiah 9:8a, "You found his heart faithful before You, and made a covenant with him."[11] Once authenticated, Abraham's covenant status

---

[9] In west Texas one can visit the McDonald Observatory located in the Davis mountain range. On most nights one can try to count the stars; for believers it can be a time for reverent awe! Sheriffs (*Friendship of the Lord*, 284) comments on the relationship between "seeing" and "believing" in Exodus–Deuteronomy, "The 'believing' the Israelites did was based on seeing a demonstration, not on propositions and concepts that are invisible or a God who is hidden" (cf. Exod 4:8, 17, 28, 30; 7:3; 8:23[19]; 10:1–2; Num 14:11, 22; Deut 6:22; 7:19; 11:3; 26:8; 29:3[2]; 34:11).

[10] Kalluveettil (*Declaration*, 188ff) finds this same meaning for הֶאֱמִן in 1 Sam 27:12, where Achish believed David on the demonstration of his fidelity after attacking his own people. The term occurs twenty-three times in the Old Testament and often conveys the sense of "believing" in the same manner as Gen 15:6 (Exod 14:31; 19:9; Num 14:11; 20:12; Deut 1:32; 2 Kgs 17:14; Jonah 3:5; Ps 78:22; 2 Chr 20:20. See also H. Wildberger, *TLOT*, 1:142–45; R. W. L. Moberly, "אמן," in *NIDOTTE* 1:427–33). Sheriffs (*Friendship of the Lord*, 19n23) notes that wholehearted loyalty in biblical and ancient Near Eastern covenant relationships demanded an inward orientation consistent with an "outward complicity" to the covenant stipulations. For the purposes of this study, the term אמן conveys the resulting status of a covenant member who has been "tested" and demonstrates fidelity in return. Thus, in our context אמן signals a turning point for Abraham, who has matured through his personal trials.

[11] Alfred Jespen ("אמן *'A¯man*," in *TDOT* 1:296) recognizes the ambiguity of Neh 9:8 but suggests that אמן there refers to the demonstrated fidelity of Genesis 22 on the basis of a similar reference in Sirach 44:20, where Abraham is tested (נסה) and found faithful (נאמן) (see also 1 Macc 2:52). Sheriffs (*DOTP*, 283) links the concept of "faith" to "loyalty" on the grounds of covenant relationship. This study recognizes that Abraham's response and the divine evaluation in Gen 15:6 anticipates the divine designation in Gen 22:12.

is confirmed as "righteous" (צדק) in Genesis 15:6b.[12] This transaction
of fidelity between suzerain and vassal is appropriately followed by
a covenant ceremony (15:9–21).[13] This authentication of faith anticipates Abraham's climactic testing in Genesis 22, where his loyalty is
revealed through his actions and affirmed in terms of his *fear*.

Genesis 20 continues Abraham's cycle of testing through hardships and conflicts in a foreign land. For example, Abraham's response
to Abimelech in Genesis 20:2 appears inconsistent with the loyalty
recently confirmed in Genesis 15:6. This episode highlights the *consistency* of Yahweh's fidelity despite Abraham's *inconsistency* and repeated
failure.[14] In contrast to Abraham, Abimelech emerges as the one who
demonstrates loyalty in response to Yahweh's visitation (Gen 20:3–8).
Abimelech's fidelity emerges as an ironic response to Abraham's statement, "Because I thought, surely there is no fear of God in this place"

---

[12] John Gibson (*Textbook of Syrian Semitic Inscriptions: Aramaic Inscriptions*
[Oxford: Clarendon, 1995], 82) cites from inscription B1 from the Barrakkab
Inscriptions line 4 רבעי ארקא בצדק אבי ובצד and notes that צדק is best translated as the loyalty demonstrated by an inferior to a superior. Moshe Weinfeld
("The Covenant of Grant in the Old Testament and Ancient Near East," *JOAS*
90 [1970]: 186n17) translates צדקה in the Panamuwa inscriptions (KAI 215:19;
216:4–7; 218:4) as "loyalty or faithfulness" in the phrase בצדק אבי ובצדקי הוש
על כרסא אבי . . . בני מראי "because of my father's and my own loyalty, the king
has established me on the throne of my father." Weinfeld finds this same idea
in 1 Kgs 3:6.

[13] Waltke (*Genesis*, 245) recognizes that the sequence of the covenant declaration coming after the demonstrated loyalty suggests a similarity to the ancient
Near Eastern land grant. For a fuller discussion of Gen 15:12–21 in light of its
ancient Near Eastern context, see Weinfeld, "Covenant Grant," 196–200; idem.,
"*Berît*- Covenant vs. Obligation," *Bib* 56 (1975): 120–28.

[14] The motif of the disruption of family loyalty is common in the patriarchal narratives and will play an important role in the Joseph narrative. There
the brother's breech of familial loyalty serves as a foil against Joseph's consistent
demonstration of loyalty toward them. This event also demonstrates the inter-
relatedness of the familial and divine components of covenant relationship.

(Gen 20:11).[15] Wenham recognizes this irony and comments, "Abraham, while explaining his motives, actually condemns himself out of his own mouth."[16] Thus, Abimelech receives the indirect designation as "God fearer." Clearly Abimelech's success serves as a foil to Abraham's failure.[17] Recognizing the dual nature of the testing for both Abraham and Abimelech, Wolff comments:

> Abraham is acquitted but at the same time condemned because he did not take into account the fear of God in that place. . . . Does not this key show that the story is now thought of as a two-fold temptation? Who was really tempted more severely, Abraham or Abimelech? The point was to test the fear of God in both parties to the action.[18]

---

[15] Claus Westermann (*Genesis 12–366: A Commentary*, 2nd ed., trans. John J. Scullion [Minneapolis: Augsburg, 1985], 322) suggests that the narrative emphasis is on Abimelech and his immediate obedient response to the divine command of v. 7.

[16] Wenham, *Genesis 16–50*, 72. Von Rad (*Genesis: A Commentary*, rev. ed., trans. John H. Marks [Philadelphia: Westminster, 1973], 229) comments, "It is humiliating for Abraham to have to be surpassed by the heathen in the fear of God." He regards "fear of God" as "reverence and regard of the most elementary moral norms" and chooses the nuance of "obedience" for the idea of "fear" both here and in Gen 22:12 and 42:18.

[17] While Genesis 22 portrays Abraham as a model of covenant fidelity, Genesis 20 portrays him as a model of covenant failure. The relationship of testing and fear in this context supports the interpretation of the phrase "fear of God" as an indirect reference to Abimelech's obedience to God. This reading of the text supports the theological and covenantal concerns in other contexts where fear and testing occur together. The interpretation of "fear of God" as general morality detracts from this theological emphasis.

[18] Hans W. Wolff ("The Elohistic Fragments in the Pentateuch," *Int* 26 [1972]: 162–63) maintains that the Elohist regards the "fear of God" as a universal obedience to the protective will of God and a respect for the rights of aliens. Against the idea of "fear of God" as "general morality," we suggest that the theological juxtaposition of Abimelech with Abraham favors the meaning of covenantal obedience.

This contrast between Abraham and Abimelech, where the failure of one is set as a foil against the success of another, parallels the Joseph narrative, where the failure of the brothers functions as a foil for Joseph's success. While Joseph received the designation as "God fearer," the narrative leaves this designation open-ended for the brothers. For Abraham the designation "God fearer," missing in Genesis 20, will soon be assigned to him in Genesis 22:12 at Mount Moriah.

The testing cycle that began in Genesis 12 reaches its climax in Genesis 22:1–19 for Abraham. The narrative signals Abraham's test in several ways.[19] First, the primary testing term נסה identifies the coming event as a *test* for the patriarch.[20] Second, the imperatives "take" and "go" in verse 2 function as the *aural* component of Abraham's test. Here blessing of the promised seed will entirely depend on the faithfulness of the patriarch (cf. Gen 12:1–3). Third, the reference to "Moriah" builds on ראה ("to see") and further emphasizes testing through the visual examination of the loyalty that will be on display from, in this example, both covenant members.[21] Thus, "Moriah" anticipates the

---

[19] For a summary of the history of exegesis on Gen 22:1–19, see Westermann, *Genesis 12–36*, 354.

[20] Following G. Gerleman ("נסה *Nsh* Pi. to Test," in *TLOT* 2:742), Waltke (*Genesis*, 304) suggests that in this context נסה means "to test another to see whether the other proves worthy." Westermann (*Genesis 12–36*, 355) recognizes the tripartite sequence for נסה in the context of Genesis 22 as follows: the assignment of a task to the one tested, the execution of the task, and the determination of whether the test was passed. Wenham (*Genesis 16–50*, 103–4) renders נסה as a test that demonstrates true character through hardship and cites the biblical examples of Sheba and Solomon (1 Kgs 10:1), Daniel and his companions (Dan 1:12, 14), Israel in the wilderness (Exod 15:25; 16:4; 20:20; Deut 8:2, 16), false prophets (Deut 13:4[3]), and foreign oppression (Judg 2:22; 3:1, 4) where this same meaning is found. Wenham suggests that Deut 8:2 defines Hebrew נסה.

[21] Moberly ("Commentary," 306–7) recognizes a link between "Moriah" and the temple at Jerusalem on two grounds. First, *places of seeing* are generally linked either to Sinai (e.g., Exod 24:9–11; 33:11–34:35; 1 Kgs 19:9–18) or to Jerusalem (2 Sam 24:15–17; Isa 6:1). Moberly recognizes the explicit link in 2 Chr 3:1, where Mount Moriah is designated as the site of the temple. Second,

visual demonstration of loyalty between two covenant members in several ways.[22] First, Abraham responds to the divine commands with a three-day journey.[23] In addition, it is on the mountain of *seeing* that Yahweh provides a lamb! Finally, Abraham demonstrates his willingness to follow through with the command that involves his son of blessing. The result of Abraham's authentication earns him the designation of "God fearer" (22:12).[24] In response Abraham confirms the event by naming the place in verse 14.

Moberly regards the phrase, "mountain of Yahweh," in Gen 22:14b, as an allusion to the temple in Jerusalem (cf. Ps 24:3; Isa 2:3). Given that the visual emphasis is repeated eight times in Gen 22:1–19, the link of "Moriah" to this same theological emphasis will be appreciated here.

[22] H. Seesemann (*TDOT* 6:256) recognizes Abraham's test as a test of faith or fidelity and makes a conceptual link to Sinai, where God's people are tested by means of Torah.

[23] The "three day" period between a stipulation and its fulfillment signals a heightened tension for the reader. Joseph will assign his brothers to confinement for three days. Waltke (*Genesis*, 307; see also Victor P. Hamilton, *The Book of Genesis,* NICOT [Grand Rapids: Eerdmans, 1995], 107) notes that a three-day period is a common duration for a preparation time prior to an important event (cf. Gen 31:22; 42:18; Exod 3:18; 15:22; 19:11, 15–16; Num 10:33; 19:12, 19; 31:19; 33:8; Esth 5:1; Hos 6:2; Jonah 3:3).

[24] See Wolff ("Elohistic Fragments," 158–73), who recognizes the "fear of God" as the major theological theme of the Elohist. Against Wolff, Westermann (*Genesis 12–36*, 362) suggests that ירא אלהים is not uniformly presented in the Elohistic texts of Gen 20:1–18; 22:1–19; 42:18; Exod 1:17–21; 18:21; and 20:18b–21. Von Rad (*Genesis*, 241–42) adds to the discussion: "Where the phrases 'fear of God' and 'fearing God' occur in the Old Testament, they refer not to a particular form of strong emotions but rather to their consequence, i.e., to obedience (Gen. 20:11; 42:18; II Kgs 4:1; Isa. 11:2; Prov. 1:7; Job 1:1, 8)." Waltke (*Genesis*, 308) comments, "The 'Fear of God' entails an obedience to God's revelation of his moral will, whether through conscience or Scripture, out of recognition that he holds in his hands life for the obedient and death for the disobedient." While "fear" certainly involves moral behavior, the meaning of covenant obedience gains support from the wider biblical context.

Abraham called the name of that place Yahweh *will see* (ראה)
as it is said to this day, "In the mount of the Yahweh *it will be
seen* (ראה)" (author's translation and emphasis).

Abraham's designation and use of ראה highlights the visual confirmation of loyalty demonstrated between two covenant partners.[25]
Genesis 22:15–18 maintains that this loyalty is grounded in *both* the
unconditionality of Yahweh's promises and the conditional response
of the patriarch. On this point Moberly comments:

> Abraham by his obedience has not qualified to be the recipient
> of blessing, because the promise of blessing had been given to
> him already. Rather, the existing promise is reaffirmed but its
> terms of reference are altered. A promise which previously
> was grounded solely in the will and purpose of Yahweh is
> transformed so that it is now grounded *both* in the will of
> Yahweh *and* in the obedience of Abraham. It is not that the
> divine promise has become contingent upon Abraham's
> obedience, but that Abraham's obedience has been incorporated
> into the divine promise. Henceforth Israel owes its existence not
> just to Yahweh but also to Abraham.[26]

---

[25] Hamilton (*Genesis*, 112) notes the intentional use of יראה ("provide=lit.
see") (v. 8) and ירא ("fear") (v. 12) as two words that sound alike and thus place
emphasis on the divine intention behind the test, that is, the name of the place
יהוה יראה, "Yahweh will *see*." This term indicates the divine intent of Yahweh
to confirm Abraham's loyalty.

[26] Moberly ("Commentary," 318) holds together the tension between the
conditionality and unconditionality of the patriarchal covenants. Moshe Weinfeld ("The Covenant Grant in the Old Testament and Ancient Near East," *JAOS*
90 [1970]:184–203) argues that the patriarchal covenants are unilateral on the
basis of their similarities to the ancient Near Eastern land grants. T. Desmond
Alexander ("Genesis 22 and the Covenant of Circumcision," *JSOT* 25 [1983]:
17–22) argues that the conditionality of the Abrahamic covenant in Genesis 22
is a continuation of the conditionality previously established in Genesis 17. It
is clear that the essence of testing requires the demonstration of fidelity on the
part of the inferior member of covenant relationship. While the covenant in

Thus, like Joseph, Abraham fulfills the role of the faithful (and tested) covenant mediator through the events of Genesis 22:1–14. The speech of the divine messenger (22:15–18) confirms that it was Abraham's loyal activity working with the loyal activity of Yahweh that mediated divine blessing to his immediate family, as well as to future generations of faithful. Significantly for Israel, Abraham functions as a model of covenant obedience and fulfills the necessary mediatorial role in Israel's salvation history.[27]

The Testing of the Midwives

The malicious command of Pharaoh in Exodus 1:16 to kill all male Israelite children at birth represents a test of disobedience for the midwives, Shiphrah and Puah.[28] The political crisis in Egypt (1:8) threatens the fulfillment of Joseph's words. Israel has long lost the political

---

its essence remains unconditional, the blessings of covenant relationship remain conditional upon the demonstrated loyalty of the inferior member.

[27] Moberly ("Commentary," 321) develops the idea of the faithful covenant mediator from the role Moses plays in Exodus 32–34, where the covenant is renewed despite a disobedient Israel. He recognizes that Moses obeys in response to the faithfulness of Yahweh despite the infidelity of the people. Thus, the obedience of one man continues the promise God has made. While there are no direct recipients of the immediate blessing as a result of Abraham's obedience in Genesis 22, it is apparent that vv. 17–18 defer the blessing to the seed of Abraham. Westermann (*Genesis 12–36*, 356) recognizes that the individual focus of Genesis 22 presupposes a corporate sense of testing. Thus, for Westermann, the testing of Abraham and the term נסה "was forged in the context of God's action in history or Israel's experiences in history."

[28] Brevard Childs (*The Book of Exodus: A Critical, Theological Commentary*, OTL [Philadelphia: Westminster, 1974], 16) acknowledges it is unclear whether these women were Egyptian or Hebrew and suggests that an Egyptian nationality would have strengthened the theological force of their designation as "God fearers." A non-Israelite status for the midwives links them with Abimelech, who as a foreigner also "feared God" by his demonstrated loyalty to God's will. An Israelite status for the midwives aligns them closer to Joseph, who as an Israelite in disguise also "fears God." This ambiguity may intentionally convey

protection Joseph provided (Exod 1:6; cf. Gen 50:19–21). This new crisis precipitates a test of loyalty for the midwives.[29] In their context disobedience to Pharaoh represented obedience to Yahweh, and God responded with his blessing to them (Exod 1:20) and to Israelite children. Like Joseph is in Egypt, the loyalty of the midwives is tested and, as in Joseph's case, obedience by means of disobedience mediates blessing to Israel. By this interpretation "God fearer" in Exodus 1:17 falls in line with both Abimelech and Joseph to describe one who acts in obedience to the will of Yahweh, even as a foreigner (cf. Gen 20:11; 42:18). Thus, the declaration of Exodus 1:17 signals the authentication of midwives fidelity to Yahweh against the aural demand of Pharaoh. By means of demonstrated loyalty, God again extends divine blessing to the sons of Israel (1:20).

The Testing of Moses

The events of the burning bush and the call to ministry in Exodus 3 suggest an implicit test for Moses who, like Joseph, also serves as mediator of covenant blessing to the sons of Israel. In addition, Moses' testing provides several parallels to Abraham's testing in Genesis 22. First, the command to "go" initiates an aural command for both Abraham and Moses (cf. Gen 22:2; Exod 3:10).[30] Further, the response הנני ("Here I am") signals the loyal disposition of the addressee that precedes the aural demands delivered to both Moses and Abraham (cf. Gen 22:1; Exod 3:4b; see also Gen 37:13). Finally, both Exodus 3:1–15

---

the point that regardless of cultic orientation the blessing of God is mediated through the fidelity of the one who is tested.

[29] Sheriffs (*Friendship of the Lord*, 71) regards the fear of the Lord in Exod 1:17 to signal a test of obedience for the Hebrew midwives.

[30] Nahum M. Sarna (*Exodus*, The JPS Torah Commentary Series [Philadelphia: JPS, 1991], 16) suggests that this charge places Moses as the pivot point and human agent for the redemption of Israel. The divine will and the human will become linked to the execution of a single command.

and Genesis 22:1–18 highlight the visual confirmation of loyalty.[31] God confirms his faithfulness on Mount Horeb (Mount Sinai), just as he did on Mount Moriah.[32] However, instead of providing a lamb, God reveals the divine name, יהוה, to Moses as a means of confirming loyalty to him (Exod 3:14–15). Thus, Exodus 3 both looks back to Mount Moriah (Genesis 22) and anticipates Mount Sinai (Exodus 20) for Israel; both mountains offer significant contexts for covenant loyalty to be both tested and confirmed.

The Testing of Israel at Sinai

The events at Sinai illustrate in climactic fashion an aural test for a new nation. Moses sets the agenda in Exodus 19:3–6 and mediates the aural commands of Yahweh to the people; they call for Israel's future and exclusive covenant loyalty and obedience. This call to obedience rests on the foundation of Yahweh's history of demonstrated faithfulness—the parting of the sea, the provision of water and manna in the desert, and protection from enemies, just to name a few.[33] The conditional language in verse 5 qualifies the Hebrew designation סגלה ("treasured possession") as an "already, but not yet" reality for Israel and suggests that Sinai's commands constitute a test that will both reveal (check) and refine (improve) Israel's national fidelity. Yahweh's commands in Exodus 19:4–6 rally the people of God, and the

---

[31] This emphasis occurs six times in Exodus (3:2, 3, 4, 7, 9, 16) and five times in Genesis (22:4, 8, 13, 14a, 14b).

[32] The promised return in Exod 3:12 anticipates the events at Mount Sinai, where Yahweh confirms fidelity and invites Israel to remain loyal covenant partners. Umberto Cassuto, *A Commentary on the Book of Exodus*, 5th ed., trans. Israel Abrahams (Jerusalem: Magnes, 1967), 32.

[33] Exodus 14:30 clearly depicts the impact of this event, where in response to the divine display of fidelity, the people both ירא ("fear") and אמן ("believe") in Yahweh. The provisions of manna, quail, and water in the wilderness of Sin (cf. Exod 16:1–17:7) provide further *visual* demonstrations of God's presence with and fidelity toward the people.

exchange of *words* (19:7–8) confirms the covenant obligations of both covenant members.[34] Israel's response in verse 8 functions similarly to the הנני ("Here I am") uttered by Abraham, Joseph, and Moses and signals Israel's willingness to obey (cf. Gen 22:1; 37:13; Exod 3:4).

More can be said regarding the contextual clues that signal Israel's testing at Sinai. For example, the reference to "three days" signals the preparation for a testing event to come.[35] Like Abraham and Jacob's sons before them, Israel emerges after three days ready to embrace the test. The *aural* nature of the test is made more emphatic for Israel as the "words" or stipulations of covenant obligations are literally *heard* as the sound of thunder and loud trumpets (cf. Exod 19:16, 19; 20:18). This aural emphasis is only matched by Yahweh's *visual* emphasis— the thunder and lightning that is *seen* operates for Israel just as it did for Abraham and confirms the extent of Yahweh's covenant commitment (cf. Gen 15:5).[36] Moses offers the theological present (and future) purpose for the Sinai experience in Exodus 20:20, "Do not be afraid; for God has come in order to test you (נסה), and in order that the fear of Him may remain with you, so that you may not sin." The testing intent specified by the key term נסה suggests that the stipulations of covenant relationship represent an ongoing means by which Israel confirms her covenant fidelity before Yahweh.[37] While Abraham's

---

[34] Kalluveettil (*Declaration*, 32–3) argues that the term דברים commonly signifies the stipulations of the treaty or covenant in ancient Near Eastern contexts.

[35] Genesis 42:17 places the sons of Jacob in prison for three days prior to the beginning of their testing period. A three-day period also preceded Abraham's testing event in Gen 22:4.

[36] Sarna (*Exodus*, 115) calls the *seeing* of sound in this context a "sense paradox" that emphasizes the overpowering presence of the divine. The event remains literally beyond words in the mind of the author. It is recognized here that both senses of "fear" (i.e., "fear" as "religious awe" and "fear" as "future obedience") will have a necessary function in Exod 20:20.

[37] John I. Durham (*Exodus*, WBC [Waco, TX: Word, 1987], 303) summarizes the different interpretations of נסה as the experience of something, a test of faith, a test of obedience, a test of respect, and a test of keeping boundaries. Moshe

"God fearing" status in Genesis 22 comes as an affirmation of loyalty demonstrated, Israel's God-fearing status must await further confirmation on the road ahead. The test (נסה) announces the beginning of Israel's opportunity to demonstrate loyalty and thus maintain the life and blessing Yahweh promises in return. On this point Wolff comments:

> God tests his people through hard trials (*nissāh* in Gen. 22:1 as here in Ex. 20:20). God's normative word from Mount Sinai to all Israel is directed toward the same goal that he had set for the Patriarchs: fear of God, which produced obedience through trust in God's promise (Gen. 22) and which obediently accepts God's assurances and which prefers to disobey human commands rather than fail to follow God's word (*ḥata'*) (Ex. 1:15ff.).[38]

In addition, the intensity of the experience, which includes both sight and sound, serves to ingrain into Israel a corporate "motivating memory" that serves as a deterrent against future disobedience and sin. There is a timeless principle here. Effective teachers and parents are those that win the discipline battle *early* with their young students.[39] From this early warning Moses immediately launches into the first

---

Greenberg ("נסה in Exodus 20:20 and the Purpose of the Sinai Theophany," *JBL* 79 [1960]: 273–76) argues for the meaning of "experience, to have experience of" and cites 1 Sam 17:39 and Deut 28:56 as examples. Seesemann (*TDOT* 6:24) maintains both religious and nonreligious nuances for the root נסה. The proximity of "test" and "fear" sets the covenant context and the meaning of "a test of obedience" for נסה in this context.

[38] Wolff ("Elohistic Fragments," 167) declares: "The most prominent theme of the Elohist is the fear of God. By means of the traditional materials from salvation history the Elohist wanted to lead the Israel of his day through the events in which they were tempted and bring them to new obedience and to new disobedience."

[39] The intensity of the event is also part of the intended purpose, that is, to provide a memory and deterrent to future disobedience.

of the Ten Commandments (Exod 20:1–20; cf. v. 3). Wolff recognizes
a significant link between Exodus 20:20 and Genesis 42:22–28 in the
way that the ideas of fear and recognition of sin motivate individuals
toward obedience.[40] The common terms, phrases, and concepts shared
between Exodus 20, Genesis 22, and the Joseph narrative inform the
theology of testing for an audience concerned with Torah obedience.
This concern was also applicable for Israel on the plains of Moab, preparing to enter a hostile land while keeping covenant fidelity. Our
study ahead will only reveal that the struggle over faith and fidelity
will remain with Israel throughout her entire spiritual history.

Testing that Authenticates and Improves Faith

On some occasions testing as refinement will involve the heat of hardships, difficulties, and even suffering for both the faithful and rebellious
alike. These testing experiences serve to bring about both authentication and improvement in the *quality* of faith and loyalty within the
covenant community. As before, we will investigate both explicit and
implicit testing in various pentateuchal contexts. This test of experience will often employ divinely assigned agents, such as thorns and
thistles, famine, hunger, thirst, marauding bands, and even invading
armies; they all serve as a means of increasing futility. Depending on
the quality of an individual's faith at the start, these experiences are
intended to agitate, frustrate, and ultimately move the individuals
to greater faith, deeper dependence, and purer loyalty. Thus, testing
proves and also *improves* the faith of the covenant member.

---

[40] Wolff, "Elohistic Fragments," 167.

Prepatriarchal Testing

Genesis 2:1–4:26 establishes a foundation for understanding the pentateuchal testing that follows. First, Genesis 2:23–24 highlights the familial basis for covenant relationship. As was already recognized in the Joseph narrative, the testing of brotherhood represents this familial basis for testing and emerges as a significant theme in the Joseph narrative. Through the lives of these patriarchal families, Israel is invited to understand her own relationship to Yahweh. Genesis 2:23 offers the basis of the familial bond common in both biblical and ancient contexts (cf. Gen 29:14; see also Judg 9:3; 2 Sam 5:1; 2 Sam 19:13–14; 1 Chr 11:1).[41] The reference to "becoming one" in verse 24 also recalls the solidarity of covenant relationship common in ancient treaty texts.[42] On the terms of their unique relationship, God extends blessings to Adam and Eve on the condition that the aural demands of Genesis 2:16–17 are met, which constitute the implicit "test" for Adam and Eve.[43] The serpent—who embodies the opposing agenda—questions the command and intensifies the test of obedience with a counterfeit command of his own (Gen 3:1). The failure of Adam and Eve to demonstrate fidelity to God's commands results in their immediate removal from God's presence, an experience common to all humanity. In the wilderness the experience of thorns and thistles work to contain, refine, and transform humanity's rebellion into faith and trust. Through Adam, Israel recognizes the basic logic of testing that

---

[41] For a brief discussion, see Kalluveettil, *Declaration*, 209n45.

[42] Ibid., 102–3.

[43] G. Liedke ("צוה" in *TLOT* 2:1063) suggests that the command (צוה) sets up a limit which has validity beyond the initial situation. He notes that צוה parallels דבר and its function to convey the demands of a special relationship. Sheriffs ("Testing," 831–32) recognizes the similarity between Eden (Gen 2:16–17; 3:11) and the testing of Abraham in that both episodes involve: (1) a divine stipulation that functions to test for obedience and (2) a demonstration of divine initiative, provision, and commitment.

works to refine rebellious humanity through a common and shared experience.

The recognition of testing in Genesis as an expression of the relational aspects of covenant supports the idea that a universal testing or refining experience is common to all. In response to Adam and Eve's failure, God enacts the futility curse in judgment against them. They will experience planting and harvesting, family relationships, and child bearing with an *increased* futility (Gen 3:16–19). Adam's rebellion will have serious relational implications. The created order established by Yahweh for the purpose of covenant expression will now be subjected to futility and will thus operate as an agent of refinement against rebel man.

Beyond Adam, in the life of Noah, the flood account offers early development of the theme of the tested patriarch (Gen 6:1–10:32). First, God commissions Noah for a massive building project (6:14–22). Noah's command to "build" parallels Abraham's aural command to "go" (Gen 12:1–3), in that demonstrated fidelity to both commands extends divine blessing to the family of each tested patriarch (Gen 6:18; cf. 12:2–3). Thus in both contexts the fulfillment of the promise depends on the faithfulness of the patriarch. Both Noah and Abraham share the designation צדק ("righteous") (see 6:9; cf. 15:6). Like Abraham, Noah demonstrates immediate fidelity to the command (6:9; cf. 12:4). Noah also shares in the struggle to maintain faith and fidelity amid the hardship of life (cf. Gen 9:20–28). This test of experience both reveals and confirms Noah's faithfulness before God.[44] Like Abraham, Noah illustrates the *tested* patriarch who extends covenant blessing in response to his testing. Thus, the three narratives of Abraham, Joseph,

---

[44] According to Sheriffs (*Friendship of the Lord*, 27–37), Enoch, Noah, and Abraham are all presented as covenantally loyal under the concept of "walking with God" (cf. Gen 5:22; 6:9; 17:1b; 24:40; 26:3b, 5; 48:15). He recognizes similar phrases that convey loyalty in second millennium Hittite treaty texts.

and Noah demonstrate the similar result that God extends and mediates blessing through the tested and faithful patriarch.[45]

The Testing at Shur and Sin

After leaving Egypt, Israel experiences a series of tests that both authenticate and refine for the faith necessary to enter the land. In route to the Promised Land, Yahweh authenticates his faithfulness toward Israel through a series of miraculous events. Along with the experience of God's miraculous provision, Israel also experiences the hunger and thirst that works to cultivate faith and trust in the Lord.[46] At both Shur and Sin, the central term נסה signals two testing events. This repetition of נסה links these testing events and works to create a progression for the divine commands. The first command issued at Marah represents a general call to covenant obedience and trust. God's continued care and protection in the wilderness are wrapped up in Israel's consistent demonstration of fidelity (cf. Exod 15:26). Thus, Marah illustrates the basic covenant exchange where Yahweh demonstrates fidelity through protection and provision and demands the faithfulness of Israel in return. After two months Yahweh increases the specificity of his command and expectation (15:26). Israel gathers manna for five days, collects a double portion on the sixth day, and then observes the Sabbath on the seventh (16:4–5).[47] Yahweh

---

[45] Weinfeld ("Covenant Grant," 185–86) links the fidelity of Noah described in Gen 6:9 and the key terms הלך, תמים, and צדק to similar phrases used to describe the fidelity of patriarchs in other contexts (cf. Gen 17:1; 24:40; 48:15; for David, see 1 Kgs 3:6; 14:8; 15:3).

[46] H. J. Helfmeyer (*TDOT* 9:450–51) recognizes that the theme of deprivation in Exodus 15 is expanded in the theological reflection of Deuteronomy (cf. Deut 8:1–5, 16), where the wilderness experience disciplines, humbles, and teaches Israel.

[47] Birger Gerhardsson (*Testing of God's Son [Matt. 4:1–11 & Par.]: An Analysis of an Early Christian Midrash*, New Testament Series 2 [Lund: Berlingska

demonstrates fidelity through the provision with the expectation of fidelity in return.[48] Together Shur and Sin anticipate the more comprehensive list of Torah instructions to be delivered at Sinai.[49]

The Testing at Massah

At Massah, Israel's testing as both authentication and refinement continues.[50] In place of quiet (faithful) resolve, the people continue to complain (Exod 17:2). The use of נסה in the question of verse 2b highlights that Israel is not yet demonstrating the faith that Yahweh requires, as Moses exclaims, "Why do you *test* the LORD?" (Exod 17:2, emphasis added; cf. Exod 15:25b; 16:4).[51] In fact, Israel's testing of

---

Bibtryckeriet, 1966], 27) suggests that 16:4 functions as a stipulation by which Israel was tested for covenant loyalty. He links this testing to Exod 20:20.

[48] The word תורתי ("my Torah") in 16:4 seems anachronistic but may also simply mean "teaching, instruction" from the root ירה. In context, "Torah" involves the specific instructions concerning the gathering of manna and the Sabbath. Deuteronomy 8:2–3 suggests that the test in this context subjects Israel to times of hunger as a means of driving them toward utter dependence and faith. See Sarna, *Exodus*, 86. For a fuller treatment of the role of Torah in Israel's covenant community, see Daniel Block, "The Grace of Torah," in *How I Love Your Torah, O LORD!: Studies in the Book of Deuteronomy* (Eugene, OR: Cascade, 2011), 1–20.

[49] Sheriffs (*Friendship of the Lord*, 78n28) comments that the conditional "test" at Marah and use of נסה links the tests in Exod 15:25; 16:4; and 20:20 to that of Abraham in Genesis 22, where נסה also links divine command to personal or corporate obedience.

[50] According to Milgrom (*Binding of Isaac*, 31–33), the water and manna in the desert in Exod 15:25 and 16:4 provide the basis for the testings of Yahweh in Exod 17:2–7 and Ps 78:18. She recognizes these events as failures in the faith and fidelity of the people. While she holds to Greenberg's meaning of "experience" for נסה, it is difficult to apply this meaning to the contexts of Exodus 15–17, where the meaning of "testing" is clearly intended. See Childs, *Exodus*, 344; see also Gerhardsson, *Testing of God's Son*, 25.

[51] Sarna (*Exodus*, 93) notes the theological emphasis of Deut 8:2, 16, where the forty years in the wilderness are interpreted as a period of "testing" (cf. Ps 81:8).

Yahweh signifies just the opposite of faith and fidelity.[52] Again, Yahweh demonstrates his loyal disposition toward the people with a visual sign (17:6). Collectively, these events represent only a portion of the "ten" testings referred to in Numbers 14:22. Thus, Israel's early history of testing God confirms that this generation was not yet capable of demonstrating the level of faith necessary to take the land. Yahweh graciously cannot allow failure as an option at this critical stage in Israel's history!

Testing in the Wilderness

The entire series of events out of Egypt signify the practical beginning of Israel's wilderness experience; Israel enters a classroom that moves the nation toward greater trust and dependence on Yahweh. At Sinai, and at several points along the way, Israel receives the commands or words of Yahweh but also amid their experience of hardship, hunger, and thirst. Israel's first significant authenticating experience occurs at Kadesh, on Canaan's southern border. At Kadesh, Israel fails to trust Yahweh and, by her infidelity, tests Yahweh instead.[53] Yahweh declares, "Surely all the men who have seen My glory and My signs which I performed in Egypt and in the wilderness, yet have put Me to the test these ten times and have not listened to My voice, shall by

---

[52] Cassuto (*Exodus*, 187) suggests that מסה ("Massah") is best translated as "proof," which highlights the testing of Yahweh by the people. Sheriffs (*Friendship of the Lord*, 79n39) identifies the reaction of Israel in Exodus 17 as an "ironic twist" to the previous testing of the people.

[53] R. K. Harrison, *Numbers*, The Wycliffe Exegetical Commentary (Chicago: Moody, 1990), 183. Gerhardsson (*Testing of God's Son*, 28) comments, "To test God is to examine him to see if he will keep his obligations, challenging him to demonstrate his fidelity to the conditions of the covenant. It is usually a query raised by the covenant son, a demand that God should show by a powerful work, by a 'proof' (מסה) or 'sign' (אות or מופת) that he really is the god of the people, is in their midst, is active as their saviour, protector and provider in accordance with his covenant promises."

no means see the land which I swore to their fathers, nor shall any
of those who spurned Me see it" (Num 14:22–23). At Kadesh the
generation who encountered Yahweh at Mount Sinai and who experienced the miraculous provision and protection out of Egypt were
authenticated and found lacking. Israel's failure at Kadesh marks a
cycle of refinement that will require nearly a generation to complete.
The designation of סגלה ("special treasure"), first pronounced at Sinai,
will signal the end of Israel's testing in the wilderness (Exod 19:5; 7:6).
The wilderness experience worked to refine Israel to take the next
step; one generation is left behind while another generation will learn
the lesson of the wilderness (Deut 8:1–3). The generation who com-
plained more than trusted would have failed in taking Canaan from
the pagan nations who occupied it. Thirty-eight years after Kadesh
where Yahweh recounted ten episodes where Israel had severely ques-
tioned (tested) the Lord (Num 14:22),[54] Moses addresses a new generation of Israelites who have emerged from the wilderness refinement.
The designation of "special treasure" confirms this transformation
(Deut 7:6). Moses addresses this new generation on the plains of Moab
in preparation to enter the land.[55]

---

[54] The number "ten" here may be best understood as a round figure. This
hyperbolic function of "ten" occurs also in Gen 31:7, 41 and Job 19:3. See Philip
J. Budd, *Numbers*, WBC 5 (Waco, TX: Word, 1984), 158. The number taken
literally may refer to ten specific incidents (e.g., Exod 14:10–12; 15:22–24; 16:1–
3; 16:19–20, 27–30; 17:1–4; 32:1–35; Num 11:1–3; 11:4–34; 14:3). See Harrison,
Numbers, 215.

[55] For a full treatment of this subject, see Daniel Block, "The Privilege
of Calling," in *How I Love Your Torah, O LORD!: Studies in the Book of
Deuteronomy* (Eugene, OR: Cascade, 2011), 152–61; see also Daniel Block, *Deuteronomy*, in The NIV Application Commentary (Grand Rapids: Zondervan,
2012), 209–14.

Testing in Deuteronomy

Deuteronomy offers a unique reflection on Israel's wilderness experience through the theological lens of testing. The key testing term נסה occurs seven times in contexts that focus on Israel's wilderness testing (cf. 4:34; 6:16; 8:2, 16; 13:4[3]; 28:56; 33:8). Deuteronomy 8 sets out the theology of testing for a generation of Israel preparing to enter the land. On this point Sheriffs comments:

> The desert journey of Israel both before and after Sinai is the
> setting for testing in two directions, God's testing of Israel and
> Israel's testing of God. The first has theological approval. The
> second is condemned. The retrospective of Deuteronomy 8
> offers us the best vantage point on God's testing of Israel.[56]

Deuteronomy's development of the theology of testing remains entirely consistent with patriarchal testing discussed previously and links Israel's recent experience with her immediate future. Our analysis will focus on the meaning of נסה as compared to other pentateuchal contexts. In addition, Deuteronomy 6:4–8:20 will be examined for its particular emphasis on the theology of testing taken from Israel's own wilderness experience.

The foundation for Deuteronomy's presentation of testing is laid out in chapter 4, where the aurally received words of the covenant constituted the basis for Israel's test of fidelity and the maintaining of one's loyal disposition (=fear) before Yahweh (Exod 20:20).[57] Deuteronomy

---

[56] Sheriffs, "Testing," 832.

[57] According to Weinfeld (*Deuteronomy 1–11*, AB 5 [New York: Doubleday, 1991], 203–4) the verbs נסה and למד ("to teach") in 4:10 link this passage indirectly to the context of Sinai in Exodus 20, where the foundational *instruction* of Torah occurs. These terms also function together in the same sense in Judg 3:1–2, where a new generation experiences or learns (למד) military strategy through the test (נסה) of war. Jeffrey Tigay (*Deuteronomy: The Traditional Hebrew Text with the New JPS Translation*, The JPS Torah Commentary [Philadelphia: Jewish Publication Society, 1996], 47n40) recognizes this link to Sinai and the

4:9–14 recounts Sinai and reminds Israel of her covenant obligations and the necessary fidelity for the next leg of her journey. Moses
addresses the generation at Moab as eyewitnesses to the events at Sinai
and commands them to pass on this collective memory to the next
generation (4:9–10a).[58] Deuteronomy assigns this didactic responsibility to the parents (4:10b). The reference to "fear" in 4:10 echoes
Exodus 20:20, where "fear" described the present (and ongoing) loyal
disposition of the nation. Thus, Israel's designation of loyalty will be
partially maintained through the instructional role of parents and the
shared activity of the entire community. Both families and community
work to preserve the memory of Yahweh's great historic salvific acts.[59]

The imperative command שמע ("hear") in Deuteronomy 6:4
also builds on Israel's experience at Sinai, where the nation first *heard*
from their King, speaking from the mountain (cf. Deut 4:12, 15, 33,
36). While Yahweh's commands were first heard then, Israel is again

---

"deterrent effect" of the theophany, suggesting that "fear" is synonymous with a
concern for ethical behavior. Tigay cites Deut 5:26; 25:18; Gen 20:11; 42:18; Exod
1:17; Lev 19:14, 32; 25:17, 36, 43; Ps 34:15; Prov 3:7; and Job 28:28 as examples of
this nuance. See also Block, *Deuteronomy*, 125–29.

[58] While 4:3 recalls the events of Num 25:1–5; 4:9 addresses the people as
if they had experienced the theophany at Sinai (Weinfeld, *Deuteronomy 1–11*,
200, 202–3). Sheriffs (*DOTP* 285) links the unbelief alluded to in Num 14:11 to
the failure of the people to accept or "see" the evidence before them. This event
informs Deuteronomy's theological development of the idea of "forgetting" as
the inability to "see" or "believe." See also Block, *Deuteronomy*, 126–42.

[59] The noun form of נסה occurs in Deut 4:34, "Or has a god tried to go to
take for himself a nation from within *another* nation by *trials*, by signs and wonders and by war and by a mighty hand and by an outstretched arm and by great
terrors, as the LORD your God did for you in Egypt before your eyes?" (emphasis
added). Here, testing is best understood as the means by which Yahweh authenticates himself loyal before his own people. The question answered by the series
of miraculous and awesome events that stretch from Egypt to Sinai is the one
asked in v. 32b, "Has *anything* been done like this great thing, or has *anything*
been heard like it?" The two remaining occurrences of נסה in Deut 28:56 and
33:8 do not contribute significantly to the theme of testing. See Block, *Deuteronomy*, 142–43.

challenged both to hear and to obey.[60] Canaan, however, will offer a
litany of distractions to the singularity of allegiance that is expected of
the nation. Israel will be tested through internal and external threats
to their fidelity. According to Deuteronomy 6:6–12, Moses warns
against the threat of simply forgetting God. Cities, houses, cisterns,
and vineyards will soon replace the hunger, thirst, and hardship of
Israel's wilderness experience. Thus, both extremes of poverty *and*
abundance may serve as a means of testing national fidelity (6:10–11).
In response to this threat, Deuteronomy 6:6–9 extends the message
of 4:9–10 and places even greater emphasis on the instructional role
of parents, who facilitate and create visual reminders and teaching
moments that integrate the commands of Torah into the routines
of everyday life (6:7–9). Moreover, families also function to preserve
the collective *memory* of the history of Yahweh's demonstrated faithfulness to the nation (6:12, 21–23).[61] Part of that collective memory
includes those times when Israel failed to demonstrate national fidelity. For example, Deuteronomy 6:16 reminds Israel of her failure at
Massah where Yahweh was tested through Israel's failure to trust him

---

[60] Seesemann (*TDNT* 6:27–28) comments, "If we love God and keep His
commandments we cannot test Him or question His power by an attitude of
doubt and unbelief (cf. Isaiah 7:12)." Daniel Block ("How Many Is God? An
Investigation into the Meaning of Deuteronomy 6:4–5," *JETS* 47 [2004]: 207)
recognizes a rhetorical strategy in the structure of Deut 6:4–8:20 that focuses on
the theme of testing. According to his scheme, the prohibition against testing
Yahweh in v. 16 parallels the call to exclusive devotion from v. 5. This interpretation places appropriate emphasis on v. 16, which recalls the event at Massah
as the antithesis of the singularity of obedience called for in v. 5. See also Block,
Deuteronomy, 180–84, 192–99.

[61] Tigay (*Deuteronomy*, 80) suggests that the future threat of prosperity in
the Promised Land anticipates a settled agricultural society. He observes Deuteronomy's concern that this anticipated prosperity is a threat to the faithfulness and fidelity of the people (cf. Deut 8:12–14; 11:14–16; 31:20; 32:15). See also
Block, *Deuteronomy*, 184–90.

(cf. Exod 17:2).[62] Israel is again reminded that whether through times of feast or famine, her ability to demonstrate covenant fidelity *authenticates* her loyal status before Yahweh and the nations. Individuals or nations who are both צדק ("righteous") and who ירא ("fear") God are those who demonstrate covenant obedience and fidelity before their King (cf. Deut 6:24–25).[63]

Deuteronomy 7:1–5 introduces yet another *test* to Israel's fidelity, that of the idolatrous influence of pagan nations. Moses both anticipates and severely warns Israel against this threat in specific terms. Israel is warned against the practice of infant sacrifice, a common feature of worship to the Ammonite national deity, Molech (cf. Lev 18:21; 20:2; Deut 18:10). What was at stake was the name and reputation of Yahweh among his people (cf. Lev 18:21; 19:12; 20:3; 21:6; Deut 12:5). Thus, the severity of this threat is matched only by the command to eliminate completely the pagan altars, pillars, and images employed by these nations (7:5). The activity of driving out these nations is also prescribed by Moses in the instruction on warfare (cf. Deut 20:1–20). Israel's valued status before Yahweh, forged and *refined* through the wilderness, balances the severity of these commands.[64] Deuteronomy 7:6

---

[62] Weinfeld (*Deuteronomy 1–11*, 346–47) links 6:16 to Exod 17:7, where the request for divine presence tests Yahweh (cf. Num 20:7–13; Ps 95:6–9). Massah represents the situation where a single event tests the fidelity of both God (cf. Exod 17:1–7; Num 20:7–13; Deut 6:16) and man (cf. Ps 81:8). He recognizes the dual nature of this testing in that, while the people test God, they are still being tested by him. Tigay (*Deuteronomy*, 81) suggests that Psalms 78 and 106 present the idea that testing God is "a consequence of forgetting His past marvels, especially those that took place during the Exodus."

[63] Weinfeld (*Deuteronomy 1–11*, 344, 349) follows the Targumim reading "merit/credit" for צדק and recognizes the link between 6:25; Gen 15:6; and Deut 24:13. He links "fear" to the Akkadian *palāḫu*, a term that refers to the loyalty before God and king. The context here supports earlier observations on the meaning of "loyalty" for צדק in Gen 15:6 and suggests this same meaning for Deut 6:24.

[64] See Block, *Deuteronomy*, 468–86.

again reminds Israel of her privileged status as Yahweh's סגלה ("special treasure"), first announced at Sinai (cf. Exod 19:5–6).[65] The paganism of the nations will remain as a continual threat—or test—against Israel's covenant fidelity (cf. Judg 2:1–5; 3:1–2).

Deuteronomy 8 offers the most extensive theological "look back" or reflection on Israel's wilderness *testing* experience.[66] Moses clarifies that the wilderness served to test (authenticate and refine) Israel's heart for the fidelity called for by covenant relationship (8:2). Yahweh's agenda for the wilderness march included the harsh experiences of thirst and hunger, *yet* amid these difficulties he also provided for the physical comfort of his people (8:3–4). Moses confirms the divine intent of their experience in verses 5–6, "Thus you are to know in your heart that the LORD your God was disciplining you just as a man disciplines his *son*. Therefore, you shall keep the commandments of the LORD your God, to walk in His ways and to *fear Him*" (emphasis added). For Israel this theological reflection looks back on her own experience and brings together the concepts of testing, suffering through hardship, fear, and the unique paternal role of Yahweh.[67] Israel's own experience now validates what she has already understood through

---

[65] Weinfeld (*Deuteronomy 1–11*, 368) finds the covenant basis for this term in the dialogue between the Hittite emperor to the last king of Ugarit, Ammurapi (ca. thirteenth century BC) where the king addresses a faithful servant as *sglt*. Tigay (*Deuteronomy*, 87) suggests that the term represents the accumulated wealth of a property owner. This meaning parallels the nontheological use of the term in 1 Chr 29:3 (cf. Eccl 2:8), which refers to royal treasures consecrated to Yahweh. The designation of Israel as the סגלה of Yahweh suggests that the wilderness experience was effective as a refining experience for Israel (cf. Deut 4:20).

[66] Tigay (*Deuteronomy*, 92) observes the chiastic structure of the chapter highlights the motif of remembering.

[67] Sheriffs (*The Friendship of the Lord*, 103–7) recognizes the theological links between Deut 8:1–5 and Prov 3:5–12 and the father-son relationship. Again, the loving father tests, reproves, and disciplines but also provides and cares for his son. See Block, *Deuteronomy*, 226–32.

the patriarchal examples of Abraham and Joseph. In this context the
verb נסה carries both the notion of revealing and the functional aspect
of refinement, for both are accomplished during Israel's wilderness
exile. In the wilderness Israel's faith or trust was enhanced through
the *experience* of deprivation (and suffering). Deuteronomy 8:3–4 confirms that this new generation has finally emerged as having learned
the lesson of the wilderness; *more* than just providing daily necessities,
covenant relationship demands passionate and exclusive obedience to
Yahweh's commands—every *word* that proceeds out of the mouth of
the King (8:3).[68] Though their experience was harsh, Israel receives
assurance that behind their hardship was the disciplinary hand of a
loving and committed Father (8:5–6). This covenant principle will
become important in Israel's later history. Thus, in covenant (family)
relationship, God is obligated to respond to Israel. The thorns and
thistles of the wilderness will be replaced by the invading armies of
Assyria and Babylon, who work as divinely assigned agents of futility against Israel's spiritual failure.[69] In sum, Deuteronomy addresses
the specific needs of the new generation of Israel preparing to apply
the lessons learned in the wilderness—a necessity for successful conquest of the land. Deuteronomy addresses this new generation as the
priceless pinnacle of God's salvific activity that began in Egypt. Having experienced the deprivation of the wilderness, Israel has finally
learned the lesson of dependence, obedience, and faith. In order to

---

[68] Deuteronomy distinguishes between the test of the manna referred to in
Deuteronomy 8 and the testing at Massah developed previously in Deuteronomy 6. While Deuteronomy 8 emphasizes the didactic aspects of God testing the
people, Deuteronomy 6 emphasizes the rebellious aspects of the people testing
God.

[69] Sheriffs (*Friendship of the Lord*, 100–104) recognizes "walking" as a metaphor used in political texts from the second millennium to convey an alliance
between two treaty partners. He applies this metaphor to his interpretation of
Enoch, Noah, and Abraham as prototypes for covenant fidelity. His approach
places a right emphasis on patriarchal testing as a journey and supports the concept of the "testing experience" developed earlier in our study.

prepare them more fully for the situation to come, Moses contributes to the theology of testing in two significant ways. First, he announces that the test of *abundance* in the land posesses the same threat to fidelity as that of Israel's experience of *deprivation* in the wilderness. The threat of forgetting Yahweh remains *equally* valid in both contexts. Second, Moses elevates the parental role and responsibility of preserving the memory of Israel's past and teaching the words of Torah as a deterrent against the future threat of forgetting—modern parents take note!

Conclusion

In the Pentateuch testing follows both the *aural* (quality check) and *experiential* (quality improvement) categories established previously. In fact, the theme of testing appears as a coherently presented theological idea throughout the *entire* Pentateuch. The terms נסה and ירא used together signaled the theological highpoints regarding the Pentateuch's presentation of testing (cf. Genesis 22; Exodus 20). While the relationship between fear and testing was more evident in contexts where נסה and ירא occurred together, this same theological relationship also occurs in implicit testing contexts. By broadening the boundaries of how the ideas of "testing" and "loyalty" are understood, we gained a greater appreciation for the Pentateuch's coherent presentation of this significant theological theme. What remains to be seen is what it might look like to extend this same theological theme across the entire corpus of biblical texts.

Practically and for the modern believer, it is helpful to see how a single theological idea or concept receives development across books, authors, and historical periods. On our theme of testing, some may be encouraged to see the examples of individual testing in the lives of Abraham and Joseph. The biblical emphasis remains that faith refined through trial often becomes the faith God uses for rather significant kingdom work! Moreover, teachers and preachers need to stress the tremendous concern that God has for the development of faith and fidelity in the lives of *all* those who call on his name. The Pentateuch presents this divine concern, illustrated through the lives of tested patriarchs, as well as the nation of Israel.

CHAPTER 4

THE TESTING
OF GOD'S SONS

This study has attempted to demonstrate how the Joseph narrative
contributes to the Pentateuch's theology of testing, particularly in
its retrospective and prospective vantage points. Moreover, it has shown
the Joseph narrative's own unique contribution to this vantage point,
helping to transition testing from the more individual patriarchal experience to the more corporate experience that began for Israel at Sinai.
Thus, the Pentateuch offers a coherent theology of testing that serves
as a significant evaluative vantage point for later biblical theological
reflection. This chapter title, "The Testing of God's Sons," conveys the
theological unity of the theme of testing in the remainder of the biblical
context. To examine more of the biblical text, Genesis will be reexam-
ined to explore more fully the basic idea of Adam as a tested patriarch.
Thus, this chapter advances along the following lines: (1) The Testing
of God's Sons: Adam, (2) The Testing of God's Sons: Patriarchs, (3) The
Testing of God's Sons: Israel, (4) The Testing of God's Sons: Jesus, and
finally (5) The Testing of God's Sons: The Church.[1]

---

[1] Birger Gerhardsson provided the inspiration behind the organizational
concept and title for this chapter.

The Testing of God's Sons: Adam

The Pentateuch presents a collection of the instructional messages that Israel's first leader, Moses, intended to prepare a new nation for success in the land promised to the patriarchs. Through their experience of testing in the wilderness, Israel gained a more practical understanding of what it really means to put feet to faith. Thus, one might expect to find this same theological emphasis throughout the Pentateuch, including the earliest chapters of Genesis. We ask if there is something implicit in Adam's experience in Genesis 1–3 that illustrates this important theological theme of testing for Israel.[2] Our analysis of Genesis 1–3 draws greatly from a recognition of the intertextual themes between Adam and Israel. More recently Seth Postell has developed these themes and comments:

> When understood as the introduction to the Torah and to the Tanakh as a whole, Genesis 1–3 intentionally foreshadows Israel's failure to keep the Sinai Covenant as well as their exile from the Promised Land in order to point the reader to a future work of God in the "last days." Adam's failure to "conquer" (Gen 1:28) the seditious inhabitant of the land (the serpent), his temptation and violation of the commandments, and his exile from the garden is Israel's story *en nuce*.[3]

In previous analysis the theological vantage point in the Joseph narrative was recognized as both retrospective (looking back) and

---

[2] Seth D. Postell (*Adam as Israel: Genesis 1–3 as the Introduction to the Torah and Tanakh* [Eugene, OR: Pickwick Publications, 2011], 55–74) argues that the Pentateuch be read through the theological lens of Israel. Our text–centered approach recognizes both text and the historical circumstances surrounding its production.

[3] Ibid., 3. Our attempt to read Genesis 1–3 theologically rests on the basic recognition of a Mosaic core of the Pentateuch, in addition to a final form that reflects later theological concerns in Israel's history.

prospective (looking forward). In Adam, Israel benefits from a similar retrospective vantage point and better understands her immediate testing circumstances.[4] Of particular interest here will be creation's role as an assigned agent of futility against the rebellion of Adam (as Israel) in the context of Genesis 1–3.

To better understand testing in Genesis, it is helpful to recognize the particular *logic* of testing applied theologically in other biblical contexts. Judges offers significant theological commentary on testing as it relates to Israel's struggle against the unconquered nations at a time just before the monarchy. Judges 2:21–22 comments, "I also will no longer drive out before them any of the nations which Joshua left when he died, *in order to test* (נסה) Israel by them, whether they will keep the way of the LORD to walk in it as their fathers did, or not" (emphasis added). This text clarifies the fact (or logic) that unconquered nations remaining in the land serve as the ongoing *means* of testing, refining, and authenticating Israel's loyalty and fidelity. Joshua 23:13 amplifies the way these nations work as agents of futility against Israel:

> Know with certainty that the LORD your God will not continue
> to drive these nations out from before you; but they will be a
> snare and a trap to you, and a whip on your sides and thorns in
> your eyes, until you perish from off this good land which the
> LORD your God has given you.

---

[4] Some scholars recognize the intertextual links between Genesis and Deuteronomy, specifically in the parallels between Jacob and Moses. Postell (*Adam as Israel*, 147) summarizes: "The Pentateuch, therefore, opens (Genesis 1) and closes (Deuteronomy 34) with a focus on the unconquered land. Second, the Pentateuch opens and closes with the problem of exile (Gen 3:23–24; Deut 34:1–5). Like Adam and Eve, Moses also must die outside the Promised Land (see Gen 5:5; Deut 34:5). The Pentateuch begins and ends with these two themes, land and exile, with a longing look to the Promised Land from an exile, somewhere east of Eden."

This passage suggests that unconquered nations operate similarly to the thorns and thistles encountered by Adam. Futility—whether through thorns, thistles, or unconquered nations—can function as a means of frustrating those in rebellion against God. This fact stems from Israel's failure to completely drive out the nations during Joshua's campaigns (Judg 1:27–36; 2:21; see also Josh 13:1–5; 23:4). Failure to drive these nations out of the land also opens the door to pagan influence. This failure incites Yahweh, who remains covenantally obligated to impose the futility curses against the nation (cf. Deut 20:1–20). The logic is simple. Disobedience in fulfilling the command to drive out opposition to God's plan in the land (ארץ) will lead to increased futility in the land.

This same logic of testing may also be applied to Genesis 1–3. Adam's prefall commands relating to his role in the land (ארץ) stem from his status as divine image bearer. God commands Adam,

> Be fruitful and multiply, and fill the earth (ארץ), and subdue (כבש) it; and rule (רדה) over the fish of the sea and over the birds of the sky and over every living thing that moves on the earth. (Gen 1:28)[5]

On this parallel, Dumbrell comments:

---

[5] Postell (*Adam as Israel*, 88–91) offers additional parallels. First, the preparation of the land in Genesis 1 parallels the preparation of the *garden* in Genesis 2. Second, Genesis 1–11 details a progressive eastward movement from the *good land* (garden of Eden) to *Babylon*. Israel's later history will recount this same movement in its exilic experience. Abraham will reverse this direction in his journey to the *land*. Third, similarities exist between the boundaries described for the garden of Eden and the Promised Land (Gen 2:10–14; cf. 15:18). Finally, and significant to our study, is the observation that both Adam and Israel are commanded to, in a broad sense, *dominate* (כבש) the land (Gen 1:28; cf. Num 32:22, 29; Josh 18:1). Deuteronomy, for example, places this same emphasis on the Promised Land as the "good land" (e.g., Deut 1:25, 35; 4:21–22; 6:18; 8:7, 10; 9:6; 11:17).

Adam, like Israel, is put into sacred space to exercise a kingly/ priestly role (cf. Exod. 19:4–6). Israel, like Adam, is given law by which the divine space is to be retained; Israel, like Adam, transgresses the law; and Israel, like Adam, is expelled from the divine space. The placement of Adam and Israel in divine space was conditional. Both parties had to obey the divine mandate to retain the sacred space.[6]

Scholars have observed that the prefall commands "rule" and "subdue" conflict with a creation that is both good and perfect.[7] These terms (כבש and רדה) suggest that an object or source of "push back"

---

[6] William J. Dumbrell (*The Faith of Israel: a Theological Survey of the Old Testament*, 2nd ed. [Grand Rapids: Baker Academic, 2002], 19–21) recognizes the ancient Near Eastern parallels that support his understanding of the garden of Eden as the sacred space or sanctuary for Adam from which the order (via stipulations and decrees) in creation is established. Just as Adam received his covenantal commands in the garden to multiply, fill, rule, and subdue the land, so too Israel receives its covenantal commands from the holy mountain at Sinai. See also Stephen G. Dempster, *Dominion and Dynasty: a Biblical Theology of the Hebrew Bible*, New Studies in Biblical Theology (Downers Grove, IL: InterVarsity, 2003), 62, 102. Davis A. Young and Ralph F. Stearley (*The Bible, Rocks, and Time: Geological Evidence for the Age of the Earth* (Downers Grove, IL: IVP Academic, 2008], 463) comment, "The Scripture repeatedly refers to God's ordinances, decrees and laws with reference to the natural world. The Old Testament, in particular, teaches that God is in a covenant relation with his creation by which he upholds the ordinances of day and night, the sun and moon, the boundaries of the sea, and so on."

[7] Kenneth A. Mathews (*Genesis 1–11:26*, NAC 1a [Nashville: B&H Academic, 1996], 140, 142–43) asks, "If the 'heavens and earth' declares existence of the well-ordered cosmos, how can it also be that the 'earth' is disorganized and incomplete as portrayed in v. 2?" Mathews suggests that "heavens and earth" refer to an incomplete universe or cosmos and that vv. 3–31 describe the completion of that having already begun in vv. 1–2. Citing Isa 45:14–25, he argues, "Thus the prophet asserted that the Lord did not create the earth to remain *tōhû* but rather to become a residence for man."

exists—that is, something prior to the fall requires ruling and sub-duing.[8] Some suggest that these commands relate to the expansion of Eden's boundaries; Adam expresses his image-bearing responsibilities by cultivating the garden so that it grows and fills the earth.[9] Certainly some kind of expansion is in order that involves Adam's multiplying and filling, as Fretheim comments,

> The commands in Gen 1:28 to be fruitful, multiply, fill the
> earth and subdue and have dominion over, are all pre-Fall and
> suggest the activity of expanding the LORD's covenant domain to
> include more than just the Garden.[10]

The analysis of the testing logic discussed previously offers some clari-fication. First, there is a snake in Eden *before* the fall.[11] While exactly

---

[8] On the Hebrew term כבש, Provan comments, "It is the language of con-quest, usually military conquest. In Num 32:22, 29 and Josh 18:1, the land is being 'subdued' before God and his people; or 2 Sam 8:11, David was 'subduing' all the nations. Warfare therefore lurks in the background of this verb" in some contexts.

[9] Douglas Green ("When the Gardener Returns: An Ecological Perspective on Adam's Return," in *Keeping God's Earth: the Global Environment in Biblical Perspective*, ed. Noah Toly and Daniel Isaac Block [Downers Grove, IL: IVP Academic, 2010], 267–75) develops the idea of Adam as the "Gardener-King" and his unique role to *subdue* and *cultivate* the uninhabitable land outside of the garden of Eden described in Gen 1:2 as "desolate and empty." He follows David Tsumura's interpretation of תהו ובהו to describe a land desolate and devoid of vegetation, contrary to the more common interpretation of "formless and void." Green argues that Adam's command as "vice-gardener" is frustrated by the effects of the covenant curse enacted in Genesis 3 and the introduced futility. He recognizes the eschatological hope in the coming "gardener king of the new creation" (cf. John 1:1).

[10] Terence E. Fretheim, *Creation Untamed: The Bible, God, and Natural Disasters*, Theological Explorations for the Church Catholic (Grand Rapids: Baker Academic, 2010), 16.

[11] For a summary of the discussion of the snake as it relates to extrabiblical and ANE sources, see Gordon J. Wenham, *Genesis 1–15*, WBC 1 (Waco, TX: Word, 1987), 72–73.

who the snake is remains open for debate, for the purposes of this investigation, the snake represents the agenda of rebellion established against God's plans. The agenda of this snake was to threaten Adam's relationship with God. This agenda is in some ways parallel to the pagan idolatry that threatened Israel's covenant solidarity. Regarding the military nature of the commands to *rule* and *subdue* in the context of Genesis, Postell comments:

> The purpose of the militaristic terminology is not to give license for the exploitation of the natural resources in the world. Rather it prepares the reader for understanding what should have been Adam and Eve's response to the serpent in Genesis 3, and also supplies Israel with their marching orders in the remainder of the Pentateuch (and in the Tanakh).[12]

In Adam, Israel recognizes that her struggle against the idolatry of the land is also a struggle to preserve the integrity of her relationship with God. Adam *rules* and *subdues* the snake. Israel *rules* and *subdues* the nations. Both activities involve expansion and the conquest of that which opposes God's agenda. Interestingly, both activities involve suffering through the experience of futility. For Israel, the land represents the domain from which she expresses and extends covenant relationship. Thus, the expansion of territory will involve both land and the human heart.

---

[12] See Postell (*Adam as Israel*, 102), who seeks a broad fulfillment of the opposition to the serpent wrapped up in Gen 3:15 and the Messianic hope (Pss 72:8; 110:2).

Excursus: The Testing of Job

Like Adam, the patriarch Job lived during a time prior to the events of Mount Sinai. However, while Job did not share in Israel's covenant relationship, his unique righteous relationship with God models for Israel what authentic covenant fidelity should look like. Clearly, Job is expected to demonstrate loyalty in a world that has already fallen (Job 1:8). A clear parallel between Job and Genesis 1–3 is that an adversary again unexpectedly shows up for the purpose of *testing* a patriarch.[13] As we have already observed for Adam, this testing occurs implicitly from the context but under the sovereignty of God. For both Adam and Job, the adversary is able (allowed) to disrupt the *good* of the patriarch's relational status with God. For Job the adversary hopes he will call into question the foundation of that relational status—God's reputation is at stake (2:10).[14] In round one the adversary is allowed—as an assigned *agent of futility*—to take away some of the blessings Job has received from God, such as

---

[13] Sam Meier ("Job 1–2: a Reflection of Genesis 1–3," *VT* 39 [1989]: 183–93) points out some of the similarities of Job to Adam as: (1) his uniqueness as a human being, (2) his obedience to the command to be fruitful and multiply and exercise dominion, and (3) his experience of a "very good" world that has been disrupted by chaos. More than Adam, Job brings attention to the loyalty that is demonstrated amid a world that has been subjected to futility. For a helpful discussion on the similar role of the adversary in both Adam and Job, see R. W. L. Moberly, "Uncomfortable Truths in Job: the Value of the Old Testament for Christian Ministry," *Covenant Quarterly* 68 (2010): 6–7.

[14] Kenneth Ngwa ("Did Job Suffer for Nothing? The Ethics of Piety, Presumption and the Reception of Disaster in the Prologue of Job," *JSOT* 33 [2009]: 360n3) explores the subject of tragedy and suffering and emphasizes the theme of demonstrated fidelity amid a violated covenant structure. We appreciate this emphasis and the way Job illustrates for Israel how a faithful covenant member continues to demonstrate loyalty amid a context that includes an intentional (but directed) experience of futility and suffering.

servants (1:15–17), livestock (vv. 16–17), and children (vv. 18–19). Job offers the appropriate response for one who *fears* Yahweh (vv. 20–22). In round two the adversary subjects Job to some kind of physical suffering (2:7). Even his wife encourages him to question the integrity of his relationship with God (2:9); however, Job responds with a theologically loaded question, "Shall we indeed accept good (טוב) from God and not accept adversity (רע)?" [2:10].[15] While the covenantal significance of the juxtaposition of the terms *good* and *bad* receives more detailed attention in an appendix of this present work, the comparison of verse 10 with the words of Moses in Deuteronomy 30:15–16 needs to be noted here:

> See, I have set before you today life and prosperity [טוב],
> and death and adversity [רע]; in that I command you
> today to love the LORD your God, to walk in His ways
> and to keep His commandments and His statutes and His
> judgments, that you may live and multiply, and that the
> LORD your God may bless you in the land where you are
> entering to possess it.[16]

The exact relationship between good and bad in this text is often established on the juxtaposition between blessing and curse in

---

[15] Ibid., 363n9. Ngwa points out the interpretive options for v. 10 as either a question or a statement of fact. He prefers the affirmative statement and translates, "Indeed, we should receive the beautiful from God, but not disaster." It seems the wider context is pressed to support this translation. It seems more evident that Job is presented as a tested patriarch, like Abraham and Joseph, who *fears* Yahweh and illustrates for Israel how covenant loyalty is demonstrated amid suffering and futility.

[16] We observe that the juxtaposition of *life* and *death* in Moses' charge aligns with the same juxtaposition of access to the tree of life and exile for Adam (Gen 3:22–24) and the advice of Job's wife "Curse God and die (Job 2:9b)!" See also Meier, "Job 1–2: a Reflection of Genesis 1–3," 190.

v. 19, thus equating the bad (רע) of v. 15 with the enacting of the covenant curses. However, we wonder if more needs to be said. In Job's world, loyalty is expressed in the midst of both *good* and *bad* (cf. Job 2:10). Moberly comments, "Job's logic is, in essence, very simple. It's no good being a fair-weather friend, being into someone when times are good and easy but opting out when they get rough."[17] Of course, any ancient Israelite reader would have known that a world of good *and* bad was the direct result of Adam's infidelity and God's subjection of Adam's world to futility (Gen 3:22; cf. Rom 8:20–21). Job has had a first-hand experience of amplified futility! Similarly, Moses charges Israel to remain covenantally loyal in a land that will contain both good *and* bad at every turn (Deut 30:15). Loyalty must be demonstrated through one's experience of this kind of futility, and this is exactly what Job illustrates for Israel—love under fire. James will recognize Job's example of loyalty under fire for the first century believer and points out that such testing produces *endurance*. He writes:

> As an example, brethren, of suffering and patience, take
> the prophets who spoke in the name of the Lord. We
> count those blessed who endured. You have heard of
> the endurance of Job and have seen the outcome of the
> Lord's dealings, that the Lord is full of compassion and *is*
> merciful (James 5:10–11; cf. Ezek 14:19–20).

The example of Job for Israel also reinforces the lesson of the wilderness, that of total and complete faithfulness and the awareness that "the life of faith is a *learning* to seek God for himself rather than for what one might get out of God."[18]

---

17 Moberly, "Uncomfortable Truths in Job," 10.
18 Ibid., 11.

But Adam failed as did Israel. What were the consequences for Israel? According to Judges, the nations assigned as agents of futility against Israel also became the *means* by which Israel was tested, authenticated, and refined. For Adam, creation will itself serve a similar purpose after the fall, as Paul explains,

> For the creation was *subjected to futility*, not of its own will, but because of Him who subjected it, in hope that the creation itself also will be set free from its slavery to corruption into the freedom of the glory of the children of God. (Rom 8:20–21, emphasis added)[19]

Covenant relationship obligates God to respond to the rebellion of his children; good parents know this principle well. According to our interpretation, the spoken *words* (statutes and commands) of covenant define the domain and location for both covenant expression and received blessing. To remain in this domain, Adam (and Israel) must demonstrate ongoing obedience as the means of authenticating loyalty. This demonstration leads to divinely given life and blessing. Disobedience to those same commands ultimately leads to exile and death (blessing removal); this is testing as refinement.[20] For Adam

---

[19] It is interesting that Paul places the subjection of creation in the same context as the suffering of the believer in Rom 8:16–25. His thesis statement in v. 17 lays claim to the fact that a true son will both suffer *with* and be glorified *with* Christ. But present suffering has no comparison to the glory that will be revealed to the believer (v. 18). Paul logically connects the climax of glory in the image bearers with the subjection of creation to the effects of the fall (v. 20). What is the exact nature of this relationship? This question relates to the apparent ambiguity of the "who" behind the phrase διὰ τὸν ὑποτάξαντα "by him who subjected it" in v. 20. Joseph Fitzmeyer (*Romans*, AB 33 [New York: Doubleday, 1992], 508) lays out the options (Adam, sinful man, God, Christ, and the Devil) but argues that God remains the subject of the verb and thus *subjects* his creation to futility in response to Adam's fall.

[20] The covenantal commands established boundaries by which certain aspects of covenant relationship were defined. Scholars have noted the intertextual link of Deut 30:15–20 and Gen 2:9, 16–17 where *good* and *bad* are linked

and his descendents outside of the garden, God subjects the created order to futility as the means of testing. Rebel man outside the garden will receive authentication and refinement through the same means. In Adam, Israel understands that her failure to *rule* and *subdue* leads to exile. Thorns and thistles, swords and spears, pain, and even suffering in both contexts all serve as assigned agents of futility against the covenant rebellion of man. Wilderness experiences can be great teachers![21] In Adam, Israel better understands the experience of futility precipitated by unconquered nations. This understanding will also

---

to covenantal commands. Adam's prohibition to eat from the tree of "good and bad," once violated, leads to an exile from the garden. Similarly, Israel's future in the land is bound up in the expectation of continued loyalty and obedience, "See, I have set before you today life and *good*, and death and *bad*" [Deut 30:15, author's translation and emphasis]. Thus, in the context of Genesis 1–3, Israel understands: the basic foundation for maintaining covenantal stability in the land, obedience to covenant commands leads to the experience of good covenant blessings; infidelity will lead to the bad and the testing of exile. See Dumbrell, *Faith of Israel*, 23. For a full discussion of the concepts of "good" and "bad" in Genesis, see Ramantswana Hulisani, "God Saw That It Was Good, Not Perfect: A Canonical-Dialogic Reading of Genesis 1–3" (Ph.D. diss., Westminster Theological Seminary, 2010), 126–29. David Snoke argues that Adam in the garden was in a "probational place of testing" and surrounded by "forces of judgment." We will suggest that after the fall, these naturally occurring aspects of the created order will be amplified against rebel man as an expression of the futility curse. See David Snoke, *A Biblical Case for an Old Earth* (Grand Rapids: Baker, 2006), 58–59. For a full discussion of the covenantal uses of Hebrew טוב to refer to covenant functionality, see "Appendix B: Covenant *Good* as Functional *Good*."

[21] Regarding the details of Gen 3:17–19 and the curse against the ground, C. John Collins (*Science and Faith: Friends or Foes?* [Wheaton, IL: Crossway, 2003], 151) points out that the text does not describe a radical change in the world outside the garden, but rather it is Adam who has radically changed. He comments, "[G]od will use the properties he gave to the ground and plants and animals to discipline his sinful creatures." We concur with this basic idea, but must also account for God's subjection of creation to futility which impacted the created order as a means of *testing* and *refining* mankind. Deuteronomy mentions pests, poverty, and captivity as specific examples of those kinds of things that will be applied with the covenantal curses (cf. Deut 28:17–18, 20, 38–46).

inform her later experience of exile at the hands of the Assyrians and Babylonians. At any time in Israel's history, assigned agents of futility work to refine the rebel heart (Judg 2:22; Deut 8:2).

This study recognizes that *good* covenants accomplish the desired will of the suzerain and that the description "good" often signals the covenant's *functional* ability to do so. Thus, in Genesis, God acting as suzerain (or king) commands, orders, and creates a world where relationship is a desired outcome.[22] Adam's violation of his relational status with God enacts the terms that require exile in a world subjected to futility. The ground (אֶרֶץ) Adam is commanded to subdue now subdues him. From this thorns and thistles, sweat, futility, and even physical death become the painful human experience—amplified by the curse and felt even more severely by a shattered image.[23] Thus,

---

[22] God declares the created order as "good" in Genesis 1 to describe the created order's functional ability to accomplish that which it was intended or designed to do (see "Appendix B: Covenant *Good* as Functional *Good*"). This meaning of "good" makes sense given the author (Moses), audience (Israel), and context (preland instruction) for the theological message of Genesis. Israel understands that at the fall God disrupts this "good" status for the created order and introduces the created order to the futility to which Paul refers in Rom 8:20. Israel would have understood the removal of "good" (blessing) as God's covenant response to Israel's infidelity. On our position, after the fall and with the introduction of this futility, the *good* in the created order that includes both the animal and plant kingdoms, as well as humanity, is removed. Thus, in this world subjected to futility, normal processes such as cell multiplication, virus and bacteria duplication can turn into harmful processes for humanity—good turns to bad (cf. Deut 30:15).

[23] Regarding the "thistles and weeds" of Genesis 3, Augustine comments: "We should not jump to the conclusion that it was only then [at the fall] that these plants came forth from the earth. For it could be that, in view of the many advantages found in different kinds of seeds, these plants had a place on earth without afflicting man in any way. But since they were growing in the fields in which man was now laboring in punishment for his sin, it is reasonable to suppose that they now became one of the means of punishing him" (author's addition). See Augustine, *The Literal Meaning of Genesis*, trans. J. H. Hammand, Ancient Christian Writers 41–42 (New York: Newman, 1982), 94. On

this futility in the created order works to test and refine the rebel heart for the purposes of establishing humility, dependence, and faith—the posture of heart demanded by covenant relationship (Deut 8:1–3). Adam, as a prefall image bearer, would have met the expectations of his prefall commands to multiply, fill, rule, and subdue the land (ארץ) created (ברא) good (טוב).[24] Adam's commands to multiply, fill, rule, and subdue also included the reality of divine presence and protection. After the fall, amplified futility remains the necessary expression of the covenant curse. Adam's (thus, humanity's) shattered image works with this futility as the means to further amplify humanity's experience of refinement. Israel's long covenant history illustrates how God works through this futility to refine the faith and fidelity of his people.

---

this same idea Collins (*Science and Faith*, 160) comments: "We have no reason to think that such natural things as animals preying on others, or earthquakes and hurricanes, or the law of increasing entropy, go against the will of God for his creation. However, we humans are infected with evil, which means that we don't have the sympathetic 'feel' for nature that would enable us to govern it to consistently good and wise purposes." On this question of what gets assigned to the design of creation as opposed to what gets assigned to the effects of the fall, we answer that natural items, such as earthquakes, hurricanes, and even cancer operate as assigned agents of testing resulting from a world subjected to futility (Rom 8:20). Thus, lightning strikes and storms may have always gone together in the created order; however, the *assignment* of lightning as an agent of futility working against the sinfulness of humanity was uniquely the result of the fall.

[24] The "push back" of the normal created order would include animal death, predation, scorpion stings, snakebites, tornadoes, typhoons, and lightning strikes. Snoke defends the basic idea of balance in the created order. He recognizes the parallels between Gen 8:22 and Gen 1:4–5, 7, 9–10, 16–18, 27 on the *balance* indicated by light and darkness, day and night, land and sea, male and female, and seed and harvest. The theme of balance is common in biblical contexts where the creation is discussed (David Snoke, *Biblical Case for an Old Earth* [Grand Rapids: Baker, 2006], 76–98). Collins looks to texts such as Ps 104:21–23, where the normal activities of gathering, hunting, or harvesting food are described for both man and lion as cause for worship and celebration of the *goodness* of the world made by God—the way, Collins claims, "he designed it to work." See Collins, *Science and Faith*, 154.

The Testing of God's Sons: Patriarchs

Just before the patriarchal history officially begins with Abraham, the tower of Babel illustrates again how God's imposed futility works against the rebellion of humanity. With the promise of no more global floods (Gen 9:11–15), Yahweh remains obligated to move decisively against the rebellion of humanity that is again spiraling dangerously out of control. The walled city and the tower represent yet another opposing agenda that now includes both defense and attack (Gen 11:3–4a). The population at Shinar remains bent on making for themselves a *name*.[25] This agenda represents an utter disregard for the creation/covenant/relational role of bearing and carrying the divine name (reputation) of the Creator and King of the universe (Gen 1:26–27).[26] Though Adam walked away from his image-bearing responsibilities as an individual, the tower of Babel event illustrates for Israel this same kind of rebellion on a corporate level. The confusion of their language and the disruption of their solidarity illustrate the divinely applied futility against their concentrated rebellion (11:7–8). This response parallels Adam's experience of increased futility, for example, in the cultivation of crops and his expulsion from the garden. Genesis 11:1–9 further clarifies how God responds to corporate defiance on a more global scale. While technically prior to any officially declared or enacted covenant, these examples serve to lay a foundation for Israel's understanding of how God will use futility to isolate and potentially remove rebellion from humanity. While later prophets will explain

---

[25] See discussion on שֵׁם in Mathews, *Genesis 1–11:26*, 482.

[26] Wenham (*Genesis 1–15*, 240) recognizes the link of Gen 11:6 and Gen 3:22. The divine response at Babel falls in line with the first preemptive strike against humanity. In both contexts human self-reliance and pride remain the focus of Yahweh's attempts to increase the futility against humanity. Mathews (*Genesis 1–11:26*, 484) recognizes that their act of defiance was met with gracious intervention and finds parallel in Adam's expulsion from the garden. Both events involve God's saving humanity from himself.

the role of invading armies in terms of assigned agents of futility (and judgment) against God's people, these early examples illustrate that it is the relational aspect of covenant that obligates God to respond in this manner to the rebellion of his people. A covenant granting king cannot be ignored for long! Thus, assigned agents of futility will be the means by which covenant loyalty is both cultivated and confirmed in God's people. Though harsh, these periods of testing are *good* in that they accomplish God's ultimate divine purpose (e.g., Gen 50:20).[27] Genesis 1–3, read with Genesis 11:1–9, thus offers an introduction to a universal testing experienced by all. In this fallen world, a world of good and bad, God desires the loyalty of his people. The way ahead recognizes yet more tower of Babel episodes for Israel, where God must work against the rebellion of his own people through the assignment of secondary agents of futility.

After Babel, the Bible introduces the patriarchs, who will illustrate for Israel the life of faith that emerges through the trials of testing. Because much has already been said about the theme of testing in the patriarchal texts, just a few observations are in order. First, the patriarchs Abraham and Joseph illustrate the experience of testing

---

[27] J. Gordon McConville (*Deuteronomy*, Apollos Old Testament Commentary 5 [Downers Grove, IL: InterVarsity, 2002], 405–6, 410) comments that the futility curses of Deuteronomy create the effect that the "proper enjoyment of something is frustrated" and bring about a covenant reversal. "Curses operate, therefore, rather like prophetic oracles of judgment, which intend, not to declare judgment inevitable and fixed, but to turn people from their sins." On the role of secondary agents as the means of delivering judgment, Fretheim (*Creation Untamed*, 53) comments: "God lets the creatures have the freedom to be what God created them to be. At the same time, the looseness of the causal weave allows God to be at work in the system in some ways without violating or (temporarily) suspending it. In these terms, God is a genuine agent. At the same time, God in judgment always works in and through nondivine agents. We learn this from a study of the prophets, such as Jeremiah, that God and God's agents (Babylon under Nebuchadnezzar) are often the subject of the same destructive verbs."

through endured hardship. Abraham, for example, leads his family out of Haran by faith. Through conflict with Egyptian kings, kidnapped nephews, and the ongoing struggle to produce an heir, Abraham's testing cycle climaxes in Genesis 22 where the patriarch's fidelity receives authentication in dramatic fashion. For Israel, Abraham illustrates the covenant (and often tested) faith and loyalty Yahweh requires.

Like Abraham, Joseph illustrates for Israel the testing that both *transforms* and *authenticates* covenant faith. For Joseph the fires of refinement even come through members of his own family, who demonstrate the antithesis of the covenant loyalty of brotherhood. In addition Joseph experiences Egyptian imprisonment and hardship—yet not outside of God's presence (Gen 39:2–3, 21). Joseph emerges from this test with a refined and authenticated faith that necessarily undergirds his new role as leader and dispenser of power and authority in a foreign land. In the climactic testing event of Genesis 42, Joseph demonstrates unexpected fidelity (brotherhood) toward the sons of Jacob and thus extends loyalty to his entire family as a tested and refined patriarch. Genesis 42 also reveals the divine concern for a transformation of the brothers. Joseph acts as a divinely assigned agent of futility and facilitates a series of authenticating events for the brothers. As a bookend to the entire testing cycle, Genesis 50:20 identifies the entire experience of testing for both Joseph and the brothers as *good*. *Before* Joseph can be a blessing to others, he must first endure hardship and suffering. *Before* the sons of Israel can be a nation, they must first learn the lesson of loyalty. The basis for national solidarity is the familial *brotherhood* that Joseph (and Yahweh) seeks. On this point Fretheim comments:

> Genesis moves from a "good" creation to the "good" that God works in Joseph's family (50:20); from family disruption to brotherly reconciliations; and from the seven days of creation to the seventy descendants of Jacob entering the land of Egypt.

> Joseph functions as a new Adam . . . and the command to be fruitful and multiply is fulfilled in this family (47:27).[28]

The patriarchs illustrate that *good* results come through testing and refinement experiences. Joseph's refinement, for example, illustrates how God uses and even allows hardship to mold and transform his saints.[29] Joseph was not spared his Egyptian experience, and the sons of Jacob follow this Egyptian refining experience with a 400-year bondage experience of their own. Eventually they too will emerge with a new opportunity to trust God and demonstrate faith and fidelity on their way to the Promised Land.

The Testing of God's Sons: Israel

God's testing agenda for Israel begins immediately upon their miraculous deliverance from Egypt. Israel begins the journey as a small child and demonstrates an immediate need for constant care and guidance. Israel will be tested but under the continuous parental oversight of Yahweh. Donald Gowan comments:

---

[28] Terence E. Fretheim, *The Pentateuch*, ed. Terence E. Fretheim, Gene M. Tucker, and Charles B. Cousar, Interpreting Biblical Texts (Nashville: Abingdon Press, 1996), 69.

[29] Another clear example of where God's faithful servants get caught in the crossfire of God's *good* covenant intentions that involve the enduring of hardship is found in the life of the prophet Jeremiah. Jeremiah preached the unpopular message that the Babylonian captivity was essentially God's plan for the faithful remnant remaining in Jerusalem. In this context the enemy and the exilic experience awaiting Judah are caused by God and are described as *good* (Jer 15:11–14). Theologically, this covenantal intent for *good* comes in Jeremiah's new covenant, which finds its foundation in the Mosaic covenant as well as David's *everlasting* covenant. Yahweh proclaims, "[I] will make with them an everlasting covenant not to turn away from them, but to do them *good*; and I will put in their hearts reverence for me so that they do not turn aside from me" (Jer 32:40; trans. Thompson; emphasis added). See J. A. Thompson, *The Book of Jeremiah*, NICOT (Grand Rapids: Eerdmans, 1980), 352, 391, 432, 590–97.

The strongest verb used with God as subject in the pre-Sinai wilderness materials is "test" (*nissah*). . . . No test results in punishment, however, for even though the theme of "murmuring in the wilderness" is introduced immediately, God's reaction to it is to hear (16:7, 8, 9, and 12) and to help, without any mention of impatience or judgment, such as we encounter in the murmuring stories in Numbers. The wilderness materials in Exodus introduce us at length to the God of grace.[30]

Along the difficult journey God authenticates himself through a series of miraculous acts that demonstrate his covenant loyalty to the nation (Exod 14:31). In response the nation is tested through a series of statutes or commands intended both to authenticate and to establish Israel's national fidelity.[31] The provision of water and manna offers just one example, "There He made for them a statute and regulation, and there *He tested them*" (Exod 15:25b, emphasis added). These early examples illustrate God's plan to develop Israel's faith in gradual steps that anticipate the more significant covenant event to come. At Sinai, Yahweh will expand Israel's testing to include ten additional "words" or commands (Exod 20:1–17). The purpose of Sinai's testing is clearly stated, "Do not be afraid; for God has come in order to *test* (נסה) you, and in order that the fear of Him may remain with you, so that you may not sin" (Exod 20:20, emphasis added). Thus, these ten *words*

---

[30] Donald E. Gowan, *Theology in Exodus: Biblical Theology in the Form of a Commentary* (Louisville, KY: Westminster, 1994), 168–69.

[31] C. Houtman (*Exodus*, Historical Commentary on the Old Testament [Kampen: Kok, 1993], 2:313) comments, "In short, the object of 15:25b, 26 is to highlight that from the start Israel knew of YHWH's requirement of obedience. It is the *charter, the constitution, for YHWH's relationship with Israel.* Before YHWH announces to Israel specific commandments and stipulations, it is informed of the only foundation on which its future can rest: faithfulness to YHWH and his commandments (cf. Jer. 7:23)."

define how Israel will express covenant fidelity to experience longevity and blessing in the land.[32]

As the wilderness testing continues, Israel also continues to demonstrate a basic unwillingness to trust in Yahweh. Israel's climax of unbelief occurs at Kadesh Barnea. There her refusal to trust Yahweh and enter the land authenticates the lack of national fidelity that God required. Entering the land at this stage would have led to spiritual disaster! Not unlike previously discussed patriarchal examples, God enacts a necessary refining experience for the entire nation (Num 14:22–24).[33] Clearly this generation of Israel could not have represented Yahweh's name and reputation in the land; too much was at stake![34]

---

[32] While the context may support an immediate test for Israel (e.g., the *test* of keeping their distance), we recognize a much broader and future context for נסות ("testings"), one that suggests an ongoing authentication for Israel's covenant loyalty. Deuteronomy 8:2 will recount that covenant fidelity was indeed the agenda of Israel's wilderness experience. See Houtman, *Exodus*, 3:77; see also Gowan, *Theology in Exodus*, 172–73; Block, *Deuteronomy*, 224–40.

[33] Yahweh recounts ten separate incidents of this kind of testing out of rebellion (Num 14:22). Deuteronomy 6:16 specifically prohibits the *kind* of testing that occurred at Massah. See also Terry L. Brensinger, "נסה," *NIDOTTE* 3:112.

[34] The taking of the land of Canaan on Yahweh's terms required the complete covenant fidelity of the people. Success involved more than just military victory but the establishment of Yahweh's name and reputation in the Promised Land. Moses called on the *name* of Yahweh, which included a list of his divine attributes (see Exod 34:5–7). *This* was the God who would win the battles for Israel for the purpose of demonstrating his great name and reputation before the nations (v. 10; cf. Josh 2:10–14). Moses' concern was for the establishment of Yahweh's name and reputation in the preparation of Israel for entering the land (see Deut 12:5, 11, 21; 14:23–24; 16:2, 6, 11; 26:2, 18–19; 28:9–10). Eventually Yahweh's name and reputation would be forgotten. Jeremiah screams against the infidelity of Judah and declares, "They have lied about the Lord and said, '*Not He*; misfortune will not come on us, and we will not see sword or famine'" (Jer 5:12, emphasis added). This Hebrew phrase לא־הוא can also be translated "He does not exist." See Allen P. Ross, "שם" in *NIDOTTE* 4:148.

Testing Assessed at Moab

On the plains of Moab, Israel emerges as *tested* and *refined* as a result of the wilderness experience. This experience has prepared Israel to better hear (and obey) Yahweh's final instructions and commands, delivered through Moses, that will allow for both blessing and success in the land (Deut 8:1–3). Deuteronomy 4:20 echoes Israel's special status first declared at Sinai (Exod 19:5).[35] To this new generation Moses offers significant theological reflection on Israel's wilderness experience as it relates to the theme of testing:

> You shall remember all the way which the LORD your God
> has led you in the wilderness these forty years, that He might
> humble you, *testing* you, to know what was in your heart,
> whether you would keep His commandments or not. He
> humbled you and let you be hungry, and fed you with manna
> which you did not know, nor did your fathers know, that He
> might make you understand that man does not live by bread
> alone, but man lives by everything that proceeds out of the
> mouth of the LORD. (Deut 8:2–3, emphasis added)[36]

Through the experience of testing, Israel learns the lesson that Yahweh demands the exclusive loyalty, dependence, faith, and obedience of his

---

[35] The fact that Moses addresses this new generation at Moab using the same unique expression from Exod 19:5 (סגלה ["special treasure"]) suggests that Israel's forty-year testing/refining experience yielded the desired results. This new generation now carries that same unique status with them into the land. Eugene Carpenter (*NIDOTTE* 3:224) comments; "Although all nations are his, Israel will become the 'crown jewel' among all the nations. Her unique quality lies in her position/function/character as his kingdom of priests and a holy nation."

[36] The LXX normally translates נסה with πειράζω as is used in Matt 4:1 to describe Satan's testing of the Lord. Christ quotes from Deut 8:3 and 6:16 in his defense against Satan. In Matthew 4, Christ embodies the theology of Israel's wilderness experience where Israel learned the lesson of complete trust and dependence. To deny this was to call into question God's fidelity. See Brensinger, "נסה," *NIDOTTE* 3:112.

people. Moses reminds Israel that the testing or refinement for this kind of covenant faith remains firmly within the grace boundaries of Yahweh's covenant commitment toward his people and declares, "In the wilderness He fed you manna which your fathers did not know, that He might humble you and that He might *test* (נסה) you, to do good (טוב) for you in the end" (Deut 8:16, emphasis added). Again the covenant will function to accomplish that for which it was intended: *good* in the end.

At Moab, Israel's special preparation for entering the land included specific identification of the potential threats to covenant solidarity. One such threat constituted the potential of failed leadership in Israel. Deuteronomy 17:14–20 set the bar for Israel's future leadership and defined the *kind* of king she would require. Israel's kings would forever be chosen and approved by her true King and function as model covenant citizens for the nation. The amassing of a large army, the exchange of women through political alliances, and any preoccupation with wealth all represent the common pursuits of pagan kings. The question of kingship will remain central in Israel's history. For example, the thesis statement of Judges raises the question of kingship, "In those days there was no king in Israel; everyone did what was right in his own eyes" (Judg 21:25; 17:6).[37] Taken with Deuteronomy 17:14–20, this question suggests that the right *kind* of king in Israel might resolve Israel's spiritual crisis amid the growing threat of paganism due to the unconquered nations. The wrong kind of king

---

[37] Judges 18:1 and 19:1 suggest that the crisis for Israel's covenant fidelity is linked to a crisis of leadership. The Danite crisis, as well as the account of the Levite's concubine, illustrate graphically the spiritual decline of the nation in the dark days of judges but also looks to the spiritual crisis ahead. Dan, for example, will function with Bethel as one of two primarily cultic sites for the establishment of pagan worship in Israel in protest to Jerusalem. King Jeroboam, of course, will lead his new nation fiercely away from devotion to Yahweh (1 Kgs 12:25–33). See Daniel Isaac Block, *Judges, Ruth*, NAC 6 (Nashville: B&H, 1999), 513–14.

only amplifies this source of futility against Israel. In fact, these unconquered nations will become a *means* for testing Israel. In addition to
the pressures from foreign invaders, Israel's kings will offer little relief
and contribute to the spiritual chaos that multiplies during the period
of the divided kingdom. Through the prophets Yahweh addresses
the nation and increases Israel's theological awareness of the growing threat of exile (Deut 28:63–68; see also 4:25–28). Amid this threat
Israel's prophets will again address the issue of Israel's kingship and
ask what *kind* of king could possibly restore covenant relationship and
blessing to the nation. The prophetic answer will be a new covenant,
a circumcised heart, and a king *like David* (again, Deut 28:63–68; see
also 4:25–28).[38]

Testing and Conquest

The transition of leadership from Moses to Joshua includes the generation of Israelites that had experienced the refinement and testing of
the wilderness. The battle over Canaan will soon involve more than
just conflict over land but also the struggle over Israel's exclusive devotion to Yahweh amid the growing pagan threat. The commands to *rule*
and *subdue*, first issued to Adam, now involve the laws of warfare first
prescribed by Moses (Deut 20:1–20). The land remains *the place* for
the establishment of the name and reputation of Yahweh among the

---

[38] McConville (*Deuteronomy*, 427) comments on Deuteronomy's recognition
of the broken covenant: "That problem could not be solved by a mere turning
back of the clock; a new thing had to be done to deal effectively with Israel's
sinful disposition. And the answer lay in Yahweh's acting in a completely new
way in order to make covenant life with him possible (cf. Jer 31:31–34; 32:39–40;
Ezek 36:24–27)." Jeremiah will develop the idea that Yahweh will do something
new among his people and proclaim, "Break up your fallow ground, and do not
sow among thorns. Circumcise yourselves to the LORD and remove the foreskins
of your heart" (Jer 4:3b–4a). Jeremiah's call for a radical repentance required an
inner transformation and the totality of the entire person (cf. Deut 10:16). For
Jeremiah, this would require a new covenant. See Thompson, *Jeremiah*, 214–15.

nations. Thus, in order to establish Yahweh's reputation in the land, Israel will first need to engage in military conflict enacted on God's terms. Moreover, Yahweh's reputation will be established through the loyalty and covenant obedience of his own people (Deut 4:5–8). As encouragement for the nation, Israel's kings would support this cause by serving as walking billboards to illustrate covenant obedience. Of course the threat will be the paganism of the nations, and Israel receives warning against this threat that would challenge the exclusive devotion called for by covenant relationship (Deut 4:15–20; 7:1–11). In the land, unlike the wilderness, Israel cannot be the one to *test* Yahweh again, for to do this would be to misrepresent his name before a watching world (Deut 5:11; Exod 20:7).[39] Thus, Israel's expression of faith and fidelity in the Promised Land illustrates to the nations the name and reputation of God himself.

In Deuteronomy, Israel receives her specific instruction on how the battle against paganism is to be fought, expressed in the theology of the ban that fully anticipates this threat (Deut 7:1–5).[40] What is at stake is Israel's valued status of *special treasure* before Yahweh (Deut 7:6; Exod 19:6).[41] Paganism threatens not only Israel's status before Yahweh but

---

[39] McConville (*Deuteronomy*, 143–44) comments, "The recollection of Massah (Exod. 17:7; cf. Deut. 9:22) fits well in the present context because Israel's 'testing' of the LORD there involved questioning whether he could take them safely through the wilderness and into the promised land."

[40] While the language of the ban (חרם) sounds harsh to the modern reader, it must be understood that Yahweh's war against the nations was a war against the threat of paganism. For example, Israel is specifically warned against accommodating to the practice of infant sacrifice as an expression of worship to Molech (Lev 18:21; 20:2–5; Deut 12:31) *before* entering the Promised Land. The result of *not* heeding this command is fully felt in texts such as Jer 7:31 and the reference to the "high places of Topeth." Worship of this Amorite god in Jeremiah's day was conducted in the valley of Ben-hinnom, just south of Jerusalem. For an excellent discussion see Daniel Isaac Block, *Deuteronomy*, NIV Application Commentary (Grand Rapids: Zondervan, 2012), 205–23.

[41] Israel's special relationship with Yahweh was not an excuse for spiritual smugness and overconfidence. Jeremiah will warn against this false sense of

also Yahweh's status or reputation before the nations. Yahweh's sentiment against this threat is described as a *consuming fire*. Paganism warrants the divine judgment that Yahweh plans to execute against these nations through the instrument of his own people (Deut 9:3–5).[42]

Under Joshua, Israel enacts the necessary plan of expelling paganism from the land. Some of the campaigns were successful, but Israel's mission was not entirely accomplished (Josh 13:13; 16:10; 17:12). Judges 1:27–2:5 brings further emphasis to territories not captured by the Israelites and their subsequent impact. These nations now substitute for the "thorns and thistles" of Genesis 3 and function to *increase* Israel's experience of military/political and spiritual futility (cf. Num 33:50–56). Judges 2:21–22 confirms the divine intent that the remaining nations function to test (refine) Israel: "I also will no longer drive out before them any of the nations which Joshua left when he died, in order to test (נסה) Israel *by them*, whether they will keep the way of the LORD to walk in it as their fathers did, or not" (emphasis added). As we suggested earlier, this role of the nations parallels the role shared by the hunger and thirst of the wilderness (Deut 8:1–5), in addition to the "thorns and thistles" of the fallen created order (Gen 3:17–19). In all cases rebellion leads to divine intervention and increased futility.

---

privilege preached by the false prophets in his day, "They heal the brokenness of the daughter of My people superficially, saying, 'Peace, peace,' but there is no peace" (Jer 8:11). Deuteronomy 8:11–20 warns of the threat of *forgetting* Yahweh by reminding Israel that their experience in the wilderness offered daily reminders of why utter dependence on Yahweh was central to her covenant fidelity! McConville, *Deuteronomy*, 155; Thompson, *Jeremiah*, 300.

[42] This fire, of course, gets turned back on Yahweh's own people and becomes the fire of refinement against Judah. Jeremiah writes, "The bellows blow fiercely, the lead is consumed by the fire; in vain the refining goes on, but the wicked are not separated" (6:29). Thompson (*Jeremiah*, 266–67) writes, "When the lead was placed in a crucible with silver ore and heated, the lead became oxidized and served as a flux to collect impurities. The bellows blew fiercely to give a high temperature, but out of the heat came only lead, copper and iron. The ore was so impure that the whole procedure failed."

Israel's new experience in the land may extend her wilderness wan-
derings as unconquered nations in the land operate as assigned agents
of futility.[43] Israel must return to the lesson of the wilderness: exclusive
loyalty is demonstrated through obedience to the *word of Yahweh*. Both
nation *and* king must demonstrate this quality of covenant fidelity if
there remains any hope of prospering in the land (Deut 8:3; cf. Judg
17:6; 21:25). Yet amid the chaos, faithfulness and loyalty emerge in the
most unassuming of places.[44] The book of Ruth reads as a contrasting
account to the book of Judges. Ruth serves as a model of fidelity for
Israel and illustrates that individual faithfulness and fidelity to covenant demands can flourish in the most difficult of times. Ruth's fierce
loyalty to Naomi reminds Israel what loyalty ought to look like, even
from the example of a non-Israelite.[45] Her entrance to Israel's faith
story adds a surprising twist as she expresses one of the most eloquent
statements of loyalty in all of Scripture:

---

[43] Block (*Judges, Ruth*, 137) comments: "The Canaanite nations represent
not only a challenge to him and his historical program, but they also remain as a
test, proving whether or not Israel will accept her status as his covenant people,
with all the privileges and obligations attached thereto. This generation needs to
learn that they have been called to a holy war, that Yahweh is the commander-
in-chief, and that the enemy is to be totally exterminated." Now that Israel is in
the land, thorns and scorpions have been replaced by pagan marauders, but the
lesson is the same."

[44] Block (*Judges, Ruth*, 610) compares the difference between Ruth and
Judges in terms of the activity of Yahweh and comments: "Unlike the book of
Judges, however, here his hand is not driving the movers and shakers in Israel.
David does not emerge because of divine manipulation of the ruling class. On
the contrary, the seeds of the great dynasty that would arise in the future are
being sown in this private family of Bethlehem. This family consists of the most
unlikely candidates for divine service: a widow left without husband or sons, an
alien in a similar state, and a bachelor from the humble town of Bethlehem."

[45] Ruth's clinging to Naomi (Ruth 1:14–17) mirrors Joshua's charge for Israel
to cling to Yahweh (Josh 23:8), as well as the call for Israel's exclusive allegiance
(Deut 6:4–5). This is the language of loyalty and fidelity! See ibid., 638–44.

Do not urge me to leave you *or* turn back from following you;
for where you go, I will go, and where you lodge, I will lodge.
Your people *shall be* my people, and your God, my God. Where
you die, I will die, and there I will be buried. Thus may the
LORD do to me, and worse, if *anything but* death parts you and
me. (Ruth 1:16–17)

Thus, Ruth falls in line with the biblical portrayal of the individual who
through great difficulty remains loyal and demonstrates great fidelity.

Testing and the Monarchy

First Samuel addresses the question of kingship raised by the book of
Judges: what *kind* of king in Israel will it take to end the cycle of spiritual and political chaos? As has been discussed, Deuteronomy 17:14–
20 offers the correct answer. The people's request for a king raises a
flag: "Now appoint a king for us to judge us *like all the nations*" (1 Sam
8:5b, emphasis added). Their request rejects Yahweh's rule as the true
King over Israel and may signal a much deeper spiritual problem
(1 Sam 8:7–8). Yahweh instructs Samuel to grant the request; however, the prophet attempts to persuade otherwise. Samuel offers details
regarding the *kind* of king that is requested by the people (vv. 10–20).[46]
This king will not be concerned with the spiritual development of
his people. Instead, his focus will be, according to Samuel, raising an
army by force (8:11–12), amassing female servants and slaves (8:13),
and amassing wealth through taxation (8:14–17). Clearly this is the

---

[46] Some scholars tend to minimize this observation. Ralph Klein (*1 Samuel*,
WBC 10 [Waco, TX: Word, 1983], 75) comments, "The law of the king in Deuteronomy (17:14) also refers to a king 'like the nations,' but it is difficult to tell
whether this expression in v. 5 expresses a negative evaluation or whether it
merely takes cognizance of the fact that kingship was a relatively late institution
in Israel (cf. Gen 36:31)."

antithesis of the king Deuteronomy prescribes.[47] Thus, in addition to
the spiritual pressure caused by Israel's unconquered pagan neighbors,
the monarchy itself now threatens to contribute to Israel's list of spiritual distractions in the land![48] The text suggests that the desire of the
people was to be *like* the nations. Thus, their kind of king would only
advance the rebel cause—a situation that warrants testing as refinement for the entire nation (cf. Judg 2:22). Israel appears to be intent on
walking away from her covenant agreement; the bride is walking out
of her marriage and is on her way to the "red light district"![49] Yet Yahweh's covenant commitment can be understood as the loyalty a groom
feels for his new bride, a love that obligates him to respond. The granting of Israel's request for a king, much like the unconquered nations,
becomes yet another means of *testing* and *refining* Israel. Increasing
futility by means of invading nations, oppressive kings, and even exilic

---

[47] One argument that does not favor our observation suggests that the details
of 1 Sam 8:10–18 do not match those described in Deut 17:14–20 point for point.
J. P. Fokkelman (*Narrative Art and Poetry in the Books of Samuel: A Full Interpretation Based on Stylistic and Structural Analyses*, Studia Semitica Neerlandica
20 [Assen, Netherlands: Van Gorcum, 1981], 4:342) reduces the implications of
their request and cautions, "And speaking of the covenant: nowhere do the people say, in conversation with Samuel, that they want to be rid of the covenant."
While it is true that ברית does not occur in the context, it is difficult to minimize
the covenantal force of the author's vantage point.

[48] Klein (*1 Samuel*, 78) comments: "In v. 20 the people's desire to be like the
nations is given a more prominent position than in v. 5, and it is presumably to
be interpreted here quite negatively. In 1 Sam 8 the people fail the test and suc-
cumb to a desire to be like the nations."

[49] Jeremiah will portray Judah in his day as a wayward wife who has left
her husband for a lifestyle of prostitution and proclaims, "If a husband divorces
his wife and she goes from him and belongs to another man, will he still return
to her?" (Jer 3:1a). Jeremiah will also relate Israel's covenant infidelity and subsequent exile as the equivalent of being issued a certificate of divorce (Jer 3:8).
Judah is now on the same path as her sister to the north. There is a beautiful
reminder here of the strength of Hosea's love for Gomer, for he sought for her
among her strange lovers and brought her back home (Hos 2:14–3:3).

experiences will all continue to serve as Yahweh's method both to contain the rebellion and to precipitate change among his people. Hosea will illustrate this same kind of tough love through the "solitary confinement" experienced by Gomer upon her return (Hos 3:2–4). The groom desires his wayward bride to return and to demonstrate a loyal heart (v. 5). Our earlier presentation of the metallurgical background for testing suggests that God assigns such *futility* as the *heat* that is necessary to refine this kind of loyalty. On this point C. S. Lewis offers an insightful and helpful comment:

> God whispers to us in our pleasures, speaks in our conscience, but shouts in our pains: it is His megaphone to rouse a deaf world. A bad man, happy, is a man without the least inkling that his actions do not "answer," that they are not in accord with the laws of the universe.[50]

God cannot remain neutral on the topic of the rebelliousness of the human heart. While the unbelieving world expects and even demands a pain-free existence, the biblical story presents the reality of living in a fallen world where loyalty (love) is demonstrated through suffering. Lewis again comments:

> No doubt pain as God's megaphone is a terrible instrument; it may lead to final and unrepentant rebellion. But it gives the only opportunity the bad man can have for amendment. It removes the veil; it plants the flag of truth within the fortress of a rebel soul.[51]

As Israel's monarchy advances, the influence of paganism continues slowly to erode the spiritual vitality and covenant devotion of the nation. Only a minority of Israel's kings will be involved in any kind

---

[50] C. S. Lewis, *Problem of Pain* (New York: Macmillan, 1962), 93.
[51] Ibid., 95–96.

of genuine attempt at covenant reform. Josiah's campaign, for example, attempts to root out the practice of child sacrifice and the worship of Molech (2 Kgs 23:10; cf. 2 Kgs 21:6). Even with added prophetic voices, such as Jeremiah, even Judah will resist change (Jer 7:31–32). An alarming number of Israel's kings remain unmoved by the prophetic voice directed at them and continue to allow (and even encourage) such abominable practices (2 Kgs 17:17; 16:3; 1 Kgs 11:7). Moses' theological warning against this extreme paganism became the theological basis for the prophetic voices and their message of judgment (and testing) against both Israel and Judah. While space will not allow a full development of the theme of testing in the Prophets, the prophets Amos, Jeremiah, and Ezekiel will serve to narrow the focus of our investigation in the next section.

Testing and the Divided Kingdom

As Israel experienced a divided kingdom and continued political failure, her spiritual life and vitality also continued to decline. The kingdom's division contributed to the spiritual fragmentation of the nation.[52] Israel's growing syncretistic religion demanded the correction that covenant relationship obligated Yahweh to deliver to his own people. For example, on the basis of Deuteronomy 17:14–20 and the warnings of 28:15–68, Yahweh puts the nation on trial for their

---

[52] The division of the kingdom was grounded in the false religion established by King Jeroboam I at Bethel and Dan (1 Kgs 12:25–33). These shrines would be thriving in the days of Amos. The prophetic message is clear, *"As for those who swear by the guilt of Samaria, who say, 'As your god lives, O Dan,' and, 'As the way of Beersheba lives,' they will fall and not rise again (Amos 8:14)."* Jeff Niehaus argues that this passage clearly refers to the pagan shrines first established by Jeroboam I at Dan and Bethel. See Jeff Niehaus, "Amos," in *The Minor Prophets: An Exegetical and Expository Commentary*, ed. Thomas Edward McComiskey (Grand Rapids: Baker, 1992), 476–77.

covenant infidelity.[53] Again God acts to test the nation. Interestingly, in Amos the concept of testing builds on the idea of futility and on the language and concepts drawn from the book of Deuteronomy. Amos draws directly from this language as he builds his covenant case against Israel. For example, Amos proclaims,

> Therefore because you impose heavy rent on the poor
> And exact a tribute of grain from them,
> *Though* you have built houses of well-hewn stone,
> Yet you will not live in them;
> You have planted pleasant vineyards, yet you will not drink
> their wine. (Amos 5:11)[54]

Like Jeremiah and Ezekiel to come, Amos draws heavily from the covenant futility language and concepts of Deuteronomy 28 as he lays out his covenant lawsuit against Israel. For example, Amos illustrates how Israel will experience increased futility in the common activities of agriculture and war. Amos charges:

> Behold, I am weighted down beneath you
> As a wagon is weighted down when filled with sheaves.
> Flight will perish from the swift,
> And the stalwart will not strengthen his power,
> Nor the mighty man save his life.
> He who grasps the bow will not stand *his ground*,
> The swift of foot will not escape,
> Nor will he who rides the horse save his life.

---

[53] Niehaus (ibid., 317–23) recognizes the "covenant-lawsuit" pattern in Amos that draws heavily from the theology of Deuteronomy, which scholars have observed is organized along second-millennium Hittite treaty forms. Amos employs the "messenger formula" as he announces his covenant lawsuit against Israel, employing a covenant ideology found in the Pentateuch.

[54] Niehaus (*Amos*, 420) recognizes the connection of this futility curse with Deut 28:39 (cf. Deut 28:30–31).

> Even the bravest among the warriors will flee naked in that day,
> declares the LORD. (Amos 2:13–16)

Regarding this futility, Niehaus comments:

> The Lord announces by a simile the punishment for his people.
> He will press down upon them, as a load of sheaves presses
> down upon a cart. The overall sense is that of a pressure from
> above that defeats the *normal function* of something—in this
> case, the cart and, by analogy, God's people. So the sense is
> broader than being "bogged down" (emphasis added).[55]

This disruption of the normal function of something parallels our discussion of God's subversion of the design and intended function of the created order by subjecting it to futility (Rom 8:20; Gen 3:16–19). From Adam's exile out of the garden to the coming exile from the Promised Land, the biblical case is that God commonly responds to the rebellion of his people through the amplification of futility. In the example just cited, Yahweh removes the blessing of victory, or *good*, in battle and soldiers struggle with their normal functional role. For Amos, increased futility also translates to frustrated weather patterns, failed harvest cycles, and even famine (Amos 4:6–11). Amos recognizes Yahweh's deliberate assignment of these agents that work to refine Israel's spiritual pride—another wilderness experience! Yet, despite the famine (4:6), inconsistent rain cycles (4:7), periods of drought (4:8), ruined crops due to insects or blight (4:9), plague (4:10), and military defeat (4:11), Israel remains deaf to the prophetic warning.[56] Niehaus comments:

_____

[55] Ibid., 371. Niehaus (ibid., 364) brings appropriate emphasis to this divine initiative.

[56] James Luther Mays (*Amos: A Commentary*, OTL [Philadelphia: Westminster Press, 1969], 79–80) comments: "Lists of curses had a fixed place within the treaty form used to organize international relationship within the ancient Near East: they functioned as divine sanctions against a possible breach of the treaty.

As Creator of heaven and earth, he has all authority in heaven
and earth to send or withhold rain, to make the earth fertile
or hard as iron from drought. The curse of drought, here
portrayed, was threatened in the original covenantal documents
(e.g., Lev 26:19; Deut 28:23–24).[57]

To the untrained these measures appear harsh. As we have attempted
to argue, God's covenant obligation moves him to enact these tough
measures in response to the rebellion of those covenantally obligated
to him. For example, Hosea illustrates Yahweh's covenant committ-
ment toward Israel as a lion attack and proclaims:

> For I *will be* like a lion to Ephraim
> And like a young lion to the house of Judah.
> I, even I, will tear to pieces and go away,
> I will carry away, and there will be none to deliver.
> I will go away and return to My place
> Until they acknowledge their guilt and seek My face;
> In their affliction they will earnestly seek Me. (Hos 5:14–15)

This particular text illustrates several important concepts that relate
to our primary discussion of testing. First, the prophetic call to repentance comes in the midst of the lion attack. In Israel's context the

---

With Israel's use of the treaty form as a way of thinking about the covenant with
Yahweh, the curses acquired theological gravity and meaning." Niehaus (*Amos*,
399–400) recognizes that שוב repeated five times in this section follows the same
idea in Deut 4:30 and 30:2 (cf. Hos 14:2–3 [1–2]), where the people of God are
called to return to Yahweh after an event of covenantal punishment. God's gracious intent is to get their attention (see Amos 4:6, 8–11).

[57] Niehaus (ibid., 399–400) points out that these curses were common in
second-millennium Hittite treaty texts. Some examples highlight that the ele-
ments of nature served as both witnesses of covenant breach and agents of
judgment (futility) against the guilty. Niehaus cites one such example: "The
mountains, the rivers, the springs, the great Sea, heaven and earth, the winds
and the clouds—let these be witnesses to this treaty and to the oath" (see also
ANET 205; cf. Deut 4:26).

lion attack comes at the hand of God through the assigned agent of futility—the Assyrians—as Israel is subsequently "dragged off" and exiled. This announced exile comes with the intended result that Israel acknowledges sin and seeks Yahweh. Moses reminds us that wilderness experiences are intended to change hearts (Deut 8:1–5).[58] Second, the immediate context suggests that the lion attack also comes with the possibility of future restoration and healing. After the announcement of the attack, Hosea proclaims:

> Come, let us return to the LORD
> For He has torn *us*, but He will heal us;
> He has wounded *us*, but He will bandage us.
> He will revive us after two days;
> He will raise us up on the third day,
> That we may live before Him.
> So let us know, let us press on to know the LORD. (Hos 6:1–3a)

The *same lion* tears *and* heals, wounds *and* bandages. Amid all these activities arises the call to a deeper knowledge of Yahweh (6:3a; cf. Deut 8:5; 30:3). Thomas McComiskey comments, "The call to repentance is based on the fact that Yahweh, who tore the nation as a lion rends its prey, is willing also to heal the people and bind up the wounds

---

[58] One cannot miss the fact that the marriage of Hosea to Gomer amplifies the significance of God's covenant obligations toward Israel. Yahweh commands Hosea, as an extension of his marriage (covenant) to Gomer, to find her and bring her home to be his wife (Hos 3:1–5). The context suggests that Hosea has gone to extreme lengths—at great sacrifice and even personal suffering—in order to bring Gomer home. The text also points to the fact of a future restoration where Yahweh is God, David is king, goodness is in the land, and fear is in the hearts of the people (v. 5). Hosea's covenant commitment (marriage) to Gomer, amplified by the personal sacrifice and suffering involved in bringing her home to be his bride, illustrates the great truth of the Messiah. The incarnation and the cross will illustrate these same divine principles.

he inflicted."[59] Thus, testing as refinement rests on the foundation of both judgment *and* grace that extends from God's covenant obligations toward his people.[60]

Finally, Amos warns Israel in the language of Deuteronomy 28 that the expensive homes and vineyards built on the backs of the poor would become vacant in the coming exile (Deut 28:30b, 39; cf. Amos 5:11; Zeph 1:13).[61] On covenant grounds God is obligated to test and refine his own people—even through suffering and exile (cf. Amos 4:2).[62] On further analysis the book of Amos demonstrates a keen awareness of the divine role in the enactment of the futility curses of

---

[59] Thomas McComiskey, *Hosea*, ed. Thomas McComiskey, vol. 1 of *The Minor Prophets: An Exegetical and Expository Commentary* (Grand Rapids: Baker 1992), 88.

[60] Hosea may be recognizing the similarity between Israel and Adam in how God responds to rebellion in both contexts, that of God's covenant obligation to increase futility against the rebel heart. Hosea 6:7 states, "But like Adam they have transgressed the covenant; there they have dealt treacherously against Me." McComiskey argues that while the covenant terminology does not appear in Genesis 1–3, the basic concepts of covenant obligation do: "The people of Hosea's day were like Adam in that they violated a covenant as did he" (See ibid., 95).

[61] Mays (*Amos*, 94) comments, "The formulations ('to build houses and not live in them; to plant vineyards and not drink their wine') are actually fixed expressions which belong to the category of futility curses. Outside the Old Testament such curses are found in treaties where the curses are the sanctions which enforce the terms of the treaty; the curses fall on those who violate the terms. These sentences appear in the curse series in Deut. 28 (cf. vv. 30, 38–40) where they are sanctions against covenant disobedience in Israel; they are used as words of judgment in Zeph. 1.13; cf. also Micah 6.14f." For similar examples of the futility curses see Deut 28:30a, 31 and Micah 6:15. See also Niehaus, *Amos*, 420.

[62] Niehaus (*Amos*, 392–93) comments on Amos 4:2: "In this passage the Lord's holiness is the guarantor of the oath because God cannot violate his holiness. He cannot lie or forsake his promise. And when the Lord swore to Abraham, he swore by himself, because there was no greater guarantor of his promise (Heb 6:13). The Lord will always be faithful to his covenant, both to purge and to restore."

Leviticus 26 and Deuteronomy 28. Just as Yahweh commands the obedience of his people, he also commands the judgment, "For even now Yahweh is *commanding*, and he will pound the large house to pieces, and the small house to bits" (Amos 6:11, emphasis added).[63] Niehaus identifies the similarity of this language and the use of מצוה ("commanding") in key covenantal contexts where Yahweh also *commands* the obedience of his people (cf. Exod 34:11; Deut 26:16). Thus, Amos emphasizes the divine hand that orchestrates judgment in response to Israel's rebellion (cf. Jer 34:22).[64] In the case of the Assyrian and Babylonian exiles, Yahweh issues the command and allows the secondary agent freedom to carry out judgment.[65] For example, in Amos 7:1–6 futility curses of Deuteronomy 28:15–68 are applied to Israel's context in a way that emphasizes Yahweh's rule and authority over the created order, which also serves to increase futility against the nation; locust swarms and crop fires increase futility and judgment against Israel (Amos 7:1, 4).[66]

As the prophetic focus moves to Judah in the south, testing continues to play an important theological role for the prophetic message. Jeremiah warns Judah with the theology of testing and the coming enemy from the north in Jeremiah 6:27, 29–30:

> I have made you an assayer (בחן) and a tester among My people,
> That you may know and assay (בחן) their way.
> The bellows blow fiercely,
> The lead is consumed by the fire;
> In vain the refining (צרף) goes on,

---

[63] Translation by Niehaus (*Amos*, 442).

[64] Niehaus (*Amos*, 445) comments, "The Lord is commanding—he is at work within time controlling events so that his judgment may fall on his rebellious people."

[65] Ibid., 445.

[66] The participle form of יצר brings emphasis to the sovereignty of Yahweh over these natural agents of futility. Niehaus (ibid., 450) comments, "Here, it is used of the Lord as the former of a locust swarm that he will use to judge Israel."

But the wicked are not separated.

They call them rejected silver,

Because the LORD has rejected them. (Jer 6:27, 29–30)

While Jeremiah acts as the *assayer* or the metallurgist through his prophetic ministry and message, the Babylonians provide the necessary *heat* for the refining (צרף) of Judah.[67] Jeremiah's description of the refining process for Judah contributes to the theological message of prophetic judgment against the nation. Judah's spiritual condition is equated to "bronze and iron" or the undesirable metals that mark the beginning of a refining process (6:28). Judah's fidelity will first be authenticated (בחן) for its quality (6:27b), and then subsequently refined (צרף) and improved (6:29b). Both activities we have suggested for testing, the quality check and the quality improvement, work together and represent the full spectrum of *testing* for Israel.[68] Michael Brown comments, "The prophetic message (and messenger) will always reveal what is in the hearts of God's people, purifying and refining

---

[67] Thompson (*Jeremiah*, 265n1) comments on the difficulty in the MT with the word מבצר, which literally translates "fortress." He proposes a revocalized מבצר as a Piel participle and the meaning "one who searches through." On this proposal, מבצר describes Jeremiah's role of assessing the quality of the ore (fidelity) in Judah. This meaning parallels בחן and the meaning of "assayer" from v. 27. William Holladay offers a full discussion of the metallurgical idea behind this text. See William Lee Holladay, *Jeremiah 1: A Commentary on the Book of the Prophet Jeremiah, Chapters 1–25*, ed. Paul D. Hanson, Hermeneia (Minneapolis: Fortress, 1986), 230–32.

[68] The aspect of quality enhancement is contained in צרף and shares the same semantic range with בחן, yet carries the more intense aspect of refining in most contexts. On our analysis Jer 6:27–30 employs the specific nuances of meaning developed previously. Jeremiah in his prophetic role executes the *touchstone* role, examining the fidelity of God's covenant people in Jerusalem (v. 27). Upon the determination of quality, Jeremiah's role moves to that of *refiner* and the task of enhancing the quality of fidelity in God's people. This task will be accomplished through the coming exilic experience announced by the prophet and his words. See ibid., 265n7; see also Michael L. Brown, *Jeremiah–Ezekiel,* The Expositor's Bible Commentary 7 (Grand Rapids: Zondervan, 2010), 156–57.

them, testing their loyalty and obedience."[69] As the intensity of refining increases, the base metals—the rebels and slanderers of 6:28—
remain inseparable from the more desirable metals (6:29). Finally, the
refining ends and leaves behind that which Yahweh rejects (6:30).[70]

Jeremiah offers additional insight into testing that is unique
among the prophets: Jeremiah experiences and endures the *suffering*
brought about by the message he delivers! From this unique vantage
point, Jeremiah invites readers to wrestle with some of the more difficult theological implications for the concept of testing, especially
the testing of the faithful. First, Jeremiah raises the timeless question
of why the righteous suffer at the hands of the wicked and declares,
"Righteous are You, O LORD, that I would plead *my* case with You;
indeed I would discuss matters of justice with You: Why has the way
of the wicked prospered? *Why* are all those who deal in treachery at
ease?" (Jer 12:1, emphasis added).[71] The wider context of Jeremiah
11:18–12:6 highlights the fact that Jeremiah gets caught in the crossfire of suffering for his divinely assigned role as *touchstone* of the people. Jeremiah presents his case before Yahweh after receiving death
threats from the men of Anathoth, Jeremiah's hometown (11:19, 21).[72]

---

[69] Ibid., 157.

[70] Terrence Fretheim comments (*Jeremiah*, Smyth & Helwys Bible Commentary [Macon: Smith & Helwys, 2002], 128), "Only the catastrophic fires of
judgment and God's creation of a new heart (see 24:7; 32:39) will make a future
possible."

[71] Robert P. Carroll relates the complaints of Jeremiah in this text to Job on
the parallel to the prosperity of the wicked (cf. Job 21) (*Jeremiah: A Commentary*,
OTL [Philadelphia: Westminster Press, 1986], 284).

[72] Jeremiah, like Joseph, receives persecution from those who know him
best. The testing (בחן) here takes us back to the pinnacle testing event for Joseph
in Genesis 42. Jeremiah, like Joseph, facilitates the testing of those who would
need it most (cf. Jer 6:27). Brown (*Jeremiah*, 209) rightly brings emphasis to the
fact that Jeremiah's message was an all-out attack against the idolatry of Anathoth. The warning of Judges—that the remaining nations become a source for
testing Israel—has now come full circle (see Judg 2:3, 22; 4:4).

Yet amid his personal struggle Jeremiah affirms Yahweh's role as the
One who *"tests* (בחן) heart and mind"* (11:20 HCSB, emphasis added;
cf. Jer 20:12).[73] In the process of proclaiming the message of *testing/
refinement* against the majority of unfaithful in Jerusalem, Jeremiah
recognizes that he too must experience the refining fire of testing,
just like everyone else. Jeremiah's question in 12:1 would have represented Jerusalem's righteous remnant. Their experience contradicts
the common theodicy of the ancient world where the gods reward the
righteous and punish the evil or wicked.[74] Jeremiah's frustration rests
on the realization that the world offers the righteous *and* unrighteous
alike equal access to suffering.[75] Thus, Jeremiah aligns with our previous discussion of Job. He questions the fact that the covenant faithful
in Jerusalem experience the *same* refining experience as the covenant
unfaithful. On this point Thompson comments:

> The problem raised is the age-old question of why the wicked
> should flourish. They were God's creatures. It lay in his power
> to bring them to judgment. But they pursued their evil ways
> unchecked and caused innocent men to suffer. Why, for
> example, should Jeremiah, God's servant, called to declare
> his word to disobedient Israel, be subjected to the treacherous
> plots of the men of his own village? Like Job and some of

---

[73] See also Pss 7:9–10; 17:3; Prov 17:3; 21:2. Jack R. Lundbom, *Jeremiah 1–20:
A New Translation with Introduction and Commentary* AB 21a (New York: Doubleday, 1999), 637–38.

[74] Brown (*Jeremiah*, 212) does not shrink back from the full force of Jeremiah's charge against the Lord and comments, "Rather, Jeremiah is saying (perhaps with some sarcasm in the opening clause): 'I lodge a complaint with you,
nonetheless, I'm going to bring charges [or, make a judgment] against you'—
specifically, 'I question the way you run your world.'"

[75] Mark E. Biddle's comments are helpful on this point. See his *Deuteronomy*, Smyth & Helwys Bible Commentary (Macon: Smyth & Helwys,
2003), 428–29.

the psalmists Jeremiah believed in God and stood under his
sovereignty but found his ways hard to comprehend.[76]

Yahweh's answer to Jeremiah's charge offers little comfort: "If you
have run with footmen and they have tired you out, then how can
you compete with horses? If you fall down in a land of peace, how
will you do in the thicket of the Jordan?" (Jer 12:5). The intensity
of Jeremiah's experience of testing gets worse before it gets better.[77]
Thompson comments:

> Instead of the wicked, who in Jeremiah's view might well have
> been punished, it was Jeremiah, the man called by God and the
> faithful servant of God, who was suffering. And God knew the
> whole story. He knew (yāda') him and saw him, and had tested
> his devotion. According to the generally accepted view it was
> Jeremiah who should have been spared. Hence the question,
> *Why do the wicked prosper?* The answer to that question belongs
> to the mystery of evil in God's creation, which has puzzled
> men of faith in every age. . . . That there might be some divine
> purpose served through his suffering or that it might prove a
> means to a deeper knowledge of God does not seem to have
> been clear to the prophet, or if it was, he did not declare it.[78]

---

[76] Thompson, *Jeremiah*, 352.

[77] While this verse may certainly imply that things are only going from bad
to worse for the prophet, Holladay (*Jeremiah*, 379) suggests that this verse also
carries with it a sense of greater expectations for Jeremiah. With the call and
divine enablement, Jeremiah will be able to keep up with and even surpass the
horsemen.

[78] Thompson (*Jeremiah*, 354n34) points out the links to other contexts where
the same issue of suffering is raised, such as Hab 1:2–4; Psalms 37; 49; 73, and
the book of Job. It is interesting that Jeremiah does not attempt to solve his pre-
dicament with any form of a "greater good" response. As we have suggested
for the context of Genesis 1–3, something is *good* in that it has been assigned
a covenantal function, enacted by the divinely spoken word, and carried out
to its fruition, accomplishing God's ultimate outcome. In the case of covenant

His experience offers insight into the common experience of
humanity; sometimes the righteous get caught in the crossfire of the
judgment of the unrighteous. While immediate relief is apparently not
in sight, Yahweh *does* respond to the covenant faithful with a message
of hope and future restoration. As we have seen, this message of future
restoration stems from the theology of exile first developed in Deuteronomy (28:58–68; 30:1–5). Jeremiah 15:11 assigns the divine purpose
behind Judah's exilic experience. Amid the prophet's own personal
struggle of suffering caused by the covenant curses activated against
Israel, Yahweh declares, "Surely I have made an enemy for you *for
good*; surely *I have laid on you*, in a time of evil and in a time of distress,
the enemy" (emphasis added).[79] The causative force of this translation
emphasizes the divine purposes behind Jeremiah's personal struggle
amid the corporate suffering of the entire nation.[80] Theologically, this

---

relationship, love or loyalty is the desired outcome, or object of refining. God is
checking for its quality, and enhancing its value, even at the expense of the suffering of his own people, and this is *good*.

[79] Thompson (*Jeremiah*, 393) offers his translation of this somewhat difficult passage. Thompson follows the MT reading and takes the root of the first
verb שׁרר as a piel participle with a causative force. Fretheim (*Jeremiah*, 236)
recognizes the difficulty of translating v. 11 and comments, "Translations of
v. 11 differ and no certainty is possible. One translation has God speaking in
entirely positive language: God will intervene on Jeremiah's behalf in his times
of trouble and distress and bring his enemies under his feet (see NEB, NIV).
In other translations (NRSV; cf. REB), God speaks of acting in Jeremiah's life
for good but at the same time recognizes that God's word has created enemies
for him as well. If the latter sense is correct, which seems likely, then Jeremiah's
experience of God has generated both blessing and bane for him, a typical reality
for the prophets and other individuals called to such a critical leadership role."
Our discussion of טוב and its covenantal function makes sense of Thompson's
translation above and echoes the same verdict of Gen 50:20.

[80] Mark Biddle (*Deuteronomy*, 429) identifies the obvious tension here and
comments: "Israel's prophets and historians who preached and wrote during
and after the Assyrian (eighth century) and Babylonian (sixth century) crises
identified the covenant curses with the military defeats dealt them by these Mesopotamian imperial powers. As might be expected, and as textual evidence from

response recalls Joseph's closing words, "As for you, you meant evil against me, *but* God meant it for *good* in order to bring about this present result, to preserve many people alive" (Gen 50:20, emphasis added). We also find a parallel in Moses' evaluation of Israel's wilderness exile, "In the wilderness He fed you manna which your fathers did not know, that He might humble you and that He might *test* you, to do good for you in the end" (Deut 8:16, emphasis added). Each context brings emphasis to individual suffering amid a testing/refining cycle. For Joseph, the suffering he endures brings both personal transformation and extends divine *good* for Joseph's family (Israel). Through Israel's experience Yahweh extends grace and allows the nation to enter the land. Like Joseph's, Jeremiah's endurance of suffering facilitates the preservation of the righteous remnant that experiences the exile and eventual return to the Promised Land. Ezekiel will bear the prophetic mantle of *touchstone* for the exiles in Babylon, where the refining of both righteous and unrighteous *together* continues.

Like Jeremiah, Ezekiel offers additional insight into the idea of prophetic testing in the parable of the sword (Ezek 21:13–22 [8–17]).[81] This parable brings together the ideas of sword (judgment) and

---

the period demonstrates (compare, for example, Lam 5), the invading armies had no interest in distinguishing between those guilty of covenant unfaithfulness and the innocent. They behaved as invading armies always do. They killed, burned, pillaged, and raped indiscriminately. Innocent people suffered the common fate. Yet Israel's theologians insisted that the Assyrians and the Babylonians were instruments of YHWH's justice."

[81] Daniel Block (*The Book of Ezekiel: 1–24*, NICOT [Grand Rapids: Eerdmans, 1997], 678) identifies the irony in this short parable in that while the people would have interpreted Yahweh's sword as a symbol representing a military victory over the Babylonians, Ezekiel quickly turns the parable on its head—the sword is coming against God's own people! Block comments: "This verse announces the delivery of the sword into another person's hand. It is at once repetitive and vague, as if the prophet hesitates to get to the point. Who hands the sword over? Probably Yahweh (so Vulg.). To whom is it given to be polished? Perhaps some smith. Who seizes it? It must be Yahweh's agent, but this identity remains undefined throughout the song."

testing in a unique manner. Yahweh commands his prophet to use a sword to illustrate divine judgment. The Lord assigns who will wield the sword against his own people (21:11, 16). This sword bearer is announced as the "king of Babylon" who wields the sword of judgment against Judah (21:19–22). This text introduces the key testing term בחן in verses 12–13, "For *there is* a testing (בחן)," and may suggest that the coming exilic experience for Judah will be one of refinement.[82] While scholars disagree over exactly who or what the object of testing *is* in this context, we suggest that it is the people.[83] This is consistent with Ezekiel's use of the language of refining to describe Yahweh's judgment against Judah and the impending Babylonian exile in verses 31–32:

> I will pour out My indignation on you; I will *blow on you with the fire of My wrath*, and I will give you into the hand of brutal men, skilled in destruction. *You will be fuel for the fire*; your blood will be in the midst of the land. You will not be remembered, for I, the LORD, have spoken (emphasis added).

Ezekiel 22:17–22 uses similar imagery of the refining process when judgment is discussed. God's people are identified as the undesired

---

[82] Scholars recognize the difficulty in translating this verse. Block (*Ezekiel 1–24*, 674n92) recognizes בחן as a Pual perfect but treats this term as a segholate noun, just as it occurs in Isa 28:16. He translates v. 18a, "For the testing [is over]," adding the additional words to his interpretation to suggest that the object of testing has been the sword. With the verbal sense preserved, scholars also regard the *people* as the subject of the verb. See Moshe Greenberg, *Ezekiel 1–20: a New Translation with Introduction and Commentary*, AB 22 (Garden City: Doubleday, 1983), 424. We prefer this particular interpretation on grounds that Ezekiel 22 continues the emphasis on the testing of the people through their coming exilic experience.

[83] Block (*Ezekiel 1–24*, 679) comments: "What is this test? Who is being tested? In view of the previous references to the sharpening and polishing of the sword, this is best applied to the weapon, which Yahweh hereby affirms to be ready for its deadly mission."

portion of the refining process, with the result that they will be gathered so that the LORD can blow on them *the fire of His wrath* (22:19–21; cf. Jer 6:27–30). Block comments, "The prophet's point is that far from being regarded as Yahweh's special treasure, the house of Israel is nothing more than slag, the waste produced in the extraction of silver from ore."[84] This text, taken with the parable of the sword, emphasizes that Judah's exilic experience acts as a sovereignly assigned testing/refining experience against the entire nation; the Babylonian siege functions as the necessary *heat* for Judah's refinement. God assigns the Babylonians as an agent of futility against Judah, who will experience testing in two basic phases. Phase one begins with the Babylonian siege of Jerusalem. For Jeremiah the siege begins with the announcement of the boiling pot that pours out its hot liquid as judgment against Jerusalem (Jer 1:13). For Ezekiel the Babylonian army, which represents the hot liquid, has now surrounded the city for a siege, thus transforming the city into a boiling pot of refinement for God's people (Ezek 22:17–22; 24:1–14). Phase two occurs in Babylon under the prophetic *word* of Ezekiel. The combination of difficult circumstances and the intensity of prophetic words serve as the refining fire for the exiles. After seventy years of refinement, not unlike Israel's experience of forty years in the wilderness, a new generation of the faithful emerges and returns to the land.

---

[84] Block, *Ezekiel: 1–24*, 718. The Hebrew term סגלה is rare and conveys the special value of covenant relationship (see Exod 19:5; Deut 7:6; 14:2; 26:18). We ask where the confirmation of Israel's status as dross may have occurred. On our interpretation of בחן in 21:18, Ezekiel's song of the sword may serve as the pronouncement of Israel's *authentication* on the metallurgical idea. Thus, an even more desperate situation exists in the land. The exilic refining begins on a metal whose value has already been determined. Greenberg (*Ezekiel*, 468) contrasts this smelting process described by both Jeremiah and Ezekiel and comments, "Moreover, in Jeremiah the lead is annihilated as a normal part of the smelting process; Ezekiel weirdly transforms the entire process into a symbol of obliteration. Here as elsewhere in Ezekiel, fire is not a purifying but a destructive force."

The Testing of God's Sons: Jesus

God's primary concern for the quality of the faith and fidelity of members of his own covenant family extends into the New Testament. This concern will involve the testing of his Son, Jesus. One cannot escape the significant parallel of Christ's experience of testing in Matthew 4:1–11 and Israel's own wilderness testing.[85] Christ's primary defense against the satanic challenge draws primarily from two passages in Deuteronomy where testing is the contextual focus. Christ's experience shares similarities with Israel's wilderness experience. First, Christ shares in the wilderness experience of deprivation; hunger (not starvation) was part of Israel's experience of futility in the wilderness (Deut 8:3a).[86] Christ responds by quoting Moses' stated theological purpose behind

---

[85] The aorist passive infinite of πειράζω conveys the basic idea of "to try, to be put to the test" and does not convey as much of the metallurgical refining idea as δόκιμος. However, Matt 4:1–11 clearly shares common ground with the testing context developed from Deut 8:2, where the piel infinite construct of נסה is translated as an aorist active subjunctive from ἐκπειράζω. On this contextual relationship, William Stegner ("The Temptation Narrative: A Study in the Use of Scripture by Early Jewish Christians," *Biblical Research* 35 [1990]: 10) writes, "In view of the parallel situation between Jesus and the wilderness generation, and in view of the fact that the first quotation from Deuteronomy is cited from Deut. 8:3b, we might infer that the point of the testing is the same." Gerhardsson (*Testing of God's Son [Matt. 4:1–11 & Par.]: An Analysis of an Early Christian Midrash*, New Testament Series 2 [Lund: Berlingska Bibtryckeriet, 1966], 26–27) argues that the language used in both contexts suggests "a testing of the partner in the covenant to see whether he is keeping his side of the agreement." Thus, according to Gerhardsson, Christ stands with Israel as a *tested covenant son*.

[86] William Stegner has recognized the relationship between the idea of testing and the concept of the "wilderness" in both Qumran texts and New Testament texts. He argues for a primeval time (*Urzeit*) and eschatological time (*Endzeit*) relationship between the wilderness generation under Moses and the self-understanding of the community at Qumran. The text of 1QS 8:1–4 refers to the "endurance of the trial of affliction (מצרף) where the idea that this particular kind of trial functions to either refine out the wicked or purify the righteous." Stegner suggests that the closest New Testament term for this idea is πειρασμος, a term common to the testing of the faithful during eschatological

the wilderness experience, "that man does not live by bread alone, but man lives by everything that proceeds out of the mouth of the LORD" (Deut 8:3b).[87] Thus, Christ's identification with suffering through *testing* brings theological emphasis to Christ's identification with the suffering of humanity. Christ's suffering in the wilderness prepares him for the suffering that will soon come, where the fullest expression and example of suffering is made available to the whole world. The invitation is that we suffer *with Christ* (Rom 8:16–17).

Satan's attack further calls into question the fidelity of God himself (Matt 4:5–6).[88] In response Christ draws from the texts of Deuteronomy 6:13 and 10:20 to respond with a statement of his firm loyalty and devotion. Matthew's account of Christ's victory over Satan not only anticipates the cross but also offers an initial glimpse into the fulfillment of the original promise of Genesis 3:15 that a future son of Adam would crush the head of the serpent. On this parallel Postell comments:

> Genesis 3:15, however, when interpreted both within the
> context of the Pentateuch and the canonical Tanakh as a
> whole, must be regarded as the promise of a royal seed from
> the tribe of Judah, a future "Adam" who defeats, not only the
> wicked inhabitants of the Promised Land, but the serpent itself,
> in the last days and takes up Adam's rule (see Gen 1:26–28;
> Num 24:19; Ps 72:8; 110:2). Israel's eschatological hope for the

---

contexts ("Wilderness and Testing in the Scrolls and in Matthew 4:1–11," *Biblical Research* 12 [1967]: 22).

[87] Gerhardsson (*Testing of God's Son*, 47) comments: "The real nature of the sin of craving is here revealed. Discontent with the divine nourishment provided during the wilderness period is characterized as unbelief, lack of trust, as a violation of the basic obligation of the covenant."

[88] Gerhardsson (ibid., 28) writes: "To test God is to examine him to see if he will keep his obligations, challenging him to demonstrate his fidelity to the conditions of the covenant. . . . To test God is thus the opposite of believing in him and therefore a very definite violation of the covenant bond."

attainment of the promise of the "land," therefore, is presented in royal terms (Gen 49:1, 8–12; Num 24:5–9, 17–24; Deut 31:28–29; 33:5, 7), and this hope is already introduced in the opening chapters of the Torah. Adam is the type set for this coming conquering king. The "king" of the ראשית ("beginning") provides the job description for the king of the אחרית ("end").[89]

Theologically, Matthew 4:1–11 focuses attention on the unity between the Old and New Testaments on the theme of testing in a way that encourages and reminds first-century believers that the testing of faith, often through difficult circumstances, remains the normal Christian experience.[90] As we will see, for Paul and other New Testament authors, the theme of testing amid suffering remains a central focus for letters written to encourage the persecuted church of the first century.

The Testing of God's Sons: The Church

In Romans 8:12–25 Paul develops a theology of suffering that applies to all believers. With Christ's example of suffering in view, Paul suggests that God's adopted sons (the church) are called to suffer through testing—and with significant eschatological implications.[91] For Paul the Christian suffers *with* Christ for the purpose of being *glorified* with him (8:17–18). Thomas Schreiner comments: "By 'suffering' Paul does not mean suffering in God's sight or in baptism but actual suffering. Suffering is the path to future glorification, and συνδοξασθῶμεν

---

[89] See Postell, *Adam as Israel*, 163.

[90] Stegner (*Wilderness and Testing*, 27) comments, "Every test that the first Israelite under Moses failed to pass, the Messiah as the new Israel successfully surmounts. This is suggested by the quotes from Deuteronomy in the story."

[91] Ernst Käsemann (*Commentary on Romans* [Grand Rapids: Eerdmans, 1980], 231) comments, "In adoption . . . those who are already set in the state of sonship, and who anticipate heavenly glory therein, are also those who wait and suffer, sharing the groaning of every creature."

is just another way of describing the future inheritance of believers."[92]
In the context of Romans 8, we observe the relationship between the
suffering of the believer and the testing of the believer on the grounds
that suffering must come with the authentication and refining of faith.
Earlier we explored the possibility that postfall creation operates as an
agent of futility against rebel humanity for the purpose of both testing and refining faith—thus, the universal testing experience for all
humanity.[93] Paul refers to creation's subjection to futility in his discussion of suffering for the early church. Testing *through suffering* accomplishes the higher purpose of authenticating and refining the faith of
all divine image bearers (8:20–21).[94] Paul's connection of Genesis 3
with Romans 8 suggests that *testing through suffering* occurs through
the created order's subjection to futility and that it was God's covenant obligation toward rebel man to do so—*just as a man disciplines his*

---

[92] Thomas R. Schreiner, *Romans*, Baker Exegetical Commentary on the
New Testament (Grand Rapids, MI: Baker, 1998), 428. See also Douglas J. Moo,
Romans 1–8, The Wycliffe Exegetical Commentary (Chicago: Moody, 1991),
551; Grant R. Osborne, *Romans*, The IVP New Testament Commentary Series
6 (Downers Grove, IL: IVP, 2004), 210–14; James D. G. Dunn, *Romans 1–8*,
WBC 38a (Dallas: Word, 1988), 470–72.

[93] Schreiner (*Romans*, 435–36) makes the argument that God is the subject
of the verb ὑπετάγη in v. 20. He comments, "Subjecting the world to frustration
connotes control over the world, whereas Adam lost dominion over the world
by succumbing to sin . . . for the same God who subjected the created order will
also set it free from its slavery (v. 21)." Regarding the "groaning" and "suffering"
of v. 22, he comments, "Both of these verbs signify that the created order has not
fulfilled its purpose; the futility, decay and frustration of the present world signal its incompleteness and failure to reach its full potential." See also Fitzmeyer,
Romans, 507.

[94] Regarding this futility, Fitzmeyer (*Romans*, 507) comments, "It denotes
the state of ineffectiveness of something that does not attain its goal or purpose;
concretely, it means the chaos, decay, and corruption (8:21) to which humanity
has subjected God's noble creation." As we have said previously, Adam's mandate to *rule* and *subdue* the earth was frustrated at the fall. Now earth *rules* and
subdues humanity for divine purposes.

son (Deut 8:5b).[95] Thus, for Paul, Adam's exile from the garden and Israel's exile from the land share a common lesson and experience for both believer and unbeliever: man must learn to live by means of every word that proceeds from the mouth of the Lord (Deut 8:3). Thus, the experience of futility can work as the divine means by which faith is both tested/refined and authenticated in the individual heart. This futility operates in much the same way as it did in the account of the tower of Babel, frustrating humanity's attempt to build towers of self-reliance and rebellion and working to refine the faith of some and establish the faith of others. On this basic idea Paul encourages believers with the eternal perspective that the suffering of the saint in the context of testing brings glory to God (Rom 8:17). Concerning this point, Schreiner comments:

> Paul encourages believers to endure temporary sufferings by
> giving them a glimpse of the beauty that awaits the children
> of God. The redemption they await is so stupendous that
> it will involve the entire created order. Just as creation fell
> when Adam sinned, so too, it will be transformed when the
> children of God experience the completion of their redemption.
> Believers should be full of hope because the sufferings of this
> age are part and parcel of a fallen creation, and the glory of the
> age to come inevitably includes a renewed creation.[96]

---

[95] In regard to the *groaning* of creation (Rom 8:22) and the implications for Christian suffering, Collins (*Science and Faith*, 158–59) comments: "The creation also groans because, as I argued already, it is the arena in which God chastises man. Hence it suffers when man is punished (as in the flood of Genesis 6–8). So the creation 'waits with eager longing' for the day when this is no longer needed."

[96] Schreiner, *Romans*, 438. Everett F. Harrison and Donald A. Hagner comment ("Romans," vol. 11 in *The Expositor's Bible Commentary*, ed. Tremper Longman and David Garland [Grand Rapids: Zondervan, 2006], 137), "Before passing to the final ministry of the Spirit in vv. 26–27, Paul lingers over the concept of future glory in relation to the present era of suffering. His presentation

Thus, Paul encourages Christians to wait *eagerly* for the final outcome of their sufferings, not in this life but in the life to come where the *good* will be found (8:23–25).[97] Perhaps *testing through suffering* is best understood as God's primary means of responding to sin and rebellion throughout the history of faith. Faith cultivation in the rebel heart and faith development in the loyal heart have been God's agenda from the beginning.[98]

Additional texts from the New Testament further expand the idea of testing through suffering. For example, Peter and James share Paul's contention that the faithful experience testing through hardship and, in the context of the early church, persecution.[99] James opens his letter with the emphasis that testing has a transformative impact on the faith of the believer. James writes: "Consider it all joy, my brethren, when you encounter various trials, knowing that the *testing* of your faith produces endurance. And let endurance have *its* perfect result, so that you may be perfect and complete, lacking in nothing" (Jas 1:2–4,

---

may be seen as an expansion of what he had already written to the Corinthians (2 Cor 4:17 NASB, 'an eternal weight of glory far beyond all comparison'). Weighed in the scales of true and lasting values, the sufferings endured in this life are light indeed, compared with the splendor of the life to come—a life undisturbed by anything hostile or hurtful."

[97] Fitzmeyer (*Romans*, 505) comments: "In the development of this topic, Paul alludes to Gen 3:17–19 and 5:29, where the earth has been cursed because of Adam's sinful transgression. But he is also thinking of the OT promises about 'a new heaven and a new earth,' the apocalyptic promises in Trito-Isaiah (Isa 65:17; 66:22)."

[98] On our analysis we should not be surprised that *testing through suffering* receives a "good" recommendation in Rom 8:28 (cf. Gen 50:20)—not *our* purpose but only *God's* purpose receives this commendation. Thus, the fullness of understanding for the believer will only be realized in the eschatological future. See Schreiner, *Romans*, 450.

[99] Walter Grundmann (*TDNT* 2:259) comments on suffering according to Jas 1:2–4: "Here there are no obstacles to understanding δοκίμιον as a means of testing. Suffering is a means of testing faith, and as such leads to patience."

emphasis added).[100] He thus encourages Christians to endure trials of faith through the realization that participation in the experience of testing through suffering is also somehow and mysteriously linked to the sufferings of Christ. Thus, testing is a transformative experience on earth that carries with it eternal benefit for Christ, as well as for those who call on his name.[101]

Peter's focus on the eternal benefits of testing through suffering draws on the metallurgical background and language for testing previously discussed.[102] He exhorts his audience,

> In this you greatly rejoice, even though now for a little while,
> if necessary, you have been distressed by various trials, so that
> the proof of your faith, *being* more precious than gold which is
> perishable, even though tested by fire, may be found to result
> in praise and glory and honor at the revelation of Jesus Christ.
> (1 Pet 1:6–9)

Peter shares the emphasis that James and Paul placed on testing through suffering, that Christians *joyfully* share in the sufferings of Christ knowing that their present sufferings impact favorably the future revelation of the glory of Christ.[103] That future revelation will include the product of the refinement of the saints! Peter further proclaims,

---

[100] James 1:2–4 and 1 Pet 1:6–7 incorporate nominal forms from both πειρασμός and δοκίμιον in their presentation of the basic idea of *testing* through *suffering*.

[101] Ralph Martin (*James*, WBC 48 [Waco, TX: Word, 1988], 15) comments: "[T]rials serve as a feature of the life of trust that refines and shapes believers' knowledge of divine providence and God's holy purpose."

[102] Thomas R. Schreiner (*1, 2 Peter, Jude*, NAC 37 [Nashville: B&H Academic, 2003], 67–68) develops this metallurgical emphasis in his commentary and asks, "Why is it God's plan to suffer? Verse 7 provides the reason. Sufferings function as the crucible for faith. They test the genuineness of faith, revealing whether or not faith is authentic."

[103] John H. Elliott (*1 Peter*, AB 37B [New York: Doubleday, 2000], 772) comments, "Since in 1 Peter *peirasmos* is interpreted positively here and is described

> Beloved, do not be surprised at the fiery ordeal among you,
> which comes upon you for your testing, as though some
> strange thing were happening to you; but to the degree that
> you share the sufferings of Christ, keep on rejoicing, so
> that also at the revelation of His glory you may rejoice with
> exultation. (1 Pet 4:12–13)

Peter here clarifies the *kind* of suffering that qualifies as suffering *with* Christ, encouraging authentic sufferers to persevere on the under-standing that it is God's will for them to endure under such difficult, though *temporary*, circumstances (vv. 14–16, 19). Peter and Paul agree that the testing/refining of believers contributes to the future glory that is to be revealed in Christ.[104] Peter offers further explanation to the believer's suffering as it relates to future glory and the coming day of the Lord (2 Pet 3:3–18). His warning of future eschatological judg-ment shares some of the language that we have already seen common to testing/refining contexts. For example, Richard Bauckham trans-lates 2 Peter 3:10 as follows:

> But the day of the Lord will come life a thief. On that day the
> heavens will pass away with a roar, the heavenly bodies will be
> dissolved in the heat, and the earth and the works in it *will be
> found* (emphasis added).[105]

Peter employs the same term in verse 14 in his warning to individual believers and writes, "Therefore, beloved, since you look for these

---

in 1:6–7 as a 'testing' or 'proving' (parallel in sense to *dokimion* and *dokimazo*, 1:7) of the genuineness of faith, it is clearly God who is envisioned as the one who tests."

[104] With such an emphasis on glory in these testing/suffering contexts, one wonders if a *fallen* world is not a better glory producer than a world with no fallenness at all.

[105] Richard Bauckham argues for the reading "will be found" from εὑρεθή-σεται as the correct reading on this textual variant. See his *Jude, 2 Peter*, WBC 50 (Dallas: Word 1990), 316–21; Schreiner, *1, 2 Peter, Jude*, 384–87.

things, be diligent to *be found* (εὑρεθῆναι) by Him in peace, spotless and blameless" (v. 14, emphasis added). The future passive sense behind Peter's use of these terms in both verse 10 and verse 14 suggests a refining process that may have its *end* result as a future eschatological fulfillment for the believer. Again, this is where the *good* will be found.[106] Thus, believers are encouraged to endure with the expected hope of an eternal value to their earthly suffering. The Lamb who has suffered will surely receive his reward! Al Wolters recognizes Peter's consistent usage of testing terminology in both 1 Peter 1:7 and 2 Peter 3:10, 14 and comments:

> It is striking that for the two occurrences of the absolute use in
> the letters of Peter the context in both cases evokes the image
> of a metal's purification in a melting pot or crucible. Could
> it be that the common Greek verb *heuriskesthai* has a precise
> technical sense in the vocabulary of the smelter and refiner? Its
> meaning would then be something like "emerge purified (from
> the crucible)," with the connotation of having stood the test, of
> being tried and true.[107]

The desired product of this refining process, for both Paul and Peter, is the pure gold that remains—the glory that is rightly due the Lord (1 Pet 4:12–13; Rom 8:18).

Finally, the author of Hebrews offers a theological reflection on testing that draws from a unique parallel between the Old and New

---

[106] Tom Schreiner (*1, 2 Peter, Jude*, 383–86) offers a detailed presentation of the difficulty of interpreting v. 10b and prefers Bauckham's reading of this verse. Here the Greek carries with it the sense of a purposeful search or examination and might refer to the climax of God's eschatological testing cycle for the entire cosmos.

[107] See Albert M. Wolters, "Worldview and Textual Criticism in 2 Peter 3:10," *WTJ* 49 (1987): 412. Wolters makes a persuasive case for the metallurgical background of εὑρίσκω, found in 1 Pet 1:7 and 2 Pet 3:10, 14, drawing from the prophetic context of Mal 3:2–4 and the theology of the coming Day of the Lord.

Testaments and emphasizes Christ's role as the perfect high priest, as well as his identification with the faithful and their sufferings through his incarnation. William Lane comments:

> The incarnation exposed the Son to the conflicts and tensions of human life, which were climaxed by the suffering of death in a final act of obedience to the will of God (cf. 4:15; 5:2, 7–8). It was at this point that his fidelity to God was put to the extreme test, and he proved to be a faithful high priest. Because he was tested in this specific sense, he is able to help those who are now exposed to the ordeal of trial.[108]

The fact and purpose of the sufferings of Christ are made clear in Hebrews 2:10, "For it was fitting for Him, for whom are all things, and through whom are all things, in bringing many sons to glory, to perfect the author of their salvation through sufferings." Furthermore, Hebrews emphasizes Christ's identification with the suffering of the believer, as well as his ability to assist those enduring testing through suffering (2:18). Finally, believers are encouraged to remain faithful through their suffering because "Christ *was faithful* as a Son" (Heb 3:6a). Thus, Christ's experience of testing through suffering *as a Son* offers hope to the believer who experiences the same. The contextualization of Psalm 95:7–11 in this text illustrates for the New Testament believer what *not* to do in response to the Lord's demonstration of fidelity.[109] In contrast to the wilderness generation, who *tested* God

---

[108] See William L. Lane, *Hebrews*, WBC 47A (Dallas: Word, 1991), 66. David L. Allen points out that this "sympathy" builds on the idea of the maternal bond between mother and child, as well as the bond shared between brothers. Christ's sympathy builds on the incarnation. Allen (*Hebrews*, NAC 35 [Nashville: B&H Academic, 2010], 283) comments, "Jesus sympathized with people by sharing their flesh and blood, suffering to deliver them (2:10–18), and offering help (4:16)."

[109] Allen (*Hebrews*, 254–59) offers several observations related to the differences between the LXX and the author's quote in 3:7–11. He suggests that these

through their unbelief (Heb 3:9), Hebrews encourages believers to remain faithful amid their difficulties, following the example of Christ, who "learned obedience from the things which He suffered" (Heb 5:8). Christ's demonstration of obedience amid testing and hardship parallels the wilderness generation, who emerge as having learned—through discipline and instruction as a *tested son*—the lesson of the wilderness, that "man shall not live on bread alone, but on every word that proceeds out of the mouth of God" (Matt 4:4; cf. Deut 8:3, 5). The exhortation of Hebrews to remain faithful amid the difficulties of testing through suffering draws from the Old Testament context and delivers its message to the suffering first-century believers. The promise of *rest* extends to every believer who experiences suffering amid testing because they are identifying with the *tested* and *perfected* High Priest, who offers mercy, grace, and help in the believer's time of greatest need (Heb 4:14–16).[110]

Conclusion

While the previous chapters developed the theme of testing from the Joseph narrative and then the Pentateuch as a whole, this chapter sought to expand the theme of testing to include the rest of the Old and New Testament contexts. Even from the first chapters of Genesis, beginning in Adam, the theme of implicit testing offers Israel a window of understanding and insight into her own experience. After Adam's fall creation itself was subjected to futility as a means of testing

---

differences reveal the author's intent to contextualize Psalm 95 for his readers with an urgent appeal for demonstrated faith and fidelity.

[110] Part of the scholarly discussion on this key text focuses on the exact meaning and theological implications of πεπειρασμένον and the meaning of "to test, assay, examine" or "to tempt." Whether it refers to Christ's temptation or testing, it seems evident that the author draws from the context of the wilderness *testing* from Psalm 95. Thus, a case can be made that the *obedience* of Christ, amid testing, is in view.

and refining humanity's rebel heart (Rom 8:20). Thus, in Adam, Israel understands the theological foundation for testing at any time in her history. Additional narratives, such as those of Abraham and Joseph, illustrate for Israel the role of the tested patriarch. The Joseph narrative particularly highlights the significance of how *suffering* through *testing* is understood as *good* (Gen 50:20; cf. Deut 8:16). Joseph, as did Abraham, endures hardship through periods of testing, emerges as refined, and subsequently acts as an agent of God's grace and extends blessing toward Israel.

Testing is also extended to corporate Israel at Sinai, where covenant stipulations establish the framework and means by which testing occurs (Exod 20:20). Upon their failure Israel experiences the testing of refinement in the wilderness. To the new generation of refined Israelites at Moab, Moses affirms that they have indeed learned the lesson of the wilderness (Deut 8:2–3). In the conquest Israel's failure to *rule* and *subdue* the Promised Land—like Adam's failure in Eden—precipitates yet another corporate testing experience. Unconquered nations now serve as agents of futility against Israel as a means of further testing and refinement in the land (Judg 2:3, 22; 4:4). While the book of Judges suggests that a king in Israel might restore spiritual stability in the land, Israel's kings will demonstrate a propensity to induce even more spiritual chaos. Throughout the period of the divided kingdom, God continues to amplify futility against Israel and Judah. Instead of proclaiming peace, the prophetic *word* works to intensify the fires of refinement against the nation (Jer 5:14). Again pagan nations serve as agents of futility against Israel through the exilic experiences of both Israel and Judah. Like the wilderness generation before them, Israel will again be tested and refined. Through the collapse of both Israel and Judah, prophets recognize that the ultimate solution to Israel's spiritual problem rests in the promised Messiah, One who will experience the fullness of testing through suffering yet will also offer a complete cure for the disease of sin.

The New Testament picks up the theme of testing in the Gospel account of Christ's own wilderness experience (Matt 4:1–11). Like the patriarchs before, Jesus represents the testing of the faithful individual and lays the theological foundation for testing grounded in Israel's own history. Moreover, other New Testament authors raise a unanimous voice and offer encouragement and hope to early Christians who are suffering for their faith. Believers are encouraged to follow the example of Jesus and suffer with him because of the future glory that is to be revealed in him.

CHAPTER 5

CONCLUSION

The Pentateuch presents a unified and coherent theology for the theme of testing and lays the foundation for this theme that stretches across both Old and New Testaments. Of particular focus in this study was the Joseph narrative and its unique contribution to the theology of testing. The goal was to find a consistent and more precise meaning for *biblical testing* by exploring the meaning of key vocabulary in testing narratives. First, we investigated the nature and function of testing in both biblical and nonbiblical texts by probing key terms and concepts. While the *basic* meaning of testing stems from the world of metallurgy, we recognized that unique nuances exist for the key testing terms. Of particular interest was the metallurgical background for בחן and the meaning of "authentication" applied to the Joseph narrative and other biblical contexts. We saw that this meaning finds support from the ancient metallurgical concept of the "touchstone." Thus, just as the ancient touchstone authenticated the purity of precious metals such as gold, בחן functions in biblical contexts where covenant loyalty (faith) requires authentication. Thus, Joseph's test (בחן) in Genesis 42 directed at the brothers carries this same nuance. From our analysis, two major categories for testing have emerged. The aural test (quality check) and the test of experience (quality improvement) emerged as the more helpful broad categories for understanding testing in its biblical context.

Through these categories of meaning, our investigation of the Joseph narrative recognized both the implicit and explicit examples of testing that applied to both the individual (Joseph) and the group (Joseph's brothers). Thus, this narrative serves as a necessary look back to the more individual patriarchal testing but also offers Israel a look ahead into the more corporate testing of Israel. The Joseph narrative brings together both types. Joseph's test (בחן) for the brothers sought to both *authenticate* and *refine* for the quality of loyalty desired in the context of familial (covenant) relationship. The metallurgical background for בחן as "touchstone" supports this more focused interpretation. Joseph's personal experience in Egypt functions to refine and parallels the Pentateuch's theme of the tested patriarch. His self-designation as "God fearer" validates this prior testing experience. Thus, the Joseph narrative offers a retrospective and prospective theological vantage point for Israel. First, the Joseph narrative looks back to Genesis 22 where Abraham was tested and was designated as a "God fearer." *Both* Joseph and Abraham serve to illustrate the example of the faithful, yet tested, mediator of covenant blessing. Second, the Joseph narrative anticipates Israel's more corporate experience of testing that begins immediately out of Egypt and will include her forty-year wilderness trek. Thus, the Joseph narrative serves as a *necessary* theological link between the patriarchal narratives and the rest of the Pentateuch for its development of the motif of testing.

As more of the biblical text was examined on the theme of testing, we discovered that God's concern for the *authentic* fidelity of the covenant faithful obligates him to test for this faith. We argued that pentateuchal testing be extended to include Adam and his *implicit* testing. Adam's failure and subsequent exile from the garden illustrates for Israel the cycle of testing, rebellion, and exile that the nation will repeat in so much of her later history. Thus, Israel's cycle of national testing included experiences of futility in the land, such as the continuous spiritual opposition of paganism, the ongoing agitation and threat of foreign invaders, the increased experience of futility through political failure, the constant refiner's fire heard through the message of the prophets, and the final exile from the land at the hands of invading nations. This theological foundation is consistent with the unified voices of the New Testament focused on Christ, who shares in humanity's experience of *testing through suffering*. Thus, by means of a fallen world subjected to agents of futility, God accomplishes the testing of *both* saint and sinner. The value of the divine currency of love is established through the suffering of the saints and authenticated through *testing*. In a fallen world God remains obligated to test the family of faith.[1] The biblical authors offer a unanimous voice that faithful sons and daughters can encounter such testing with joy, as James affirms: "Consider it all joy, my brethren, when you encounter various trials, knowing that the testing of your faith produces endurance. And let endurance have *its* perfect result, so that you may be perfect and complete, lacking in nothing" (Jas 1:2–4).

---

[1] William Dembski (*The End of Christianity: Finding a Good God in an Evil World* [Nashville: B&H Academic, 2009], 23) said it best: "In a fallen world, the only currency of love is suffering." Over many lunch conversations on the topic of the problem of evil and suffering, I deeply benefitted from Bill's appreciation for Christ's ministry and this problem (see his chap. 1, "The Reach of the Cross"). I gained greater insights into the overlap of my topic of "testing" and the subject matter dealt with in his book. The overlap is simply that testing involves suffering and that *some* of the suffering experienced in the world comes from the hand of a *good* God who shares a paternal concern for both the refinement and authentication of the faith of his adopted sons amid a fallen world. As Bill pointed out, Christians can rest in the fact that the *reach* of the cross extends to include their experience of this kind of suffering. Our study has offered at least an initial explanation for *why* pain and suffering must occur amid this two-sided coin of divine activity and *why* such activity could possibly be considered *good*.

TESTING AS "TOUCHSTONE"

The Hebrew term בחן remains central to our discussion due to its primary role in Genesis 42 where Joseph tests his brothers. The unique metallurgical background for this term has not received the attention it deserves and requires closer examination. While this section may appear a bit cumbersome in its technicality, the details are necessary. The basic meaning of בחן as "touchstone" contributes a unique category of meaning to the semantic range under development in this study. Practically, the basic idea of "touchstone" helps one understand the divine purposes behind testing. God seeks to authenticate the faith and fidelity of his people through touchstone experiences. That this term and its metallurgical background found its way into the Hebrew language at some point in Israel's history will be the primary focus of this excursus.

One early lexical theory for the term בחן builds on the ancient Near Eastern use of the touchstone.[1] The touchstone was used in ancient

---

[1] Samuel P. Tregelles, *Gesenius' Hebrew and Chaldee Lexicon to the Old Testament Scriptures* (Grand Rapids: Eerdmans, 1949), 111. Maximillian Ellengoben

Babylonia for testing gold. The term also finds expressions in ancient
Aramean, Hebrew, and Greek.² While any historical reconstruction
is feasible, the *metallurgical function* of the touchstone in the ancient
Near East and its *literary function* remain the primary focus of our
investigation.³

John Brown argues for the literary function of the touchstone
and the link between the Lydian stone and βάσανος in the following
seventh- to sixth-century BC Greek texts:

> You will find me in all my works like *refined gold*, red to see
> when rubbed with the *touchstone*, on whose surface black rust
> and mold never seize, but which forever has its pure bloom
> (emphasis added).

> The *Lydian stone* proclaims gold; wisdom and omnipotent truth
> show the virtue of a man (emphasis added).

(*Foreign Words in the Old Testament: Their Origin and Etymology* [London: Luzac
and Company, 1962], 48) cites Koehler, who argues for בחן as an Egyptian loanword. Ellenbogen incorrectly identifies the Egyptian בחן as a "stone of very fine
grain, and dark-grey and grey-greenish color, which was extensively used by
Egyptian sculptors."

² The touchstone ("lapis Lydius") suggests a meaning of *proving by means
of rubbing* for בחן. See Tregelles, *Lexicon*, 111. Thomas O. Lambdin ("Egyptian
Loan Words in the Old Testament," *JAOS* 73 [1953]: 148) proposes the link of
the "stone of testing" (אבן בחן cf. Isa 28:16) to the Egyptian *bḥn*, "touchstone."

³ Touchstones are difficult to identify in the field and isolate to specific
archaeological contexts. Andrew Oddy ("Assaying in Antiquity," *Gold Bulletin* 16 [1977]: 56) attributes the earliest literary references to the Greek poet The-
ognis of the sixth century BC and the Greek historian Herodotus of the fifth
century BC. See also W. A. Oddy, "Gold in Antiquity: Aspects of Gilding and
of Assaying," *Journal of the Royal Society of Arts* 130 (1982): 740–41. R. Bogaert
("L'Essai Des Monnaies dans l'Antiquité," *Revue Belge de Numismatique* 122
[1976]: 8–10) proposes a twelfth-century BC Egyptian origin for the touchstone.
J. H. F. Notton ("Ancient Egyptian Gold Refining: A Reproduction of Early
Techniques," *Gold Bulletin* 7 [1974]: 50) recognizes a period as early as 2000 BC
as possible for early gold refining in ancient Egypt. The problem is not whether
touchstones where used in metallurgy in the ancient Near East but *when*.

When you test it, gold shines out on the *touchstone*, and also right wisdom (emphasis added).

[T]o make his lips like the Lydian stone by which moneychangers test the true gold lest it be false.[4]

These texts demonstrate early examples in which the metallurgical function of the touchstone had become a literary metaphor for the *testing* or *visual examination* of the deeds or character of an individual. A text from Pliny explains the metallurgical function of the touchstone or Lydian Stone:

The discussion of gold and silver suggests the stone called *coticula*. This used to be found only in the River Tmolus, as Theophrastus says, but now it is found in many localities. Some call them Heraclean stones, others Lydian. They are of moderate size, not more than four inches long and two wide. The side that has been exposed to the sun is better than the lower side. Those who understand the use of these touchstones, when they have taken a specimen from a piece of ore as they would with a file [i.e. by rubbing] tell you at once how much gold there is in the ore, how much silver or how much copper. They are so skillful that the maximum error is less than a scruple.[5]

---

[4] Translated by John Brown ("Proverb-Book, Gold-Economy, Alphabet," *JBL* 100 [1981]: 181). Brown suggests that the text refers to the function of the moneychangers authenticating pure gold from counterfeit.

[5] Translated by Louis E. Lord, "The Touchstone," *The Classical Journal* 32 (1936): 429. Oddy ("Assaying in Antiquity," 55) cites Pliny (AD 23–79) who calculated that the touchstone was accurate to one part in twenty-four, or about 2 percent; G. P. Goold, ed., *Pliny: Natural History*, trans. D. E. Eichholz, The Loeb Classical Library (Cambridge, MA: Harvard University Press, 1962), 33:126. Theophrastus (371–288 BC) placed the standard of the touchstone to one part in 144.

Some scholars credit the Lydians, who were the inventors of coined money, with this technology in the seventh century.[6] Old texts that refer to the visual examination of precious metals increase the likelihood of the touchstone's early existence in the ancient Near East.[7] First, texts from the Neo-Babylonian Period allude to the visual examination of gold; for example,

> When the first-class gold has arrived I shall examine [rêša našû]
> it in their presence and whatever is of bad quality I shall muster
> (out); then I shall send an exact report to the king my lord.[8]

The idea of the *examination of gold* has been linked to the Akkadian idiomatic phrase *rêša našû* ("to raise, to lift the head").[9] While the term is not directly linked to the idea of the touchstone, the activity described by the phrase "lifting of the head" equates to the activity of how a touchstone was used in the ancient world. The idea of "lifting" is close to the nondestructive work of authenticating that a touchstone

---

[6] Brown, "Proverb-Book," 181. D. T. Moore and W. A. Oddy ("Touchstones: Some Aspects of Their Nomenclature, Petrography and Provenance," *Journal of Archaeological Science* 12 [1985]: 60, 67) investigate the history of the nomenclature for "touchstone" and suggest from petrographic evidence the terms "Lydian Stone" or "touchstone" as better terms for the stone typically described "lydite, basalt and basanite." Oddy recognizes a stela from Athens that describes a decree enacted in 375–374 BC describing the activity of slaves testing gold coins.

[7] Walo Wälchi ("Touching Precious Metals," *Gold Bulletin* 14 [1981]: 154) refers to the fifth- to fourth-century BC treaty attributed to Kautilya that describes the use of touchstones in ancient India. He argues that touchstones were also used in ancient Egypt.

[8] Translated by A. Leo Oppenheim, "Idiomatic Accadian," *JAOS* 61 (1941): 253. Peter R. S. Moorey (*Ancient Mesopotamian Materials and Industries: The Archaeological Evidence* [Oxford: Clarendon, 1994], 219) observes the three descending levels of gold quality as pure gold (yellowish gold), mixed gold, and normal gold. Martin Levey ("The Refining of Gold in Ancient Mesopotamia," *Chymia* 5 [1959]: 31) presents evidence that suggests refined gold was known in ancient Mesopotamia as early as the fourth millennium BC. He provides a full discussion of the color descriptions of gold in ancient Mesopotamia.

[9] Oppenheim, "Idiomatic Accadian," 252.

accomplishes. This specific activity of the visual examination of gold is further observed in several texts from the Amarna period. For example:

> Every one of my messengers that were staying in Egypt *saw* the gold for the statues with their own eyes. Your father himself recast the statues [i]n the presence of my messengers, and he made them entirely of pure gold. [M]y messengers *saw* with their own eyes that they were recast, and they *saw* with their own eyes that they were entirely of pure gold (emphasis added).[10]

> *They were* sealed, but the gold [. . .]. They were full of [. . .], and they wept very much, saying, "Are all of these gold? They do not *lo[ok* (like gold)]."
> . . . I said, "I cannot say [be]fore you, as I am used to sa[ying], 'My [brother], the king of Egypt, loves me very, much'" (emphasis added).[11]

> But now when I sent a messenger to you, you have detained him for six years, and you have sent me as my greeting-gift, the only thing in six year, 30 minas of gold that *looked like silver*. That gold was melted down in the presence of Kasi, your messenger, and he was a witness (emphasis added).[12]

---

[10] EA 27:19–27, trans. William L. Moran, *The Amarna Letters* (Baltimore: Johns Hopkins University Press, 1992), 87.

[11] EA 20:46–58, trans. Moran, *Amarna Letters*, 47.

[12] EA 3:13–22. This Amarna letter (1385–61 BC) explains the complaint of King Burraburiash of Babylon to the Egyptian king that only a fourth of his gold shipment survived the process of fire assaying gold. Oddy ("Assaying in Antiquity," 53–54) finds this reference common in texts from the second and first millennia BC. Compare trans. Samuel A. B. Mercer (*The Tell El-Amarna Tablets* [Toronto: Macmillan, 1939], 11), "This gold, [in] the presence of Kasi, thy messenger, was *tested*, and witnessed it." This reference combines the Akkadian *amāru* ("to examine") and the activity of *testing* or authenticating gold.

These texts suggest an inexpensive and rapid means of inspecting gold existed in cultures where gold mining was the primary industry.[13]

The connection of the Hebrew term בחן and the ancient concept of the touchstone is supported by additional examples. First, some evidence suggests that בחן, Syriac baḥen ("to examine"), and the noun form of the same term all derive from the older Egyptian root bḥn ("touchstone").[14] Thomas Lambdin argues that בחן is an Egyptian loanword that stems from the original verb bḥn, which in noun form refers to the touchstone.[15] Lambdin relates the reference in Isaiah 28:16, "stone of testing," to the Egyptian touchstone.[16] This etymological suggestion for בחן parallels the metaphorical use of "touchstone" in the Greek texts of the seventh to sixth centuries previously discussed.[17] Two texts serve as examples:

---

[13] R. J. Forbes, "Extracting, Smelting and Alloying," in *A History of Technology*, ed. Charles Singer, E. J. Holmyard, and A. R. Hall (London: Oxford University Press, 1954), 1:582. Oddy ("Gold in Antiquity," 740) locates the refining of gold in Egypt to the Amarna letters during the reign of Amenhophis IV of Egypt (1377–1358 BC). T. G. H. James ("Gold Technology in Ancient Egypt: Mastery of Metal Working Methods," *Gold Bulletin* 5 [1972]: 38–42) suggests that the earliest evidence of gold working in Egypt dates to the tombs of the First Dynasty (c. 3000 BC) and the height of gold working to the reign of Tutankhamun (c. 1500–1300 BC).

[14] According to Lambdin ("Loan Words," 148), this link is "more than a likelihood." J. R. Harris (*Lexicographical Studies in Ancient Egyptian Minerals*, Deutsche Akademie der Wissenschaften zu Berlin Institut fur Orientforschung 54 [Berlin: Akademie-Verlag, 1961], 78–82) suggests that bḥn refers to the "greywacke" of the Wadi Hammamat, which supports the basic conclusion of Sethe. He also cites evidence from Ptolemaic texts that refer to hard stones used in building shrines with bḥn. Pliny (cited in Goold, *Pliny*, 10:45) was the first to link the Egyptian bḥn to the *greywacke* of the Wadi Hammamat. This evidence strongly links hard stones from the Wadi Hammamat, typically called "*greywacke*," to touchstones used in this same region.

[15] Lambdin, "Loan Words," 148.

[16] Ibid.

[17] Moorey (*Materials and Industries*, 219) makes this same link to the sixth century BC and the work of Theophrastus, who links the touchstone to a river

Callicles, if I happened to have a soul made of gold, don't you
think that I would be glad to find one of those stones with
which they *test* gold, the best kind; and that when I rubbed my
soul on it, if it should assert that my soul had been well taken
care of, I would be assured that I was in good shape, and would
need no other touchstone (emphasis added)?

[T]esting [the young men] much more than gold in the fire.[18]

This same metaphorical use parallels biblical texts, such as
Proverbs 17:3 and Zechariah 13:9a:

The refining pot is for silver and the furnace for gold,
But the LORD tests hearts.
And I will bring the third part through the fire,
Refine them as silver is refined,
And test them as gold is tested.

The evidence thus far supports a broad use of touchstones in both
gold mining and literary contexts as early as the seventh century BC.[19]
While these observations appear to hold great promise for the biblical
interpretation of בחן as "touchstone," this position is not without its
critics.

Tmolus in Turkey. Moorey recognizes the archaeological difficulty of identifying found stones at digs and claiming absolute certainty as to their function as
"touchstones." See also Oddy, "Assaying in Antiquity," 55.

[18] Translated by Brown, "Proverb-Book," 182.

[19] In addition and primary to the processes involved in the refining and
removing of impurities (i.e., cupellation and amalgamation), Forbes ("Extracting," 582) identifies three distinct tests for the authentication of gold in the
ancient Near East: (1) the weight of gold compared to an external measure,
(2) the brightness of gold when it is hot and fused in contact with cold air, and
(3) the residual color of gold when assayed on a *touchstone*. Oddy ("Assaying in
Antiquity," 52–59) identifies three distinct processes known by the Greeks as fire
assaying, the Archimedes method (a method of weighing using the standard of
specific weights), and the touchstone.

Matitiahu Tsevat, for example, argues against *any* link between the early Egyptian or ancient Near Eastern touchstone and the Hebrew root בחן.[20] He objects on two grounds. First, he claims the idea that ancient man both understood and used the touchstone as a means for authenticating gold is only inferential.[21] Second, he claims that the purity of gold in the ancient Near East was determined by melting/smelting *alone* and would not have continued as a process had the touchstone existed as an *early* established technology in the ancient Near East.[22]

The following arguments may be raised against these objections. First, a distinction must be made between the nondestructive process of *authenticating* gold and the destructive and more costly processes of *purifying* and *refining* gold. Several of the texts examined thus far appear to maintain this distinction and affirm the touchstone as a *distinct* process and that the visual inspection of gold was a preliminary step employed *prior to* the refining of gold in the ancient Near East. Thus, the visual authentication (by use of the touchstone) determined the need for refining as a secondary step in the overall process of gold refining.[23] Further evidence suggests that the ancients were well aware of a variety of processes used in the testing and refining

---

[20] M. Tsevat (*TDOT* 2:69, 71–72) prefers the etymological links of the Arabic *mḥn* and the Aramaic *bḥr* to Hebrew בחן over Sethe's "otherwise untenable assumption" that it was borrowed from the Egyptian. He still finds a possible link of the term אבן בחן ("testing stone") in Isa 28:16 to an Egyptian loanword.

[21] Tsevat (*TDOT* 2:72) argues that the earliest textual reference to a "touchstone" is found in the Greek literature of the sixth century BC. Admittedly, while the archaeological evidence for ancient touchstones is scant, the ancient literary evidence cited here for the visual inspection of gold increases the likelihood that such technology was widespread and old in the ancient Near East.

[22] *TDOT* 2:71–72.

[23] The ancient Greeks wrote of three quantitative methods of testing both gold and silver: assaying by fire, the measurement of specific gravity, and the touchstone. Oddy, "Assaying in Antiquity," 53.

of gold.[24] For example, the Greeks of the seventh to sixth century BC knew of three distinct methods for assaying/testing gold, all of which are still used in modern times.[25] Thus, Tsevat's claim that smelting and touchstone processes could not have existed simultaneously in the ancient world may be overstated. Such assaying technologies have existed simultaneously for nearly three millennia. Oddy comments,

> In view of the rapid advances made in the techniques of
> chemical analysis in the past thirty years it is very surprising
> that the three techniques known to the Greeks of 2500 years ago
> are still in use.[26]

Though more investigation is certainly in order, the evidence thus far suggests the broad use of touchstone technology in the ancient world, including the mining operations of ancient Egypt.

Some have explored this Egyptian connection further and advanced historical and linguistic evidence in support of the theory that links the two terms: Hebrew בחן and Egyptian bḫn. Support for the Egyptian bḫn stone of the Wadi Hammamat as a touchstone is found in the fact that the Egyptian bḫn stone is referred to as a stone used for monuments in a text that maps out ancient Egyptian gold mines.[27] Sethe observes that the pictograph, bḫn, is written with the

---

[24] These include the gold mines of the Nubian Desert, which produced an estimated thirty kilograms of gold annually, and the hieroglyphs and maps of gold mines discovered in the Wadi Hammamat dating to the fourteenth century BC. See Forbes, "Extracting," 580–81; T. G. H. James, "Gold Technology in Ancient Egypt: Mastery of Metal Working Methods," *Gold Bulletin* 5 (1972): 38–39.

[25] These are fire assay, the touchstone, and the specific gravity method of Archimedes. Oddy, "Assaying in Antiquity," 53.

[26] Ibid., 58.

[27] K. Sethe, "Die Bau-und Denkmalstein des alten Agyptes und ihre Name," in *Sitzungsberichte der Preussischen Akademie der Wissenschaften* (Berlin: Akademie-Verlag, 1933), 894–97. Adolf Erman and Hermann Grapow (*Wörterbuch der Aegyptischen Sprache* [Berlin: Akademe-Verlag, 1926–71], 1:471) support this

sign of an eye, the Egyptian symbol that conveys the basic idea of sight or observation.[28] This close proximity of the term *bḥn* and the Egyptian symbol for "seeing" in the context of gold mining suggests a possible link of the Egyptian *bḥn* stone to a hard black stone also used for the visual authentication of gold—*the touchstone*.

One final argument offered in favor for the link between בחן and Egyptian *bḥn* comes from the historical development of the Egyptian, Hebrew, and Greek terms for "touchstone." Sethe argues for a consonantal link between the Egyptian *bḥn* and the Greek βάσανος by connecting the Greek β and ν with the Egyptian *b* and *n*, respectively. He explains the Greek ς on the basis of the shift from *ḥ* to *š* in later Egyptian.[29] On these grounds Sethe argues for the following linear etymological theory: (1) *bḥn* ("touchstone"; nominal Egyptian form describing a particular stone or the function of a stone), (2) Hebrew בחן ("to test"; borrowed verbal use), (3) *bšn* (Hittite borrowing reflecting the Egyptian shift of *ḥ* to *š*), and (4) βάσανος (Lydian to Greek application, describing a black, hard stone used as a "touchstone").[30] Taken with the evidence from seventh- to sixth-century Greek texts, Sethe's etymological proposal strengthens the

---

position and translate *bḥn* as "the dark hard stone which was used for monuments." They suggest the origin of the stone is the Wadi Hammamat in Egypt. These same processes are represented in a tomb relief dating from 2000 BC. The processes described may represent an ancient form of cupellation or cementation. Notton, "Ancient Gold Refining," 51–54; see also Forbes, "Extracting," 581–82.

[28] This observation is further supported by the Hamito-Semitic root *'ir* ("eye") and its link to the root *'er* ("to see, know") found in many proto-Semitic forms. See Vladimire E. Orel and Olga V. Stolbova, *Hamito-Semitic Etymological Dictionary: Materials for a Reconstruction* (Leiden: E. J. Brill, 1995), 21.

[29] Sethe ("Die Bau-und Denkmalstein," 908) dates this shift no later than the mid-first century, where the old *h* is still attested in personal names. Pierre Chantraine (*Dictionnaire Étymologique de la Langue Grecque Histoire Des Mots* [Paris: Editions Klincksieck, 1990], 166) confirms Sethe's conclusions on this shift in his discussion on the Greek word βασανος.

[30] Sethe, "Die Bau-und Denkmalstein," 909.

suggested historical development of the Egyptian *bḥn* into later Semitic languages.[31] Although this lengthy discussion offers a plausible Egyptian metallurgical background for Hebrew בחן, it must also be said that this theory remains open to further investigation.

In sum, granted the coexistence and uniqueness of the *authentication* and *refining* stages involved in ancient processing of gold and the observation that touchstone technology was likely available to ancient peoples involved in the trading and processing of gold, it is highly probable that the use of בחן with the meaning "to test" or "to authenticate" is early.[32] This conclusion is further supported by the fact that seventh- to sixth-century BC Greek texts attest the verbal idea of the authentication of one's inner person. This meaning of *authentication* finds further support in the biblical texts previously investigated.[33]

---

[31] The idea of Egyptian influence on Israelite culture is a matter of debate in scholarship. Kenneth A. Kitchen (*On the Reliability of the Old Testament* [Grand Rapids: Eerdmans, 2003], 241–312) provides an excellent summary of the most recent evidence suggesting an Egyptian influence in the fourteenth and thirteenth centuries.

[32] Christfried Baldauf ("Läutern und Prüfen im Alten Testament. Begriffsgeschichtliche Untersuchung zu *srp* und *bhn*," *Theologische Literaturzeitung* 103 [1978]: 917–18) suggests the figurative meaning of a nonviolent testing of the truth of a person's word for בחן in the biblical texts. He supports the linkage of בחן with the Egyptian *bḥn*, which refers to the testing of gold for purity by means of the visual examination of the streak left on a touchstone (*probierstein*). He notes that in theological speech, the בחן test involves *seeing* and *recognizing* the internal parts of a person.

[33] Two preliminary observations support the meaning of *authentication* for בחן. The term בחן is commonly used in "seeing" contexts (cf. Pss 17:2–3a; 11:4b; 139:23b–24a; Job 7:17–19a). The term is also used in contexts where the condition of an individual's heart is exposed (cf. Jer 11:20; 12:3; 20:12; 17:9–10).

COVENANT *GOOD* AS FUNCTIONAL *GOOD*

G enesis speaks of a world created by God and declared *good*. On this point theologians and modern scientists continue to debate how the creation account and the observations of modern science can be reconciled. For example, Gerald Schroeder comments on the tension that is held by one who holds that the world is created, designed, and declared as *good*:

> The opening chapter of the Bible, in a brief thirty-one
> sentences, describes the development of our universe from
> chaos at its creation to the culminating symphony of life. Seven
> times in those few sentences we're told "God saw it is good." At
> the end of the process God was so pleased that the creation was
> described as "very good." Sounds as if at times it might not have
> been so good. What we learn from these biblical events is that
> intelligent design can be complex design, but it is not necessarily
> flawless design, even when that design is the work of the
> Creator. If your image of God is based on a simplistic model of
> the Divine, don't expect that image to rest easily with the Bible's
> concept of God or with the real world. Out there on the street,

175

the innocent are often the victims and the guilty at times merely walk away.[1]

Schroeder's comment reflects the common scientific suspicion of a world created and designed as perfect. C. S. Lewis wrestled with this same tension:

> He had set Himself when He created the world, the problem of expressing His goodness through the total drama of a world containing free agents, in spite of and by means of, their rebellion against Him. . . . The symbol of a drama, a symphony, or a dance, is here useful to correct a certain absurdity which may arise if we talk too much of God planning and creating the world process for good and of that good being frustrated by the free will of the creatures. This may raise the ridiculous idea that the Fall took God by surprise and upset His plan, or else—more ridiculously still—that God planned the whole thing for conditions which, He well knew, were never going to be realized. In fact, of course, God saw the crucifixion in the act of creating the first nebula.[2]

While the intersection of the biblical text with the discoveries of modern science is certainly a topic of interest, it will have to be bracketed out for another time. Our primary concern here is for the message of Genesis 1:1–31 and the rather significant theological concerns that it must have raised for its original audience. How did that original audience understand the fact of a world described as *good*? Genesis (as does the entire Pentateuch) carries with it the theological concerns for a nation poised on entering a new land. Moses prepares the young nation, Israel, on the plains of Moab for the first leg of her journey into the land. Thus, Deuteronomy assumes an audience who had

---

[1] Gerald L. Schroeder, *The Hidden Face of God: How Science Reveals the Ultimate Truth* (New York: Free, 2001), 15.

[2] C. S. Lewis, *The Problem of Pain* (New York: Macmillan, 1962), 84.

experienced both Sinai and a forty-year wilderness experience. We ask what the theological concerns were for *that* audience. Clearly, covenant relationship remains a central theme for the entire Pentateuch. It was Israel's primary concern at Moab. Regarding Genesis, this same primary covenantal concern is evident from the beginning, with the emphatic use of the divine covenant name, "This is the account of the heavens and the earth when they were created, in the day that the LORD [Yahweh] God made earth and heaven" (Gen 2:4). Moses makes emphatic for Israel that God who created the entire cosmos is the *same* God who extended the right hand of covenant relationship at Sinai—his name, Yahweh (Exod 3:14). This link between Genesis and Exodus on the covenant name suggests a theological emphasis as well (Exod 3:14; 20:2). While there is no clear indication of an official ratified covenant or ceremony signaled by the term ברית ("covenant") in the Genesis account, perhaps other signals indicate an authorial concern for an audience who knew Yahweh in a covenant context. One clue, recognized by some scholars, is the function of the term טוב ("good") in contexts where treaty or covenant relationships are discussed. For example, Sheriffs comments:

> "Good" (Hebrew *ṭōb*) is a concept linked with the benefits of a covenant relationship. The suzerain offers blessings for obedience. What is it that Yahweh will categorize as "good"? What is it that is in the interests of the questioning Israelites that is "good"? The answer is covenant loyalty and becoming conduct. . . . When covenant relationship with Yahweh is refused, this can be summed up in the words "Israel has rejected the good" (Hos 8:3).[3]

In addition to the use of the covenant name "Yahweh," the creation account may intend to reinforce the idea that God is not only the

---

[3] Deryck Sheriffs, *The Friendship of the Lord* (Eugene, OR: Wipf & Stock, 2004), 108n36.

Author and Sustainer of life but also the King (suzerain) who seeks to extend the benefits (good) of creation to Adam. For Israel, on the verge of entering the land, this theological emphasis supports the words of Moses, who charges Israel, "See, I have set before you today life and prosperity [good], and death and adversity" (Deut 30:15, author's addition). For Israel, the land will become the new means by which Yahweh extends this benefit (good) to his people.

The central creation terms, ברא and טוב, also function together in Genesis to strengthen the covenant idea. While the common understanding of טוב is the sense of "perfection" in Genesis 1, the discussion ahead seeks to explore the broader meaning of טוב, in addition to ברא, and the relationship of these terms to the idea of *functionality*—how a world outside the garden would exist as *good*, in the sense that it is fully capable of functioning and operating, and thus fulfilling the beneficial purpose for which it was designed to do.

This functionality went from good to bad as a result of the application of the covenant curse in response to Adam's fall (Rom 8:20). Thus, in response to rebellion, the suzerain removes the *good* (טוב) and replaces it with *bad* (רע)—the implications of the futility curse. The potential for both good and bad is evident in Moses' declaration to Israel, "See, I have set before you today life and *good*, and death and *bad*" (Deut 30:15, author's translation). This is one of the clearest biblical examples of where the "good/bad" language is used in a covenant context. This use of "good" in the language of covenant or treaty language is quite common in both biblical and extrabiblical contexts. On Israel's national rejection of her covenant obligations, covenant *good* is removed and replaced with *bad*—the increased futility often associated with the covenant curses. In a later example the prophet Hosea declares in response to Israel's rejection of her covenant obligations, "Israel has rejected the good; the enemy will pursue him" (Hos 8:3). Here the example of the assigned agent of futility works against the rebellion of the covenant member; good is replaced with the assigned agent of futility.

W. L. Moran laid the initial groundwork for this idea from ancient treaty texts and concluded that the cognate "good" signals "friendship, good relations with specific reference to the *amity established* by the treaty."[4] To this Dennis McCarthy added, "The essential meaning remains: relations are defined and settled (by custom and agreement), and these relations *are good* in a special, technical sense."[5] One such example from Mari states, "We will establish 'good things' between me and between him, the divine oath and binding stipulations."[6] In this example *good* signals the permanent stipulations of the treaty that anticipate a favorable outcome between loyal covenant participants. Alan Millard recognized the frequent link between טוב and common covenant terms such as חסד in biblical contexts. He cites, for example, the return of the ark (1 Chr 16:34), the dedication of the temple (2 Chr 5:13; 7:3), and the setting of the temple foundations after the return (Ezra 3:11) as texts that demonstrate the relationship between *good* and the fidelity of covenant relationship.[7] This "good" of covenant relationship is also set as the frequent focus of praise in Israel's history (Pss 25:8, 10; 100:5; 135:3–4).[8] Another biblical example illustrates that the doing of *good* in the

---

[4] W. L. Moran, "A Note of the Treaty Terminology of the Sefire Stelas," *JNES* 22 (1963): 173. Moran establishes the frequency of "good" with other common ANE covenant terminology, such as "friendship," "peace," "brother," and "brotherhood." See also A. Malamat, "Additional Aspects of the Covenant and Covenant Terminology," *Biblical Archaeologist* 28 (1965), 63–65.

[5] Dennis J. McCarthy, "Covenant 'Good' and an Egyptian Text," *BASOR* 245 (1982): 63. McCarthy cites the example from the "Egyptian Story of Sinuhe" that describes the travels of Sinuhe out of Egypt and the "good" things that he experienced along the way from an Asiatic herdsman chief and an Amorite ruler. McCarthy suggests that each of these individuals was in some sense obligated by treaty or covenant to respond to Egyptians in the kind or *good* way that they did.

[6] Ibid., 174–75. See also *NIDOTTE* 2: 355–56.

[7] Alan R. Millard, "For He Is Good," *Tyndale Bulletin* 17 (1966): 115–17.

[8] Ibid., 116.

Promised Land results in the experience of covenantal blessing, "You shall do what is right and good in the sight of the Lord, *that it may be well with you*" (Deut 6:18, emphasis added).[9]

Numerous scholars identify this technical meaning of *good* in a variety of biblical contexts where relational benefits are extended (or withheld) in response to demonstrated loyalty. Delbert Hillers recognizes two texts that demonstrate this meaning of טוב:

> You shall not seek their *peace* and their *good* all your days forever. (Deut 23:6[7], emphasis added)

> And now, may Yahweh do with you *lovingkindness* and truth; and also, I myself will do with you this *good* because you have done this thing. (2 Sam 2:6, emphasis added)[10]

A. Malamat offers additional examples that illustrate this same meaning. For example, 2 Samuel 7:28 states, "And now, Lord, Yahweh, You are God, and your words, they will be truth, that you spoke to your servant *this good*."[11] In this verse the "words" spoken by Yahweh are described as "good" and point to the future blessing of relationship that will be experienced by the king. Additional biblical texts illustrate this same basic pattern:

> Then they spoke to him saying, "If today you will be a servant for this people and you will serve them, and answer them and speak to them *good* words, then they will be for you servants forever." (1 Kgs 12:7, emphasis added)

---

[9] Ibid., 116. Dennis McCarthy identifies this same covenantal use of "good" in an Egyptian treaty text. See Dennis J. McCarthy, "Covenant 'Good' and an Egyptian Text" *BASOR* 245 (1982): 63–64.

[10] Delbert R. Hillers, "A Note on Some Treaty Terminology in the Old Testament," *BASOR* 176 (1964): 46. Author's translation and emphasis.

[11] Translation by Malamat, "Additional Aspects," 64.

> And it shall be that Yahweh will do for my Lord according to
> all the *good* which He spoke over you and commanding you for
> a ruler over Israel. (1 Sam 25:30, emphasis added)

> Behold days are coming, declares Yahweh, that I will cause to
> rise up the *good word* which I spoke to the house of Israel and
> unto the house of Judah. (Jer 33:14, emphasis added)[12]

Each of these texts illustrates that the spoken *good* word leads to positive results that benefit the loyal and, in these specific examples, covenant member. Biblical authors ground encouragement to the faithful through God's faithful word made evident through the created order. For example, at a moment of international crisis in Judah, Jeremiah grounds the everlasting promises of the new covenant in the everlasting promises made to King David and the everlasting promises made to creation itself (Jer 33:20–21, 25–26; cf. Gen 8:22). Just as God encouraged Abraham with the fixed and immeasurable pattern of the night sky in Genesis 15, Jeremiah also regards the *fixed patterns* (statutes) of heaven and earth as a means to encourage the faithful:

> Thus Yahweh has said, "If my covenant of day and night is not,
> *then* the *statutes of the heavens and the earth* I did not establish."
> (Jer 33:25, emphasis added)

These texts suggest that God's promises and intentions are sure to the faithful. Jeremiah 31:35–37 further illustrates this same emphasis:

> Thus says the LORD,
> Who gives the sun for light by day,
> And the *fixed order* of the moon and the stars for light by night,
> Who stirs up the sea so that its waves roar;
> The LORD of hosts is His name:

---

[12] Malamat, "Additional Aspects," 64. See also 2 Kgs 25:28 and 2 Chr 24:26.

"If this *fixed order* departs from before Me," declares the LORD,
"Then the offspring of Israel also will cease
From being a nation before Me forever." (emphasis added)

These prophetic texts suggest that the same Creator and King who
spoke the worlds into existence also *spoke* Israel's covenant relationship
into existence; both are guaranteed and made sure on the unchanging
nature of God himself. For the faithful in exile, this was good news
indeed. For example, Jeremiah offers additional encouragement to
the faithful of his day by describing the future restoration for Israel
as *good*:

> And they shall come and shout for joy on the height of Zion,
> And they shall be radiant over the bounty (טוב) of the LORD—
> Over the grain, and the new wine, and the oil, And over the
> young of the flock and the herd; and their life shall be like a
> watered garden, and they shall never languish again. (Jer 31:12,
> emphasis added)[13]

These texts demonstrate that "good" covenants carry out that which
they were designed to do.

This functional idea finds support from other terms that occur
in the creation account. We find additional support from ברא in the
context of Genesis. John Walton has expanded the semantic background for ברא from his investigation of ancient cosmology texts. He
observes that texts discussing origins focus on an object's functionality. Walton suggests a similar functional role for טוב in Genesis 1:1–31
and comments:

---

[13] Jeremiah 33:11 links Hebrew טוב with the common covenant term חסד.
Other contexts where creation informs later theological and covenantal reflec-
tion include: Pss 89:28–37; 8:3; 19:1ff; 136; Jer 5:22; 33:20–26; Isa 40:12, 26;
Job 28:26; 38:31, 33; and Exod 15:25.

Throughout Genesis 1 any number of possible meanings has
been proposed for "good." In the history of interpretation it has
often been understood in moral/ethical terms or as a reference
to the quality of the workmanship. While the Hebrew term
could be used in any of those ways, the context indicates a
different direction.[14]

Walton concludes that the intended (and more ancient) audience of
Genesis 1 would have better understood a created order that was
good, and thus properly *functioning* and ready for humanity.[15] For
Walton, a *very good* world is one that: (1) operates on the design
and under the sovereignty of God, and (2) functions on behalf of
humanity created in the image of the Creator.[16] On Walton's view
ברא with טוב places even greater emphasis on the functionality of
the created order. This functionality is reduced on the enactment
of the futility curses included in the stipulations of covenant. For
the ancient person this experience is only recognized as punishment. However, for the biblical context futility is the divine means
by which the faithful (and unfaithful) are tested. In the context of
Deuteronomy, for example, Israel is reminded of the function of
this futility that worked as the means of testing the nation (Deut

---

[14] John H. Walton (*The Lost World of Genesis One: Ancient Cosmology and
the Origins of Debate* [Downers Grove: InterVarsity, 2009], 51) finds evidence in
the immediate context as to what the author of Genesis 1 means by asking the
question of what it means for a thing *not to be good*. He finds his answer in Gen
2:18, where the discussion focuses not on the issue of moral perfection or the
standard of God's workmanship in creation but on the incomplete *functionality*
of the world to accommodate Adam's need.

[15] See ibid., 51.

[16] Ibid., 151.

8:1–3).[17] Moses declared that Israel's experience—a *covenant* experience—was *good* (v. 16).

---

[17] Lewis (*The Problem of Pain*, 84–98) argues that God's *goodness* is expressed
to the world "in spite of, and by means of" humanity's rebellion against him.
While Lewis attributes natural prefall evil to Satan's fall, Lewis still maintains
that God's agenda to allow this evil to continue precipitates the experience of
pain and suffering in such a way that it either drives men to utter dependence
on God (the surrender of the self) or drives them farther away. Thus, God is in a
battle against the "illusion of self-sufficiency" in mankind through his sovereign
allowance of pain and suffering. On this basic idea we find basic agreement, as
it parallels the lesson Israel learned in the wilderness (Deut 8:1–5). This is the
purpose of refinement—a generation of Israelites coming out of the wilderness,
a generation of Israelites coming out of Babylonian captivity, all for the purpose
of cultivating a deeper covenant commitment/love in God's people.

BIBLIOGRAPHY

Aejmelaeus, Anneli. "Function and Interpretation of 'Ki' in Biblical Hebrew." *JBL* 105 (1986): 193–209.

Aistleitner, Joseph. *Wörterburch der Ugaritischen Sprache*. Berlin: Akademie Verlag, 1963.

Alexander, T. Desmond. "Abraham Re-Assessed Theologically: The Abraham Narrative and the New Testament Understanding of Justification by Faith." Pages 7–28 in *He Swore an Oath: Biblical Themes from Genesis 12–50*. Edited by R. S. Hess, G. J. Wenham, and P. E. Satterthwaite. Grand Rapids: Baker, 1994.

———. "Genesis 22 and the Covenant of Circumcision." *JSOT* 25 (1983): 17–22.

Alexander, T. Desmond, and Brian S. Rosner, eds. *New Dictionary of Biblical Theology*. Downers Grove: InterVarsity Press, 2000.

Allen, David Lewis. *Hebrews*. Nashville: B&H, 2010.

Alter, Robert. *The Art of Biblical Narrative*. New York: Basic, 1981.

Anderson, F. I. *The Hebrew Clause in the Pentateuch*. Journal of Biblical Literature Monograph Series 14. Nashville: Abingdon, 1970.

Arayaprateep, Kamol. "A Note on YR' in Jos IV 24." *VT* 22 (1972): 240–42.

Astour, Michael C. "Two Ugaritic Serpent Charms." *Journal of Near Eastern Studies* 27 (1968): 13–36.

Augustine. *The Literal Meaning of Genesis*, 2 vols. Ancient Christian Writers, vols. 41–42. Translated by J. H. Hammand. New York: Newman, 1982.

Baldauf, Christfried. "Läutern und Prüfen im Alten Testament. Begriffsgeschichtliche Untersuchung zu *Srp* und *Bḥn*." *Theologische Literaturzeitung* 103 (1978): 917–18.

Bamberger, B. "Fear and Love of God in the Old Testament." *Hebrew Union College Annual* 6 (1929): 39–53.

Barr, James. *Comparative Philology and the Text of the Old Testament*. 2nd ed. Winona Lake: Eisenbrauns, 2001.

———. "The Problem of Israelite Monotheism." *Transactions of the Glasgow University Oriental Society* 17 (1957–58): 52–62.

———. *The Semantics of Biblical Language*. London: Oxford University Press, 1961.

Barth, Karl. "'Fear of the LORD' Is the Beginning of Wisdom." *Interpretation* 14 (1960): 433–39.

Barton, John. *Reading the Old Testament*. Louisville: Westminster, 1996.

Bauckham, Richard. *Jude, 2 Peter*. WBC. Dallas: Word 1990.

Bayer, Bing B. "The Testing of God in the Hebrew Bible." Ph.D. diss. Louisville: The Southern Baptist Theological Seminary, 1987.

Becker, Joachim. *Gottesfurcht Im Alten Testament*. Analecta Biblica. Rome: Pontifical Biblical Institute, 1965.

Beckman, Gary. *Hittite Diplomatic Texts*. 2nd ed. Society of Biblical Literature Writings from the Ancient World Series. Atlanta: Scholars, 1996.

Beyerlin, Walter. *Near Eastern Religious Texts Relating to the Old Testament*. Translated by John Bowden. Philadelphia: Westminster, 1978.

Biddle, Mark E. *Deuteronomy*. Smyth & Helwys Bible Commentary. Macon: Smyth & Helwys, 2003.

Block, Daniel Isaac. *The Book of Ezekiel: 1–24*, 2 vols. NICOT. Grand Rapids: Eerdmans, 1997.

———. *Deuteronomy*. The NIV Application Commentary. Grand Rapids: Zondervan, 2012.

———. "The Grace of Torah," Pages 1–20 in *How I Love Your Torah, O LORD!: Studies in the Book of Deuteronomy*. Eugene, OR: Cascade, 2011.

———. "How Many Is God?: An Investigation into the Meaning of Deuteronomy 6:4–5." Pages 73–97 in *How I Love Your Torah, O LORD!: Studies in the Book of Deuteronomy*. Eugene, OR: Cascade, 2011.

———. "How Many Is God? An Investigation into the Meaning of Deuteronomy 6:4–5." *JETS* 47 (2004): 193–212.

———. *Judges, Ruth*. The New American Commentary, vol. 6. Nashville: B&H, 1999.

———. "The Privilege of Calling," Pages 140–61 in *How I Love Your Torah, O LORD!: Studies in the Book of Deuteronomy*. Eugene, OR: Cascade, 2011.

———. "To Serve and to Keep: Toward a Biblical Understanding of Humanity's Responsibility in the Face of the Biodiversity Crisis." Pages 116–40 in *Keeping God's Earth: The Global Environment in Biblical Perspective*. Edited by Noah Toly and Daniel Isaac Block. Downers Grove: IVP Academic, 2010.

Brensinger, Terry L. "בחן." In *NIDOTTE*. Edited by Willem A. VanGemeren. Grand Rapids: Zondervan, 1997.

———. "נסה." In *NIDOTTE*. Edited by Willem A. VanGemeren. Grand Rapids: Zondervan, 1997.

Breytenbach, A. "The Connection Between the Concepts of Darkness and Drought as Well as Light and Vegetation." In *De Fructu*

Oris Sui: Essays in Honour of Adrianus Van Selms. Vol. 9 of Pretoria Oriental Series. Edited by I. H. Eybers and A. van Selms. Leiden: Brill, 1971.

Bright, John. *A History of Israel.* Philadelphia: Westminster Press, 1981.

Brockelmann, Carolo. *Lexicon Syriacum.* Edinburgh: T&T Clark, 1895.

Brown, John P. "Proverb-Book, Gold-Economy, Alphabet." *JBL* 100 (1981): 169–91.

Brown, Francis, S. R. Driver, and Charles Briggs. *Brown-Driver-Briggs Hebrew and English Lexicon.* Peabody: Hendrickson, 1997.

Brown, Michael L. "Jeremiah." In Expositor's Bible Commentary, vol. 7: *Jeremiah-Ezekiel.* Edited by Tremper Longman and David E. Garland. Rev. ed. Grand Rapids: Zondervan, 2010.

Brueggemann, Walter. *Genesis.* Interpretation. Atlanta: John Knox, 1982.

Buber, Martin. "Abraham the Seer." Pages 22–43 in *On the Bible.* Edited by N. N. Glanzer. New York: Schocken, 1982.

Budd, Philip J. *Numbers.* WBC. Waco: Word Books, 1984.

Budge, E. A. Wallis, trans. *The Book of the Dead: The Hieroglyphic Transcript of the Papyrus of ANI.* New York: Bell Publishing, 1960.

Carroll, Robert P. *Jeremiah: A Commentary.* OTL. Philadelphia: Westminster, 1986.

Carson, D. A. *Exegetical Fallacies.* 2nd ed. Grand Rapids: Baker, 1996.

Carter, Warren. "Tempt, Temptation." In *The New Interpreter's Dictionary of the Bible.* Nashville: Abingdon, 2006.

Cartledge, Tony. *Vows in the Hebrew Bible and the Ancient Near East.* JSOT Supplement Series 147. Sheffield: JSOT Press, 1992.

Cassuto, U. *A Commentary on the Book of Exodus.* 5th ed. Translated by Israel Abrahams. Jerusalem: Magnes Press, 1967.

———. *A Commentary on the Book of Genesis.* Vol. 2. Jerusalem: Magnes, 1949.

Chantraine, Pierre. *Dictionnaire Étymologique de la Langue Grecque Histoire Des Mots*. Paris: Editions Klincksieck, 1990.

Childs, Brevard. *The Book of Exodus: A Critical, Theological Commentary*. OTL. Philadelphia: Westminster, 1974.

Clines, David J. A. *The Theme of the Pentateuch*. JSOT Supplement Series 10. Sheffield: JSOT Press, 1978.

Coats, George W. "Abraham's Sacrifice of Faith: A Form-Critical Study of Genesis 22." *Interpretation* 27 (1973): 389–400.

———. *From Canaan to Egypt: Structural and Theological Context for the Joseph Story*. Catholic Biblical Quarterly Monograph Series 4. Washington: Catholic Biblical Association of America, 1971.

———. "The Joseph Story and Ancient Wisdom: A Reappraisal." *CBQ* 35 (1973): 285–97.

———. "Redactional Unity in Genesis 37–50." *JBL* 93 (1974): 15–21.

Collins, C. John. *Genesis 1–4: A Linguistic, Literary, and Theological Commentary*. Phillipsburg: P&R Publishing, 2006.

———. *Science and Faith: Friends or Foes?* Wheaton: Crossway Books, 2003.

Cowley, A. *Aramaic Papyri of the Fifth Century B.C.* Oxford: Clarendon Press, 1923.

Crawford, Timothy G. *Blessing and Curse in Syro-Palestinian Inscriptions of the Iron Age*. American University Studies 120. New York: P. Lang, 1992.

Crenshaw, J. L. "Method in Determining Wisdom Influence upon 'Historical' Literature." *JBL* 88 (1969): 129–42.

———. *Whirlpool of Torment*. OBT. Philadelphia: Fortress Press, 1984.

Cross, F. M. *Canaanite Myth and Hebrew Epic*. Cambridge, MA: Harvard University Press, 1973.

———. "Yahweh and the God of the Patriarchs." *Harvard Theological Review* 55 (1962): 225–59.

Dahlberg, B. T. "On Recognizing the Unity of Genesis." *Theology Digest* 24 (1977): 360–67.

Dembski, William A. *The End of Christianity: Finding a Good God in an Evil World*. Nashville: B&H Academic, 2009.

Dempster, Stephen G. *Dominion and Dynasty: A Biblical Theology of the Hebrew Bible*. New Studies in Biblical Theology. Downers Grove: InterVarsity, 2003.

Donner, H., and W. Rollig. *Kanaanäische und Aramäische Inschriften*. Weisbaden: Otto Harrassowitz, 1964.

Dumbrell, William J. *The Faith of Israel: A Theological Survey of the Old Testament*. 2nd ed. Grand Rapids: Baker Academic, 2002.

Dunn, James D. G. *Romans 1–8*. WBC, vol. 38A. Dallas: Word Books, 1988.

Durham, John. *Exodus*. WBC, vol. 3. Waco: Word Books, 1997.

Eichrodt, Walther. *Theology of the Old Testament*. OTL. Vol 2. Translated by J. A. Baker. Philadelphia: Westminster, 1967.

Eissfeldt, Otto. "Zwei verkannte militär-Technische Termini Im Alten Testament." *VT* 5 (1955): 232–38.

Ellenbogen, Maximilian. *Foreign Words in the Old Testament: Their Origin and Etymology*. London: Luzac and Company, 1962.

Elliott, John H. *1 Peter*. The Anchor Bible, vol. 37b. New York: Doubleday, 2000.

Erman, A., and H. Grapow. *Wörterbuch der Aegyptischen Sprache*. Berlin: Akademe-Verlag, 1926–71.

Eslinger, C. "Knowing Yahweh: Exodus 6:3 in the Context of Genesis 1–Exodus 15." Pages 188–98 in *Literary Structure and Rhetorical Strategies in the Hebrew Bible*. Edited by L. de Regt, J. de Waard, and J. P. Fokkelman. Winona Lake: Eisenbrauns, 1996.

Even -Shoshan, Abraham, ed. *A New Concordance of the Old Testament Using the Hebrew and Aramaic Text*. 2nd ed. Jerusalem: Kiryat Sefer, 1990.

Fishbane, Michael. *Biblical Interpretation in Ancient Israel*. Oxford: Clarendon, 1985.

———. *Text and Texture*. New York: Schocken, 1975.

Fitzmyer, Joseph A. *Romans*. The Anchor Bible. New York: Doubleday, 1993.

Fokkelman, J. P. *Narrative Art and Poetry in the Books of Samuel: A Full Interpretation Based on Stylistic and Structural Analyses*. Studia Semitica Neerlandica 20. Assen, The Netherlands: Van Gorcum, 1981.

———. "Time and Structure of the Abraham Cycle." *Oudtestamentische Studien* 25 (1989): 96–109.

Forbes, R. J. "Extracting, Smelting and Alloying." Pages 573–98 in *A History of Technology*. Edited by Charles Singer, E. J. Holmyard, and A. R. Hall. London: Oxford University Press, 1954.

Fox, E. *In the Beginning: A New English Rendition of the Book of Genesis*. New York: Schocken, 1983.

Fretheim, Terence E. *Creation Untamed: The Bible, God, and Natural Disasters*. Theological Explorations for the Church Catholic. Grand Rapids: Baker Academic, 2010.

———. *Jeremiah*. Smyth & Helwys Bible Commentary. Macon: Smith & Helwys, 2002.

———. *The Pentateuch*. Interpreting Biblical Texts. Edited by Terence E. Fretheim, Gene M. Tucker, and Charles B. Cousar. Nashville: Abingdon Press, 1996.

Gaffin, Richard B. "The Usefulness of the Cross." *Westminster Theological Journal* 41, no. 2 (1979): 228–46.

Garrett, Duane. *Rethinking Genesis: The Sources and Authorship of the First Book of the Pentateuch*. 2nd ed. Grand Rapids: Baker, 1991.

Gelb, Ignace J. *The Assyrian Dictionary of the Oriental Institute of the University of Chicago*. Chicago: Oriental Institute, 1964–56.

Gerhardsson, Birger. *The Testing of God's Son (Matt. 4:1–11 & Par.): An Analysis of an Early Christian Midrash*. New Testament Series 2. Lund: Berlingska Bibtryckeriet, 1966.

Gerleman, G. "נסה Nsh Pi. to Test." Translated by Mark Biddle. In
    TLOT. Edited by Jenni Ernst and Claus Westermann. Peabody:
    Hendrickson, 1997.

Gerstenberger, Erhard. "Covenant and Commandment." *JBL* 84
    (1965): 38–51.

Gibson, John C. L. *Textbook of Syrian Semitic Inscriptions: Aramaic
    Inscriptions*. Oxford: Clarendon Press, 1995.

Goetze, Albrecht. "Fifty Old Babylonian Letters from Harmal."
    Sumer 14 (1958): 3–78.

——. *Yale Oriental Series: Babylonian Texts*. New Haven: Yale Univer-
    sity Press, 1947.

Goldingay, John. "The Patriarchs in Scripture and History." Pages
    11–42 in *Essays on the Patriarchal Narratives*. Edited by A. R. Mil-
    lard and D. J. Wiseman. Leicester: Intervarsity, 1980.

Goold, G. P., ed. *Pliny: Natural History*. Translated by D. E. Eichholz.
    The Loeb Classical Library. Cambridge, MA: Harvard University
    Press, 1962.

Gordon, Cyrus. *Ugaritic Textbook*. Analecta Orientalia 38. Rome:
    Pontificium Institutum Biblicum, 1965.

Gowan, Donald E. *Theology in Exodus: Biblical Theology in the Form
    of a Commentary*. Louisville: Westminster, 1994.

Green, Douglas. "When the Gardener Returns: An Ecological Per-
    spective on Adam's Return." Pages 267–75 in *Keeping God's
    Earth: The Global Environment in Biblical Perspective*. Edited by
    Noah Toly and Daniel Isaac Block. Downers Grove: IVP Aca-
    demic, 2010.

Greenberg, Moshe. *Ezekiel 1–20: A New Translation with Introduction
    and Commentary*. The Anchor Bible, vol. 22. 1st ed. Garden City:
    Doubleday, 1983.

——. "The Hebrew Oath Particle Ḥay/Ḥe." *JBL* 66 (1957): 35–39.

——. "נסה in Exodus 20:20 and the Purpose of the Sinai Theoph-
    any." *JBL* 79 (1960): 273–76.

Groom, Sue. *Linguistic Analysis of Biblical Hebrew*. Carlisle: Paternoster, 2003.

Gruber, Mayer I. "Fear, Anxiety and Reverence in Akkadian, Biblical Hebrew and Other North-West Semitic Languages." *VT* 40 (1990): 411–22.

Gunkel, Hermann. *Genesis*. Translated by Mark Biddle. Mercer Library of Biblical Studies. Macon: Mercer University Press, 1997.

Hallo, William W., gen. ed. *The Context of Scripture: Archival Documents from the Biblical World*. Vol. 3. Leiden: Brill, 2003.

—————. *The Context of Scripture: Canonical Compositions from the Biblical World*. Vol. 1. Leiden: Brill, 2003.

—————. *The Context of Scripture: Monumental Inscriptions from the Biblical World*. Vol. 2. Leiden: Brill, 2003.

Hamilton, Victor P. *The Book of Genesis*. NICOT. Grand Rapids: Eerdmans, 1995.

Haran, M. "The Religion of the Patriarchs." *Annual of the Swedish Theological Institute* 4 (1965): 30–55.

Harman, Allan M. "בשׁל." In *NIDOTTE*. Edited by Willem A. VanGemeren. Grand Rapids: Zondervan, 1997.

Harris, J. R. *Deutsche Akademie der Wissenschaften zu Berlin Institut Fur Orientforschung*. Vol. 54, *Lexicographical Studies in Ancient Egyptian Minerals*. Berlin: Akademie-Verlag, 1961.

Harrison, Everett F., and Donald A. Hagner. "Romans." In *The Expositor's Bible Commentary*, vol. 11. Edited by Tremper Longman and David Garland. Grand Rapids: Zondervan, 2006.

Harrison, R. K. *Numbers*. The Wycliffe Exegetical Commentary. Chicago: Moody, 1990.

Hayward, C. T. R. "The Present State of Research into the Targumic Account of the Sacrifice of Isaac." *Journal of Jewish Studies* 32 (1981): 127–50.

Healy, John F. "Greek Refining Techniques and the Composition of Gold-Silver Alloys." *Revue Belge de Numismatique et de Sigillographie* 120 (1974): 19–33.

Heimpel, Wolfgang. *Letters to the King of Mari: A New Translation, with Historical Introduction, Notes and Commentary*. Winona Lake: Eisenbrauns, 2003.

Helfmeyer, H. J. "נסה *Nissa*." In *TDOT*. Edited by G. Johannes Botterweck and Helmer Ringgren. Grand Rapids: Eerdmans, 1977.

Hillers, Delbert R. "Delocutive Verbs in Biblical Hebrew." *JBL* 86 (1967): 320–24.

———. *Treaty-Curses and the Old Testament Prophets*. Rome: Pontifical Biblial Institute, 1964.

Hoftijzer, J., and K. Jongeling. *Dictionary of the North-West Semitic Inscriptions*. Leiden: E. J. Brill, 1995.

Holladay, William Lee. *Jeremiah 1: A Commentary on the Book of the Prophet Jeremiah, Chapters 1-25*. Hermeneia. Edited by Paul D. Hanson. Philadelphia: Fortress Press, 1986.

Houtman, C. *Exodus*, 4 vols. Historical Commentary on the Old Testament. Kampen: Kok, 1993.

Huffmon, H. B. "The Treaty Background of Hebrew Yāda." *Bulletin for the American Schools for Oriental Research* 181 (1966): 31–37.

———, and S. B. Parker. "A Further Note on the Treaty Background of Hebrew Yāda." *Bulletin for the American Schools for Oriental Research* 184 (1966): 36–38.

Hugenberger, Gordon. *Marriage as a Covenant: Biblical Law and Ethics as Developed from Malachi*. JSOT Supplement Series 52. Leiden: E. J. Brill, 1994.

Hulisani, Ramantswana. "God Saw That It Was Good, Not Perfect: A Canonical-Dialogic Reading of Genesis 1–3." Diss., Westminster Theological Seminary, 2010.

Humphreys, W. Lee. "A Life-Style for Diaspora: A Study of the Tales of Esther and Daniel." *JBL* 92 (1973): 211–23.

_____. *Joseph and His Family: A Literary Study*. Columbia: University of South Carolina Press, 1988.

James, T. G. H. "Gold Technology in Ancient Egypt." *Gold Bulletin* 5 (1972): 38–41.

Jastrow, Marcus. "בחן." In *A Dictionary of the Targumim, the Talmud Babli and Yerushalmi, and the Midrashic Literature*. New York: Judaica Press, 1996.

Jenni, Ernst. "בחן *Bḥn* to Test." Translated by Mark Biddle. In TLOT. Edited by Ernst Jenni and Claus Westermann. Peabody: Hendrickson, 1997.

Jespen, Alfred. "אמן *'Āman*." In *TDOT*. Edited by G. Botterweck, H. Ringgren. Grand Rapids: Eerdmans, 1975.

Johnson, Dennis E. "Fire in God's House: Imagery from Malachi 3 in Peter's Theology of Suffering (1 Pet 4:12–19)." *JETS* 29, no. 3 (1986): 285–94.

Joüon, Paul, and T. Muraoka. *A Grammar of Biblical Hebrew*. Subsidia Biblica 14/1–14/2. Rome: Editrice Pontificio Istituto Biblico, 1996.

Kaiser, Walter C. *Toward an Old Testament Theology*. Grand Rapids: Zondervan, 1978.

Kalluveettil, Paul. *Declaration and Covenant*. Analecta Biblica 88. Rome: Biblical Institute Press, 1982.

Keiser, Thomas. "Genesis 1–11: Its Literary Coherence and Theological Message." Ph.D. Diss., Dallas: Dallas Theological Seminary, 2007.

Kikiwada, Isaac M., and Arthur Quinn. *Before Abraham Was: A Provocative Challenge to the Documentary Hypothesis*. Nashville: Abingdon, 1985.

Kitchen, Kenneth A. *Ancient Orient and Old Testament*. Chicago: InterVarsity, 1966.

————. *Egypt and Israel During the First Millenium B.C.* Supplements to Vetus Testamentum 40, 1988.

————. "Genesis 12–50 in the Near Eastern World." Pages 67–92 in *He Swore an Oath: Biblical Themes from Genesis 12–50*. Edited by Gordon Wenham, Richard Hess, and Phillip Satterthwaite. Grand Rapids: Baker, 1994.

————. *On the Reliability of the Old Testament*. Grand Rapids: Eerdmans, 2003.

Klein, Ernest. *A Comprehensive Etymological Dictionary of the Hebrew Language for Readers of English*. New York: Macmillan, 1987.

Klein, Ralph W. *1 Samuel*. WBC, vol. 10. Waco: Word, 1983.

Kline, Meredith G. "Abram's Amen." *Westminster Theological Journal* 31 (1968): 1–11.

Knudtzon, J. A. *Die El-Amarna-Tafeln*. Vorderasiatische Bibliothek. Leipzig: Otto Zeller Verlagsbuchhandlung, 1964.

Köhler, Ludwig. "Zwei Fachworter der Bausprache in Jesaja 28,16." *Theologische Zeitschrift* 3 (1947): 390–93.

————, and Walter Baumgartner. "נסה." In *HALOT*. Edited and translated by M. E. J. Richardson. New York: Brill, 1995.

————, and Walter Baumgartner. "בחן." In *HALOT*. Edited and translated by M. E. J. Richardson. New York: Brill, 1995.

Kraeling, Emil. *The Brooklyn Museum Aramaic Papyri: New Documents of the Fifth Century B.C. from the Jewish Colony at Elephantine*. New Haven: Yale University Press, 1953.

Labuschagne, C. J. *The Incomparability of Yahweh in the Old Testament*. Pretoria Oriental Series 5. Leiden: E. J. Brill, 1996.

Lambdin, Thomas O. "Egyptian Loan Words in the Old Testament." *JAOS* 73 (1953): 145–55.

Lambert, W. G. *Babylonian Wisdom Literature*. Oxford: Clarendon, 1960.

Landy, F. "Narrative Techniques and Symbolic Transactions in the Akedah." Pages 1–40 in *Signs and Wonders: Biblical Texts in Literary Focus*. Edited by J. Cheryl Exum. Atlanta: Scholars, 1989.

Lane, Edward W. *Arabic-English Lexicon*. New York: Frederick Ungar, 1956.

Lane, William L. *Hebrews 1–8*. Vol. 47a. WBC. Dallas: Word, 1991.

Lete, Gregorio, and Joaquín Sanmartin. *Handbook of Oriental Studies*. Vol. 67, *A Dictionary of the Ugaritic Language in the Alphabetic Tradition*. Edited and translated by G. E. Watson. Leiden: Brill, 2004.

Levey, Martin. "The Refining of Gold in Ancient Mesopotamia." *Chymia* 5 (1959): 31–36.

Lewis, C. S. *The Problem of Pain*. New York: Macmillan, 1962.

Lichtheim, Miriam. *Maat in Egyptian Autobiographies and Related Studies*. Orbis Biblicus et Orientalis. Göttingen: Vandenhoeck and Ruprecht, 1992.

Lipiński, Edward. *Semitic Languages: Outline of a Comparative Grammar*. Orientalia Lovaniensia Analecta 80. Leuven: Peeters, 1997.

Loader, J. A. "The Concept of Darkness in the Hebrew Root 'Rb/'Rp." In *De Fructu Oris Sui: Essays in Honour of Adrianus Van Selms*. Vol. 9 of Pretoria Oriental Series. Edited by I. H. Eybers and A. van Selms. Leiden: Brill, 1971.

Long, V. Phillips, *The Art of Biblical History*. Grand Rapids: Zondervan, 1994.

Longacre, Robert E. *Joseph: A Story of Divine Providence: A Text Theoretical and Textlinguistic Analysis of Genesis 37 and 39–48*. Winona Lake: Eisenbrauns, 1989.

Lord, Louis E. "The Touchstone." *The Classical Journal* 32 (1936): 428–31.

Lucas, Alfred. *Ancient Egyptian Materials and Industries*. London: Edward and Arnold, 1948.

Lundbom, Jack R. *Jeremiah 1–20: A New Translation with Introduction and Commentary*. Vol. 21a. The Anchor Bible. 1st ed. New York: Doubleday, 1999.

Martin, Ralph. *James*. WBC, vol. 48. Waco: Word, 1988.

Mathews, K. A. *Genesis 1–11:26*. Vol. 1a. New American Commentary. Nashville: B&H, 1996.

Mays, James Luther. *Amos: A Commentary*. OTL. Philadelphia: Westminster, 1969.

McCarthy, Dennis J. "Notes on the Love of God in Deuteronomy and the Father-Son Relationship Between Yahweh and Israel." *CBQ* 27 (1965): 144–47.

———. *A Study in Form in the Ancient Oriental Documents and in the Old Testament*. Analecta Biblica 21a. Rome: Biblical Institute Press, 1978.

———. "Three Covenants in Genesis." *CBQ* 26 (1964): 179–89.

McComiskey, Thomas. *Hosea*. Vol. 1. The Minor Prophets: An Exegetical and Expository Commentary. Edited by Thomas McComiskey. Grand Rapids: Baker 1992.

McConville, J. G. *Deuteronomy*. Apollos Old Testament Commentary, vol. 5. Downers Grove: InterVarsity Press, 2002.

———. *Law and Theology in Deuteronomy*. JSOT Supplement Series 33. Sheffield: JSOT Press, 1984.

McCree, Walter. "The Covenant Meal in the Old Testament." *JBL* 45 (1926): 120–28.

Meier, Sam. "Job 1–2: a Reflection of Genesis 1–3." *VT* 39, no. 2 (1989): 183–93.

Mendenhall, G. E. "Covenant Forms in Israelite Tradition." *The Biblical Archeologist* 17 (1954): 50–76.

Mercer, Samuel A. B., ed. *The Oath in Babylonian and Assyrian Literature*. Paris: Paul Geuthner, 1912.

———. *The Pyramid Texts in Translation and Commentary*. New York: Longmans, Green, 1952.

———. *The Tell El-Amarna Tablets*. Toronto: Macmillan, 1939.

Milgrom, Jacob. *Numbers*. The JPS Torah Commentary. Philadelphia: JPS, 1990.

Milgrom, Jo. *The Binding of Isaac: The Akedah—a Primary Symbol in Jewish Thought and Art*. Berkeley: BIBAL Press, 1988.

Millard, Alan R. "Abraham, Akhenaten, Moses and Monotheism." Pages 119–29 in *He Swore an Oath: Biblical Themes from Genesis 12–50*. Edited by Gordon Wenham, Richard Hess, and Phillip Satterthwaite. Grand Rapids: Baker, 1994.

———. "Methods of Studying the Patriarchal Narratives as Ancient Texts." Pages 43–58 in *Essays on the Patriarchal Narratives*. Edited by A. R. Millard and D. J. Wiseman. Leichester: InterVarsity Press, 1980.

Moberly, R. W. L. "Abraham, Akhenaten, Moses and Monotheism." Pages 119–29 in *He Swore and Oath: Biblical Themes from Genesis 12–50*. Edited by Gordon Wenham, Richard Hess, and Phillip Satterthwaite. Grand Rapids: Baker, 1994.

———. "Abraham's Righteousness (Gen. Xv 6)." Pages 103–30 in *Studies in the Pentateuch*. Edited by J. A. Emerton. New York: Brill, 1990.

———. *At the Mountain of God*. JSOT Supplement Series 22. Sheffield: JSOT Press, 1983.

———. *The Bible, Theology, and Faith: A Study of Abraham and Jesus*. Cambridge: Cambridge University Press, 2000.

———. "Christ as the Key to Scripture: Genesis 22 Reconsidered." Pages 143–73 in *He Swore an Oath: Biblical Themes from Genesis 12–50*. Edited by Gordon Wenham, Richard Hess, and Phillip Satterthwaite. Grand Rapids: Baker, 1994.

———. "The Earliest Commentary on the Akedah." *VT* 38 (1988): 302–23.

———. *Genesis 12–50*. Old Testament Guides. Sheffield: Sheffield Academic Press, 1995.

———. *The Old Testament of the Old Testament: Patriarchal Narratives and Mosaic Yahwism*. Minneapolis: Augsburg, 1992.

———. "Story in the Old Testament." In *From Eden to Golgotha: Essays in Biblical Theology*. Supplements to Vetus Testamentum 52. Atlanta: Scholars Press, 1992.

———. "Uncomfortable Truths in Job: the Value of the Old Testament for Christian Ministry." *Covenant Quarterly* 68, nos. 3–4 (2010): 3–12.

———. "אמן." Pages 427–33 in *NIDOTTE*, vol. 1. Edited by Willem A. VanGemeren. Grand Rapids: Zondervan, 1997.

Moo, Douglas J. *Romans 1–8*. The Wycliffe Exegetical Commentary. Chicago: Moody Press, 1991.

Moore, D. T., and W. A. Oddy. "Touchstones: Some Aspects of Their Nomenclature, Petrography and Provenance." *Journal of Archaeological Science* 12 (1985): 59–80.

Moorey, P. R. S. *Ancient Mesopotamian Materials and Industries: The Archaeological Evidence*. Oxford: Clarendon Press, 1994.

Moran, William, ed. and trans. *The Amarna Letters*. Baltimore: Johns Hopkins University Press, 1992.

———. "The Ancient Near Eastern Background of the Love of God in Deuteronomy." *CBQ* 25 (1963): 77–87.

Ngwa, Kenneth Numfor. "Did Job Suffer for Nothing? The Ethics of Piety, Presumption and the Reception of Disaster in the Prologue of Job." *JSOT* 33, no. 3 (2009): 359–80.

Niehaus, Jeff. "Amos." Pages 315-494 in *The Minor Prophets: An Exegetical and Expository Commentary*. Edited by Thomas Edward McComiskey. Grand Rapids: Baker, 1992.

Notton, J. H. F. "Ancient Egyptian Gold Refining: A Reproduction of Early Techniques." *Gold Bulletin* 7 (1974): 50–56.

Oddy, W. A. "Assaying in Antiquity." *Gold Bulletin* 16 (1977): 52–59.

———. "Gold in Antiquity: Aspects of Gilding and of Assaying." *Journal of the Royal Society of Arts* 130 (1982): 730–43.

Ogden, Jack. "Metals." Pages 66–68 in *Ancient Egyptian Materials and Technology*. Edited by P. T. Nicholson and I. Shaw. Cambridge: Cambridge University Press, 2000.

Oppenheim, A. Leo. *Ancient Mesopotamia: Portrait of a Dead Civilization*. Chicago: University Press, 1964.

————, ed. *The Assyrian Dictionary of the Oriental Institute of the University of Chicago*. Chicago: University of Chicago, 1956–.

————. "Idiomatic Accadian." *JAOS* 61 (1941): 251–71.

Orel, Vladimire E., and Olga V. Stolbova. *Hamito-Semitic Etymological Dictionary: Materials for a Reconstruction*. Leiden: E. J. Brill, 1995.

Osborne, Grant R. *Romans*. The IVP New Testament Commentary Series, vol. 6. Downers Grove: InterVarsity Press, 2004.

Parrot, Andre, and Georges Dossin, eds. *Archives Royales de Mari*. Paris: Impriemerie Nationale, 1949.

Pierce, Richard. "Egyptian Loan-Words in Ancient Greek." *Symbolae Osloenses* 46 (1971): 96–107.

Postell, Seth D. *Adam as Israel: Genesis 1–3 as the Introduction to the Torah and Tanakh*. Eugene: Pickwick, 2011.

Pratico, Gary D., and Miles V. Van Pelt. *Basics of Biblical Hebrew*. Grand Rapids: Zondervan, 2001.

Priest, John. "The Covenant of Brothers." *JBL* 84 (1965): 401–6.

Pritchard, James B., ed. *Ancient Near Eastern Texts Relating to the Old Testament*. 3rd ed. Princeton: Princeton University Press, 1969.

Provan, Iain W. "Creation and Holistic Ministry: A Study of Genesis 1:1 to 2:3." *Evangelical Review of Theology* 25, no. 4 (2001): 292–303.

Redford, Donald. *A Study of the Biblical Story of Joseph (Genesis 37–50)*. Supplements to Vetus Testamentum 20. Leiden: Brill, 1970.

Renn, Stephen D., ed. *Expository Dictionary of Bible Words*. Peabody: Hendrickson, 2005.

Richards, Larry. *Expository Dictionary of Bible Words*. Grand Rapids: Regency Reference Library, 1985.

Rogerson, J. W., R. W. L. Moberly, and William Johnstone. *Genesis and Exodus*. Sheffield: Sheffield Academic Press, 2001.

Ross, Allen. P. *Creation and Blessing: A Guide to the Study and Exposition of the Book of Genesis*. Grand Rapids: Baker, 1988.

Ross, Hugh. *A Matter of Days: Resolving a Creation Controversy*. Colorado Springs: NavPress, 2004.

Saggs, H. W. F. *Jordan Lectures in Comparative Religion*. Vol. 12, *The Encounter with the Divine in Mesopotamia and Israel*. London: Athlone Press, 1978.

Sailhamer, John. *Genesis*. Vol. 2. The Expositor's Bible Commentary. Edited by Frank Ely Gaebelein and Richard P. Polen. Grand Rapids: Zondervan, 1990.

————. *Introduction to Old Testament Theology: A Canonical Approach*. Grand Rapids: Zondervan, 1995.

————. *The Pentateuch as Narrative: A Biblical-Theological Commentary*. Library of Biblical Interpretation. Grand Rapids: Zondervan, 1992.

Sarna, Nahum M. *Exodus*. The JPS Torah Commentary Series. Philadelphia: JPS, 1991.

————. *Genesis*. Philadelphia: JPS, 1989.

Schmidt, Werner H. *Exodus*. Biblischer Kommentar Altes Testament 2. Neukirchen Vluyn: Neukirchener Verlag des Erziehungsverein, 1988.

————. *The Faith of the Old Testament*. Oxford: Blackwell, 1983.

Schoeps, Hans J. "The Sacrifice of Isaac in Paul's Theology." *JBL* 65 (1946): 385–92.

Schreiner, Thomas R. *Romans*. Baker Exegetical Commentary on the New Testament. Grand Rapids: Baker, 1998.

————. *1, 2 Peter, Jude*. The New American Commentary. Nashville: B&H, 2003.

Schroeder, Gerald L. *The Hidden Face of God: How Science Reveals the Ultimate Truth*. New York: Free Press, 2001.

Seesemann, H. "πεῖρα, πειράω, πειράζω, πειρασμός, ἀπείραστος, ἐκπειράζω." *TDNT*. Edited and translated by G. W. Bromiley. Edited by G. Kittel and G. Friedrich. Grand Rapids: Eerdmans, 1964–76.

Segert, Stanislav. *A Basic Grammar of the Ugaritic Language*. Berkeley: University of California Press, 1984.

Selms, Adrian van. "Yammu's Dethronement by Baal: An Attempt to Reconstruct Texts UT 129, 137 and 68." *Ugarit-Forschungen 2* (1970): 251–68.

Sethe, K. "Die Bau-und Denkmalstein des alten Agyptes und ihre Name." Pages 894–909 in *Sitzungsberichte der Preussischen Akademie der Wissenschaften*. Berlin: Akademie-Verlag, 1933.

Sheridan, Mark, and Thomas C. Oden, eds. *Ancient Christian Commentary on Scripture*. Vol. 2. Downers Grove: InterVarsity Press, 2002.

Sheriffs, Deryck. "Faith." *DOTP*. Edited by T. Desmond Alexander and David W. Baker. Downers Grove: InterVarsity Press, 2003.

———. *The Friendship of the Lord*. Carlisle: Paternoster, 1996.

———. "Testing." Pages 830–34 in *DOTP*. Edited by T. Desmond Alexander and David W. Baker. Downers Grove: InterVarsity, 2003.

Smith, R. Payne. *Syriac Dictionary*. Edited by J. Payne Smith. Oxford: Claredon, 1903.

Smith, Sidney, trans. *Babylonian Historical Texts Relating to the Capture and Downfall of Babylon*. London: Metheun and Co., 1924.

Snoke, David. *A Biblical Case for an Old Earth*. Grand Rapids: Baker Books, 2006.

Soden, Wolfram von. *Akkadisches Handwörterbuch*. Wiesbaden: Otto Harrassowitz, 1959-81.

Speiser, E. A. *Genesis*. Anchor Bible. New York: Doubleday, 1964.

Spiegel, Shalom. *The Last Trial*. New York: Behrman, 1979.

Stähli, H. –P. "ראּ *yr'* to fear." Translated by Mark Biddle. *TLOT*. Edited by Ernst Jenni and Claus Westermann. Peabody: Hendrickson, 1997.

———. "פחד *phd* to shake." Translated by Mark Biddle. *TLOT*. Edited by Ernst Jenni and Claus Westermann. Peabody: Hendrickson, 1997.

Sternberg, Meir. *The Poetics of Biblical Narrative: Ideological Literature and the Drama of Reading*. Bloomington: Indiana University Press, 1987.

Taylor, S. S. "Faith, Faithfulness." *New Dictionary of Biblical Theology*. Edited by T. Desmond Alexander and Brian S. Rosner. Downers Grove: InterVarsity, 2000.

Thompson, J. A. *The Book of Jeremiah*. NICOT. Grand Rapids: Eerdmans, 1980.

Tigay, Jeffrey H. *Deuteronomy*. The JPS Torah Commentary. Edited by Nahum M. Sarna. Philadelphia: JPS, 1996.

———. *Deuteronomy: The Traditional Hebrew Text with the New JPS Translation*. The JPS Torah Commentary. Philadelphia: JPS, 1996.

Torrance, Thomas F. "One Aspect of the Biblical Conception of Faith." *The Expository Times* 68 (1957): 111–14.

Tregelles, Samuel P. *Gesenius' Hebrew and Chaldee Lexicon to the Old Testament Scriptures*. Grand Rapids: Eerdmans, 1949.

Tsevat, M. "בחן." In *Theological Dictionary of the Old Testament*. Edited by G. Botterweck and H. Ringgren. Grand Rapids: Eerdmans, 1975.

Tsumura, David Toshio. *Creation and Destruction: A Reappraisal of the Chaoskampf Theory in the Old Testament*. Winona Lake: Eisenbrauns, 2005.

Van Leeuwen, Raymond C. "A Technical Metallurgical Usage of Yṣ'." *Zeitschrift für die alttestamentliche Wissenschaft* 98, no. 1 (1986): 112–13.

Van Seters, John. *Abraham in History and Tradition*. London: Yale University Press, 1975.

———. "The Religion of the Patriarchs in Genesis." *Biblica* 61 (1980): 220–33.

von Rad, Gerhard. "The Form-Critical Problem of the Hexateuch." *The Problem of the Hexateuch and Other Essays*. Translated by E. W. T. Dicken. London: SCM, 1966.

————. *Genesis: A Commentary*. OTL. Rev. ed. Translated by John H. Marks. Philadelphia: Westminster, 1973.

————. "The Joseph Narrative and Ancient Wisdom." Pages 292–300 in *The Problem of the Hexateuch and Other Essays*. London: SCM Press, 1984.

Wakely, Robin. "צרף." In *NIDOTTE*. Edited by Willem A. VanGemeren. Grand Rapids: Zondervan, 1997.

Wälchi, Walo. "Touching Precious Metals." *Gold Bulletin* 14 (1981): 154–58.

Waltke, Bruce. *Genesis: A Commentary*. Grand Rapids: Zondervan, 2001.

————, and Yu Charles. *An Old Testament Theology: An Exegetical, Canonical, and Thematic Approach*. Grand Rapids: Zondervan, 2007.

————, and M. O'Connor. *An Introduction to Biblical Hebrew Syntax*. Winona Lake: Eisenbrauns, 1990.

Walton, John H. *The Lost World of Genesis One: Ancient Cosmology and the Origins Debate*. Downers Grove: IVP Academic, 2009.

Weinfeld, Moshe. "*Berît-* Covenant vs. Obligation." Biblica 56 (1975): 120–28.

————. "Bund and Grace." Lešonenu 36 (1972): 83–105.

————. "Covenant Making in Anatolia and Mesopotamia." *Journal of the Ancient Near Eastern Society* 22 (1993): 135–39.

————. "The Covenant of Grant in the Old Testament and Ancient Near East." *JAOS* 90 (1970): 184–203.

————. "Covenant Terminology in the Ancient Near East and Its Influence on the West." *JAOS* 93 (1973): 190–99.

————. *Deuteronomy and the Deuteronomic School*. Winona Lake: Eisenbrauns, 1992.

————. *Deuteronomy 1–11*. Anchor Bible 5. New York: Doubleday, 1991.

————. "The Loyalty Oath in the Ancient Near East." *Ugarit-Forsc-hungen* 8 (1976): 379–413.

Wenham, Gordon. "The Face at the Bottom of the Well: Hidden Agendas of the Pentateuchal Commentator." Pages 185–209 in *He Swore an Oath: Biblical Themes from Genesis 12–50*. Edited by Gordon Wenham, Richard Hess, and Phillip Satterthwaite. Grand Rapids: Baker, 1994.

————. *Genesis 1–15*. WBC. Waco: Word 1987.

————. *Genesis 16–50*. WBC. Dallas: Word, 1994.

————. "The Religion of the Patriarchs." Pages 157–88 in *Essays on the Patriarchal Narratives*. Edited by A. R. Millard and D. J. Wiseman. Leichester: InterVarsity, 1980.

Westermann, Claus. *Genesis 12–36: A Commentary*. 2nd ed. Translated by John J. Scullion. Minneapolis: Augsburg, 1985.

————. *Genesis 37–50: A Commentary*. Minneapolis: Augsburg, 1982.

Whybray, R. N. "The Joseph Story and Pentateuchal Criticism." *VT* 18 (1968): 522–28.

Wildberger, H. "אמן *'mn* Firm, Secure." Translated by Mark Biddle. In *TLOT*. Edited by Ernst Jenni, Claus Westermann. Peabody: Hendrickson, 1997.

Wilson, J. A. "The Oath in Ancient Egypt." *Journal of Near Eastern Studies* 7 (1948): 129–56.

Wiseman, D. J. "Abraham Reassessed." Pages 139–56 in *Essays on the Patriarchal Narratives*. Edited by A. R. Millard and D. J. Wiseman. Leichester: InterVarsity Press, 1980.

Wolff, Hans W. "The Elohistic Fragments in the Pentateuch." *Interpretation* 26 (1972): 158–73.

————. "The Kerygma of the Yahwist." *Interpretation* 20 (1972): 131–58.

Wolters, Albert M. "Worldview and Textual Criticism in 2 Peter 3:10." *Westminster Theological Journal* 49, no. 2 (1987): 405–13.

Wurthwein, Ernst. "Egyptian Wisdom and the Old Testament." Pages 113–33 in *Studies in Ancient Israelite Wisdom*. Edited by Harry M. Orlinsky. New York: KTAV, 1976.

Young, Davis A., and Ralph F. Stearley. *The Bible, Rocks, and Time: Geological Evidence for the Age of the Earth*. Downers Grove: IVP Academic, 2008.

Zimmerli, Walther. *Ezekiel: A Commentary on the Book of the Prophet Ezekiel*, 2 vols. Hermeneia—a Critical and Historical Commentary on the Bible. Edited by Frank Moore Cross and Klaus Baltzer. Translated by Ronald Clements. Philadelphia: Fortress Press, 1979.

"נסה." In *DCH*. Edited by David J. A. Clines. Sheffield: Sheffield Academic Press, 2001.

NAME INDEX

INDEX

SUBJECT INDEX

SCRIPTURE INDEX

Note: Where Masoretic and English versification differs, the English verses are given in brackets.